MW01067875

IN THE CENTER OF THE FIRE

A Memoir of the Occult

IN THE CENTER OF THE FIRE
A Memoir of the Occult
1966–1989

James Wasserman

*I must Create a System
or be enslav'd by another Mans
I will not Reason & Compare:
my business is to Create*

—William Blake
Jerusalem

IBIS PRESS
Lake Worth, FL

First edition published in 2012 by Ibis Press
An imprint of Nicolas-Hays, Inc.
P. O. Box 540206
Lake Worth, FL 33454-0206
www.ibispress.net

Distributed to the trade by
Red Wheel/Weiser, LLC
65 Parker St. • Ste. 7
Newburyport, MA 01950
www.redwheelweiser.com

We gratefully acknowledge the cooperation of Ordo Templi Orientis, whom
we thank for permission to quote correspondence throughout the text and
materials in the appendices, copyright © Ordo Templi Orientis.

"Analysis by a Master of the Temple of the Critical Nodes in the Experience
of His Magical Vehicle" by Jack Parsons, copyright © Cameron
Parsons Foundation, reproduced with permission.

ISBN 978-0-89254-201-7

Library of Congress Cataloging-in-Publication Data

Wasserman, James, 1948–
    In the center of the fire : a memoir of the occult, 1966/1989 / James Wasserman.
-- 1st ed.
        p. cm.
    Includes bibliographical references and index.
    ISBN 978-0-89254-201-7 (alk. paper)
    1. Wasserman, James, 1948– 2. Occultists--United States--Biography. 3. Ordo
Templi Orientis. 4. Occultism--United States--History--20th century. I. Title.
    BF1997.W37 A3 2012
    130.92—dc23
    [B]   2012012912

Every effort has been made to determine the ownership of all photos and
secure proper permissions. If any errors have inadvertently occurred,
we apologize and will correct such in subsequent printings.

For additional papers, photographs, audio, and video, please visit
our dedicated website *www.inthecenterofthefire.com*

Book design and typography by Studio 31
www.studio31.com

10 9 8 7 6 5 4 3 2
Printed and bound in the United States of America. (mv)

This book is dedicated to

RICHARD GERNON

ANGUS MACLISE

GRADY MCMURTRY

HARRY SMITH

Contents

Photo inserts follow pages 112, 176, and 240

INTRODUCTION

Do what thou wilt shall be the whole of the Law.

I THANK JAMES STRAIN AND CASSIE TSIRIS (Past Master and current Lodgemaster, respectively of TAHUTI Lodge) for inspiring me to finally tackle this book. I had tried for decades to make a record of my experiences with Marcelo Motta, Grady McMurtry, and the O.T.O. copyright battle of 1976 through 1985, but had succeeded in writing just two lonely pages. Cassie and James made clear that this history was my obligation.

The support that Donald and Yvonne Weiser of Ibis Press have demonstrated for this project has been especially humbling. I was twenty years old when I first met Donald. Little did we realize a lifetime friendship lay before us.

American philosopher Jeff Cooper wrote that, if one does not write something down, it never happened. Well, it happened. And here is the record.

I include the period beginning when I left home for college at age eighteen in 1966 to the death of Richard Gernon (Gurney) in 1989. I would have ended it at Grady McMurtry's death in 1985 for personal reasons that will become more obvious as this narrative proceeds. However, James and Cassie asked for more information about the early days of TAHUTI Lodge, especially Gurney's tenure as Lodgemaster and E.G.C. Bishop of New York City.

I pay my respects to Aleister Crowley. I don't think I've ever appreciated his Magical Diary practice more than when I had reached some 35,000 words of this manuscript from memory and realized I was helpless without the diary to identify proper sequencing. I had begun the diary practice in earnest in 1970 at Crowley's direction. This book would not have been possible without it.

Bill Heidrick compiled an extensive record of the documentation and evidence of Order history that was submitted to the courts. His efforts to assemble and preserve this history not only helped us win the crucial 1985 copyright court battle in California, but helped me to make this book more accurate. He also generously provided additional materials and reviewed, supplemented, and corrected my text.

Tony Iannotti did me the favor of accepting the box of my letters with Motta around 1990. It had sat with me for some fifteen years until I couldn't take it anymore and gave it to him for safekeeping. He graciously returned the letters at my request ten years later. They remained in the sealed box in which he gave them to me for another ten years before I finally opened them in July 2011. Tony returned more than I had given him, including depositions of mine, Motta, Grady, and Donald Weiser, along with additional material that Heidrick had assembled, including early letters between Karl Germer, Grady, Crowley, and others.

Dan Gunther has been invaluable in reviewing the Motta-period history. Dan and Gurney rushed out to California in 1976 in answer to my call for help after Grady and I had secured the Germer Library. We three took our Minerval initiation into O.T.O. together. Dan and I are the only two left from that beautiful evening. Both of us lived through much confusion and I so appreciate the ability to be able to discuss it with him.

I thank Bill Breeze for his decades of friendship and for helping me clarify a number of memories from our shared past, as well as the intricacies of our legal efforts. I remain an unashamed partisan in support of his leadership of O.T.O. this past quarter century. I don't think he's ever been unaware of either my disagreements or grousing about, but I think the length of both our friendship and my membership speaks volumes about my baseline opinion of him.

This is as thorough and honest a record of what happened as I can make it. There are obviously many personal experiences and individual practices not recorded in this book. I worked on building a regular set of spiritual exercises for decades. While I more often than not fell short of my goals, I kept at it. In Brazil in 1976, somewhat disillusioned by what I read in the diaries and correspondence of those who went before me, I wrote: "The secret must be in continuously increasing the Will to overcome the inertia of the flesh again & again & again & more." That was an accurate assessment.

I have never publicly spoken of these events before and have watched for years as lies, slanders, and inaccuracies were piled on top of each other by people who did not know what they were talking about, and whose hostility toward O.T.O. is palpable. I do not expect my detractors to believe everything written here. But I am the only living person who was there during the critical moment in July 1976 between Motta, Grady, and the Germer Library. I hope this record will be of assistance to future historians. I do not pretend to understand why I was chosen to play such a seminal role in the development of the modern Thelemic movement. But I was. The title of this book is neither an accident nor an afterthought. You may accept or reject this record as you will. It is the truth insofar as I am able to understand and express it.

This is also the story of the birth and early years of TAHUTI Lodge. TAHUTI is the second oldest O.T.O. lodge in the world, and the oldest to have experienced successful transitions of leadership and remain flourishing and functioning as a full-fledged operation. As the New York City lodge, we are at the crossroads of the civilized world. I look back at some of the overall New York occult scene during the 1970s, the New York O.T.O. prior to the founding of TAHUTI, my six years as TAHUTI Lodgemaster, and Gurney's leadership after me. Kent Finne picked up the mantle from Gurney at a crucial moment in the history of the lodge and that is discussed here as well.

Finally, I was a participant in the occult publishing renaissance of the 1970s—for which we have to thank Donald Weiser, Carl Weschke, Herman Slater, and their students and successors Ehud Sperling and David Young. These were the heady days when Crowley's books came flying off printing presses in the U.S. and U.K., along with the writings of Israel Regardie, Dion Fortune, Frater Achad, Kenneth Grant, Francis King, Stephen Skinner, and so many others.

The past is indeed another country. In order to get myself into the rhythm of recall and give the reader a sense of the times and who I was when these events transpired, I begin with some stories of my late adolescence and early twenties in Part One. Here is a tiny glance, through a series of vignettes, into a period in modern American history that seems long gone. I was part of a generation that lived with the ideals we learned from Jack Kerouac and his circle of friends and fellow writers. I read *On the Road* at thirteen and it was a major influence in my life thereafter.

A rapidly shifting intermixture of sacred and profane runs throughout these pages. Without the flow of the personal mixed with the spiritual and the historical, it would be an artificial creation. If one moment finds me poised on the edge of the empyrean and the next in a pratfall of comedic error, that's the way it happened. (I've often said, "I don't make the rules, I just work here.") To paraphrase Crowley's *Liber Aleph*, the paper on which this book is written is my skin and the ink my blood. There is a degree of self-exposure here that is way out of my comfort zone. However, I determined that, unless I was willing to share my life as my memory and diary reveal it, I would leave the reader no basis for the conclusions and criticisms I draw regarding Marcelo Motta and others. Similarly, in writing about TAHUTI Lodge history, my business efforts are often discussed. As a book designer and devotee of the Lord of the Word, it somehow fits.

Drugs and alcohol figure large in my story. They were long a part of my life that I have since moved beyond. Would that that had occurred earlier. My mind was opened by drugs. I turned on, tuned in, dropped out, and nearly killed myself in the process. I hope the opening of the psychic barriers of the post-WWII materialism of the 1950s culture that my generation helped advance—continuing the work of our beatnik progenitors in lightening the girders of the soul—has freed modern spiritual seekers from the need to damage their health and sanity as much as we did. If I have spent too much time detailing the last year of my drug use, I apologize in advance. Since it resulted in Gurney's death, it is important. I know it is ridiculous to hope that our story may serve as a warning to others—nonetheless I hope it does.

I have tried to respect the privacy of living friends who are not in the public eye or widely known as members of O.T.O. by using first names only. This is especially true of women friends and members of the Order. Throughout the text, I follow the convention of beginning each season at either the Equinox or the Solstice in my subheads; thus "Winter" includes both the Solstice and the New Year through the Spring Equinox. I have included a short glossary to clarify some terms in the text that will undoubtedly be unfamiliar to the general reader.

It is impossible to share the extent of the love and gratitude I feel for the many people and life experiences recorded here. I know there is also much negativity in the pages to follow. I only hope, on balance, that the reader will experience a stronger sense of optimism and inspiration—as I do.

Love is the law, love under will.

PART ONE

1966 TO 1973

✦

* * *

CHAPTER 1

ANTIOCH COLLEGE
AND THE WORLD OF THE SPIRIT

SUMMER 1966

WHEN I WAS A BOY OF EIGHT OR TEN, my parents took me to the Cafe Figaro at the corner of Macdougal and Bleecker Streets in Greenwich Village. I proclaimed that I wanted to be a beatnik, one childhood ambition I seem to have realized. When I visited Antioch College in Yellow Springs, Ohio during my high school college-search period, I was sold. Long hair and beards on the boys and the coolest looking girls I'd seen since Greenwich Village.

I met my cousin Paul during that visit. We had not known each other previously because of my parents' discomfort with his parents' overt Communist affiliation. While my parents had been Depression-era socialists, and later committed Roosevelt/Stevenson Democrats, they were not Communists. Paul's parents apparently were and my red-diaper baby cousin was a committed radical activist and SDS campus leader. Students for a Democratic Society, founded in 1960, was the most successful of the New Left groups of the decade. Its socialist ideology spread like wildfire on college campuses, fueled in large part by the unpopular war in Vietnam and the mandatory military draft. Carl Oglesby, to be mentioned later, served as president from 1965 to 1966.

Paul had trampled a flag, perhaps accidently, in a demonstration and gotten himself in some trouble at school. But I liked him.

He was bright and had a sense of humor. He introduced me to his friend Jeff Jones, a year younger than Paul and a year older than I. Jeff was another charismatic student who later became a fugitive in the violent Weather Underground. He would emerge decades later as an environmental activist and consultant to the New York State governor's office. Go figure.

I entered Antioch just after my high school graduation and eighteenth birthday in June 1966, chomping at the bit to get on with my life. I took a class from famed civil rights activist Larry Rubin. I liked him. Soft-spoken and humble, he carried the scars of the beatings he had received from Southern sheriffs. He opened up racial consciousness to white, middle-class kids who knew few blacks, and to black kids who knew few whites. I think we all learned a lot from him.

Antioch was set up on the quarter system as a five-year work/study program. Since I had entered in the summer quarter, I would go off to my first co-op job in the fall. A civil rights attorney named Bill Higgs came to campus to recruit. He was the last white lawyer working for SNCC, the Student Non-Violent Coordinating Committee. (Stokely Carmichael had proclaimed Black Power that spring.) Higgs had been a courageous civil rights activist and suffered greatly before leaving Mississippi, ca. 1963, to continue his work in Washington, D.C. During his inspiring talk, he asked for volunteers, promising room and board and $15 a week or something like that, and I leapt at the opportunity along with three or four other students.

That summer, I also smoked pot for the first time. Like many of the ideas and experiences of that period, pot was wrapped in a messianic mystique. It seemed a real path to Higher Consciousness. For me, it required several sessions to begin to get the more in-depth effect of the drug.

Jesse Colin Young and the Youngbloods came to campus for a concert that summer. It's difficult not to smile when considering the lyrics of their most popular song, which expressed the idealism and innocence of my generation to perfection: "Come on people, smile on your brother, everybody get together, try to love one another right now." A few short years after these touching sentiments were embraced and hymned by many thousands of flower-power advocates, a bomb-making factory located in a Greenwich Village townhouse exploded. Three Weathermen (named after Bob Dylan lyrics, "you don't need a weatherman to tell which way the wind blows") were killed, while several others—including Jeff Jones—fled into hiding for over a decade.

FALL 1966

I went to work for Bill Higgs in Washington, D.C. doing legal research at the Library of Congress. I met some of the real luminaries of the contemporary civil rights movement—including William Kunstler, whom I despised, and Fannie Lou Hamer, for whom I had a great deal of respect. Some of the people who walked through that door should have been in a zoo. I was becoming increasingly uncomfortable, realizing that I was essentially working to substitute one group of power-mad sociopaths for another. Things were going from bad to worse with Higgs. He was a depressive and totally disorganized in the food and money department. I started selling hot dogs and beer at the local football stadium to earn money to eat. One day, I had a rare conversation with him while we stopped in a park and sat on a bench together. I asked him if he was concerned that our efforts against the Vietnam War might really be helping the Communists as many people were saying. He told me that he didn't care and that he did not automatically reject Communism. I did.

During the summer of 1966, I had written a statement to my parents about my acceptance of socialism as a means of achieving social justice. I wrote them again to say that I now rejected politics as the way to improve the human condition. Instead, I believed the only true means of redeeming humanity and ending suffering was through individual spiritual development with meditation and inner-directed awareness. I left Higgs under less than ideal circumstances and went to visit friends at nearby St. John's College in Annapolis, Maryland—a small school devoted to a true classical education. At the time, it was inhabited by a lot of very brilliant potheads, many of whom would be expelled as the college sought to hold back the cultural tide of the Sixties.

WINTER 1966–1967

I returned to Antioch after the Christmas break and took one of the most important intellectual and philosophical excursions of my life with visiting professor Carl Oglesby. A past president of SDS, Oglesby was teaching a class on Existentialism called Absurdist Morality. We read Camus, Sartre, Borges, and De Sade. Oglesby was brilliant, if troubled. He described himself as a Marxist.

Oglesby posed a question for the class: Imagine we are given a personal audience with U.S. Secretary of State Dean Rusk, who tells us America is in Vietnam because of the resources it holds. Forget about stopping the spread of Communism or helping the people. It is simply about greed and power. We are there because we *can* be. The class assignment was to give Rusk one absolute moral principle to convince him we should withdraw. Well, I tried amphetamine that night for the first time, drinking it mixed in a glass of water. I stayed up all night pondering the assignment. I realized that, even though I knew what the "right" thing to do was, there was no absolute principle I could quote to Rusk that everyone agreed upon—one that could make an evil or cynical person do the right thing. It was that simple. Oglesby then took us to the next level by explaining that the Existentialist accepts this position of absurdity as a given, then decides on a moral principle for himself and lives his life passionately *as if* it were true. This has been my position ever since.

Later in that quarter, I took LSD for the first time with my good friend Brian Crawford. We read *The Joyous Cosmology* by Alan Watts at the more experienced Brian's suggestion. Brian was the quintessential long-haired hippie and something of an acid evangelist. I had some difficulty with the trip. Acid was a mixed blessing for me. While I took it several hundred times, I was never particularly comfortable. I did make continuous progress in self-awareness with the drug, but often at the cost of considerable personal agony. When I was offered STP by someone years later—smiling and telling me it was like a three-day acid trip—I shuddered and politely declined.

That winter, I met Dennis Deem, another significant character in this story who long remained a friend. (He died during the writing of this book.) Dennis was visiting from California and had some very pure acid. He dressed in a corduroy sport jacket with leather-patched elbows, carried a carved walking stick, and sported a beret atop a shaved head. I was intrigued. I left campus soon after for my co-op job in New York.

SPRING/SUMMER 1967

The next period at Antioch was made up of six-month stints, either at work or school, alternating each year. As I had entered in the summer quarter, my first double-quarter rotation was a work session. I was majoring in psychology and began working at Wiltwyck School for Boys, a residential treatment center for disturbed eight-to-fourteen-year-olds sent there by the courts. The boys could not be either homicidal or suicidal, but were otherwise a severely damaged bunch. Their personal stories of abuse were absolutely heartbreaking. The book *Manchild in the Promised Land* by Claude Brown describes the school. I was assigned to work with the chief psychiatrist, Dr. Mishikian, to write a paper on psychological defense mechanisms in order to help the counselors better understand the boys' often erratic behavior. I was also to pay particular attention to one extremely troubled boy named Julian, who had been institutionalized since the age of five.

Julian was a brilliant youngster who had just turned fourteen. The staff was concerned because he was becoming too old for the program. Julian and I did become friends quickly and talked about many things. Among these were his psychic powers. He had been at a dance, met a girl, and felt that they could communicate at a distance. I was a firm believer in such matters, with some little amount of experience at this time. The problem was that Julian was also deeply schizophrenic and prone to hallucinations. It was a fine line, but I was honest with him. I unfortunately lost touch with him after I left Wiltwyck.

I was living in an apartment on Jones Street and West 4th in Greenwich Village with three fellow Antioch student roommates. One worked at *Newsweek,* another at *Time,* and the third at Wiltwyck with me.

I saw the Fugs, one of the all-time great bands, at the Players Theater on Macdougal Street. They represented a transition between the beat and hippie phenomena. Ed Sanders and Tuli Kupferberg ran the Peace Eye Bookstore on the Lower East Side and were involved in *The East Village Other* underground newspaper. Many years later, I found myself riding in the same subway car as Tuli and reflected on just how much I loved living in New York. (Many years after that, in 1992, Ed Sanders and Tuli Kupferberg, along with Allen Ginsberg, Peter Orlovsky, and other bohemian luminaries, would attend the Gnostic Mass we performed to honor Harry Smith at Saint Mark's Church.) During that long-ago summer, I sat no more than fifteen feet from the stage when Jerry Garcia and the Grateful Dead played at the small and intimate club, The Bitter End on Bleecker Street.

On my nineteenth birthday, I took a very strong acid trip. I was accompanied by my friend Charlie, who was deeply involved in psychology. Charlie was a brilliant but extremely neurotic person with many deep-seated conflicts. He was my "guide" for the trip, but was really more like a babysitter protecting me from the urban environment of New York City than a Leary-like leader through the byways of LSD. There was an underlying tension between us concerning his girlfriend, Jean. She and I had met at school the previous summer and there was a mutual attraction. But we had each gone off to our co-op jobs and she had hooked up with Charlie.

Charlie and I wandered around the Village—me in a rather ecstatic positive state, possibly wearing on his nerves as I proclaimed my newfound birthday unity with the cosmos. We entered a tourist head shop and I saw a distorted glass novelty Coca-Cola bottle. It set off a paranoid reaction because it mimicked reality in an unnerving way. My state of joy darkened. We left the store and began walking down the street. Things grew worse. Every aspect of the street began to repeat itself in my perception. I began to feel as if I were in an endless loop and would never get off that street—with the same people forever passing me in both directions.

We returned to my apartment. Everyone was gone. Charlie and I walked into the kitchen. My fear was growing out of all proportion. He tried to help me analyze it. That only seemed to deepen it. We discussed it as fear itself, rather than as fear "of." At one point, I was leaning against the stove, with my back pressed to it and hands placed behind me gripping the edge. I fell. The logical explanation is that I slipped, but I am not sure that is what happened. I believe I was in so much terror that I ceased to believe in the solidity of matter. If that is true, it would not be technically inaccurate. Matter is made up of atoms and molecules separated by relatively enormous distances. Reality is a common agreement between each of us and three-dimensionality. I believe I may have entered a state of cellular consciousness in which my agreement with reality was momentarily superseded by my fear. The many stories in mystic literature of people who walk through walls is exactly what I think happened to me—the drug and the fear substituting for the firmly disciplined, calm concentration necessary to achieve that state on purpose.

After that trip, I moved out of the communal apartment and took a place by myself on 7th Street between Avenues C and D, a sixth-floor walk-up. The Lower East Side was a part of town that was definitely not the gentrified neighborhood it is today. My rent was $46.75 a month—bathtub in the kitchen with a living room and bedroom. As I was lugging my cartons of books up the stairs, a neighbor named Junky George asked why I kept books I had already read. How often I've reflected on that question! He was part of a scene that turned the disappearing remnants of the middle-class kid from New Jersey on his ear. I remember George standing in front of a mirror picking at his face with a Bowie knife when his jacket parted to reveal a revolver tucked in his waistband.

My new neighbors included Leo, a long-haired Puerto Rican, living with Janie, a leather-jacketed, hard-edged woman with an infectious laugh that melted her roughness. And I won't forget

Rita, who used to be Ronnie, walking into Leo's apartment one day and offering anyone a case of the clap with which she had just been diagnosed. Adam, an efficient dealer and student from the University of Colorado in Boulder, was another member of the scene whom I would meet again in Boulder. He seemed to hover above the turbulence that engulfed his many customers.

It was an amphetamine universe with opiates liberally thrown in the mix. One day, I was in Leo's apartment and he was in a fury trying to find a vein to inject himself. The scene was so appalling and incoherent that I can only defer to the memory of anyone who has ever witnessed anything like it. It is virtually impossible to describe the chaos. In any case, Leo's ordeal went on for over an hour. Finally, he achieved his goal. An older black junky named Brother John stood near him with a calm look on his face and a melodious richness in his voice. He gave an approving nod, and intoned: "Drive on in, Brother, drive on in."

I was terrified of needles in that spider-to-fly modality. I arranged to get the materials together to inject myself for the first time, having carefully observed the technique. I did it alone in the kitchen at the Jones Street apartment. The horror reversed into obsession.

One night, when I was tripping alone in my apartment, I heard a sound at the door. I opened it to see the diminutive but beautiful Barbara, wearing a black-and-white dress with a huge black hat on her head. She told me she was just passing by (on the sixth floor!). I invited her in and we spoke for hours. The acid angel left, but I felt much affection for her. She was intimately entwined with the Andy Warhol crowd at the Factory on St. Mark's Place. I learned that she had been a student at Antioch. She was deeply involved with amphetamines. I developed a very protective sense toward her. I invited her to return to Antioch with me as my work/study period was nearing its close, but she did not come.

FALL 1967

This was an especially pivotal period. I was assigned to a very small college dorm off campus in Marshall Hall, a student residence more like a private house. Brian and I were roommates. This quarter was particularly laced with drugs, women, and spiritual seeking. School was simply off the radar. Brian and I were good friends and equally committed to the psychedelic lifestyle. We were very different philosophically, in that he was and is a committed atheist, and we aired our differences constantly (we still do although less frequently).

This was long before the scourge of AIDS brought an end to the free and open sexual experimentation of that long-ago era. The conjoining of sexuality and psychedelics opened the early stages of what I would later begin to understand as sexual magick. The expansion of consciousness beyond the boundaries of the ego was the first key.

An unusual group of students and non-students came together, all of us committed to spiritual seeking, drugs—particularly amphetamines and LSD—and what we perceived as the personal messages in Bob Dylan's newly released album *John Wesley Harding*. The critical messenger was a traveler named Jesse. He looked so much like Dylan that I introduced him as such to several people on campus who believed it. He was a heavy amphetamine user and the first vegetarian I'd ever met. I became a vegetarian through his influence and have remained so.

Jesse had a pure energy that surrounded him with a mysterious aura, an inner kindness, and sincerity. I have no diaries from this early period so it is hard to be more specific, but he had an aerial quality about him—thin, otherworldly, as if not fully present in three dimensions, wise beyond his years. There was also some delusion, as I remember him describing the band Pearls Before Swine as a cryptic musical group led by an old speed freak who anonymously dropped off their first album at a record company. I learned instead, decades later, that the leader was a young guy who ultimately became a lawyer.

Jesse also had an ego. We went shopping for boots in New York City once and I learned that he was very particular about his image. Yet he is the first person in my life I can clearly identify as my spiritual teacher. Jesse manifested the dying god archetype. Dylan's lines, "And picking up Angel who just arrived here from the Coast/Who looked so fine at first but left looking just like a ghost," describe him perfectly. I never even learned his last name and wonder how long he lived after he left Yellow Springs.

Susan was an important elder within our group. She was a full-blown psychic who had had a terrible accident as a child and been blinded for a time. The experience opened her inner vision. She was the most developed medium I have known. Dennis was the Magus, deeply involved with Aleister Crowley and obsessed with Yoga and Qabalah. He taught me mechanical drawing or drafting, which we would do for hours at a time while on methedrine. The drugs were so pure it was ridiculous.

Claire was sixteen. She had run away from home (although her parents lived in town) and was living with Dennis. While she was painfully shy, an occasional disarming smile would escape her disquiet. She has since grown into a woman of great character, courage, and resilience, and is one of the most important people in my life. Her brother, Louis, was a master guitarist. He once confided that he used self-hypnosis to learn to play along with Jimi Hendrix albums. He is the best guitarist I have known.

I don't believe I had ever heard of Crowley before meeting Dennis in February 1967. The only Crowley book that was even reasonably available back then was the Castle edition of *Magick in Theory and Practice*. Everything else had yet to be reprinted or was limited to the rare-book market and/or specialty occult bookstores like Samuel Weiser's in New York City. The foundation for the Crowley resurgence was being laid, however, as Jerry Kay of Xeno Publications put out an edition of *The Book of the Law* in 1967 and the Beatles included Crowley's photo on the cover of their *Sgt. Pepper's Lonely Hearts Club Band* album. The Crowley floodgates really began to open in 1969, when John Symonds and Kenneth Grant released their edition of *The Confessions* and it was reviewed in *The New York Times Book Review*. In that same year, Weiser's published Crowley's bestselling study of the Tarot, *The Book of Thoth*, which was the precursor for a slew of additional reprints released in 1970 and subsequently.

I read Herman Hesse's *Siddhartha* around this period and learned about the Bodhisattva Vow. In essence, one swears to reject the fruits of one's own spiritual labor—personal liberation or Nirvana—until every blade of grass is prepared to achieve Enlightenment as well. I was determined to take it properly.

Another obsession that later bore fruit was my desire to become a Roman Catholic priest. Now this was really weird, because, first, I was Jewish—a faith with no recent tradition of either priests or communion—and, second, I was and am so far from believing in Christ and Catholicism it is a joke. I couldn't understand the apparently absurd desire, however, nor could I rid myself of it. A dozen years later, I became a priest of the Gnostic Catholic Church (E.G.C.), with which I have been passionately involved ever since.

I was exposed to A. E. Waite's book, *The Pictorial Key to the Tarot* at this time.

I went on a New York City drug-buying run from Yellow Springs during that fall quarter. I had told some lunatic—I don't remember how I met him—that I could help him score through Leo and Janie. During the drive, I learned that he had brought a gun with him. I was terribly disturbed, but there was nothing I could do. Fortunately, it all worked out peaceably. While waiting for the deal to be set up, I ran into Barbara. I again suggested that she come live with me and said I would try to help her clean up. (I'm sure there is a note of irony here, but I was dead serious about rescuing her.) She said she might stop by Leo and Janie's later. I did some heroin while waiting for the deal to conclude. Janie told me afterward that Barbara did come by to speak with me, but I was passed out from junk. This plagued me for years; it still does. I finally saw her on the street nearly a decade later. We spoke for a short time and she appeared to be doing well. But something was lost because of my unavailability that night.

Back at school, a non-student who had been released from a mental institution was brought to Brian's and my room to beg for drugs. We shared some with him and he later came back and stole the rest. As angry as this made us, we were lucky. An undercover narcotics agent named Tony was trolling the campus for what would become a huge drug bust. He was the roommate of a friend of ours—the nicest kid, quite straight. Tony asked him, as a favor, to help him buy some grass. They came to our room together. We told them we had just been robbed and couldn't help. The narc busted our friend later, after he helped find some other kids with pot. It was a travesty. Over thirty students were arrested. What part of private, non-violent behavior do these busybodies not understand? I was not saddened to learn that "Tony" was killed some years later in a drug deal gone bad in California. Apparently he had found some real criminals.

I remember one day looking out over my fellow students in the cafeteria and realizing that my use of drugs was not normal, even for the drug-besotted Sixties culture and bohemian Antioch campus. I attempted to attend a class like a normal college student, but rushed out in the middle to throw up from dope. Ultimately, I decided to drop out of all my fall 1967 classes and just repeat the quarter. Walking over to the administration offices to withdraw, I learned that school had already been closed for a week for the Christmas break.

My brother came to pick me up for the vacation. On the way home, I had a psychotic break from amphetamines. I experienced a state of complete disassociation and depersonalization, in which I narrated a third-person biography of myself to my brother, including my choice of parents and natal family, early experiences, and subsequent life events all leading up to the car ride we were on. As unusual as this was, it was part of a continuum of out-of-the-ordinary experiences of the time, and I do not remember doing anything more than reflecting on it (as I still do). A decade later, Grady McMurtry gave me copies of some of Jack Parsons' writings, including a paper called "Analysis by a Master of the Temple of the Critical Nodes in the Experience of His Magical Vehicle." My eyes almost popped out of my head when I read it, because it mirrored the mysterious event that had happened during the hours of that drive from Yellow Springs to Youngstown. (I do not pretend to understand what either his or my experience meant, but Parsons' text is included in the appendices.)

Winter 1967–1968

I don't remember much of what happened during the Christmas vacation at home. I took my next co-op job at the Antioch bookstore, feeling way too raw to uproot myself and leave Yellow Springs again for three months. While working at the cash register, I met Mary. A pretty student, she was quite nervous. We'd have these funny interactions in which she would pay and drop her money and I would drop her change. One thing led to another and we began living together, my first experience with that depth of relationship. Then all of us in the group mentioned above came down with serum hepatitis for obvious reasons. The campus doctor explained that, fortunately, we were not contagious, save through further misbehavior with needles, so Mary was safe.

I went home to my parents and entered the hospital. I had an interesting experience with Jean, now Charlie's ex-girlfriend. I woke in the night in the hospital room and saw her flying through the window in the exact form of a Ba spirit (although I did not know this until years later when exploring Egyptian iconography). I phoned her in the morning and she told me she had been writing a late-night letter to me while listening to an album I had given her— *Changes* by Jim and Jean. The attending physician despised me as a "dirty hippie"—the generational culture war being in full bloom by 1968. He wrote my draft board assuming it was his patriotic duty to keep me out of the army and I received a 1Y classification. Mary dropped out of school and came to live at my parents' home during my convalescence.

CHAPTER 2

ON THE ROAD

SPRING 1968

RECEIVING A CLEAN BILL OF HEALTH, I accompanied Mary to her mother's house in northern New Jersey. Mother Joan was a gardener with a green thumb. Among the lush and exotic plants in her garden were some very rare oriental poppies. I would go out early in the morning to scrape the top of the plants and then head to work as a car-stereo installer at Gem Electronics, drilling holes for speakers in doors and bolting 4- and 8-track tape decks into customers' cars. Then home to my now-dried, if rather weak, opium.

After a couple of months, we headed off to Boulder, Colorado on our way farther west. Mary and I lived in a closet in a house on Marine Street with some students from the university and some non-students. We both read Leonard Cohen's *Beautiful Losers*. The book has a complex and confusing ending. One day, puzzling over it in my bed in the closet, I felt a personal merging with Cohen's consciousness, a theophany of sorts, in which I understood that he had subtly merged the two main characters into a composite figure. It was an extraordinary act of literary virtuosity.

I reconnected with Adam, the dealer mentioned earlier from the Lower East Side. While visiting his house in a small mountain town outside Boulder, we met and smoked some excellent grass with folksinger Judy Collins and musician Stephen Stills. I'm afraid I acted inconsiderately with her. She had recorded many of Leonard Cohen's songs. I camouflaged my natural sense of intimidation at meeting such a famous celebrity by questioning her about Cohen, while pretending that meeting her was not as significant to me as it actually was. If I had been able to be more honest, I would have told her how much I loved her work and how honored I was to meet her and Stephen Stills, and then politely tried to satisfy my obsessive curiosity.

Summer 1968

After a few months in Boulder—which had a more homogenous population of tanned, blond, healthy-looking white people than I had ever seen—we were on our way to San Francisco. I remember being really high on some powerful grass at a Black Panther rally in Golden Gate Park soon after we arrived. (The Panthers were a revolutionary organization of the late 1960s and 70s. They initially appeared to be a civil rights group proclaiming Black Power as a necessary consciousness-raising ideology for blacks. However, they either degenerated into, or revealed themselves as, a violent Maoist Communist movement.) When I "came to," I found myself raising my fist in the famous Black Panther salute, yelling "F*ck you, Alioto" with the rest of the mob. I realized in a flash that Jewish people should not be mimicking the National Socialist salute on general principles, that publicly cursing was really distasteful behavior, and that I had no idea who Alioto was, other than that he was the mayor of the city I had just come to visit. My knee-jerk left-wing political participation, such as it was, came to a screeching halt at that moment. On the other hand, the end of my time in San Francisco coincided with the election of Richard Nixon as president. I remember learning of his victory from a radio broadcast and becoming aware of a sense of complete alienation.

We were staying with a college friend of Mary's in the Fillmore District. I ran into an old friend of mine, a former lover from the Lower East Side who had visited me at Antioch. Coming by to see her one day, I walked into her apartment during a robbery and was ripped off by a black burglar. I resisted. He grabbed a piece of wood and struck me in the head. Luckily it turned out to be driftwood.

I was exposed to Scientology. Someone approached me on the street and asked if I wanted to take a personality test. It turned out to be a modified Minnesota Multiphasic Personality Inventory

(MMPI) with Scientology's own method of scoring. After the test, they showed a vanilla film of L. Ron Hubbard that became tedious, so I got up to leave. Someone grabbed hold of me and, after my saying I wasn't interested in pablum, brought me to a small office where I met a woman named Janice. She was about to join the Sea Org, the inner corps of the group that lived on ships and pledged their souls to Hubbard's work. She went over a fascinating chart of the Scientology system of attainment, which struck me as thorough and intelligent. (I later learned of the extraordinary influence Crowley had in the development of Hubbard's thought.) I told her I would join and was taken to the Morals Officer. He went through a song and dance about drugs. I explained that I was willing to quit in order to start the program, but that I had one joint of exceptional marijuana that I had saved for months and would be sharing with Charlie when I went home. He said I couldn't start classes. I told him fine, I'd do it in New York. He was very displeased. Janice was powerless to intervene. Pot saved me from Scientology.

FALL/WINTER 1968–1969

I was experiencing a mysterious cycle of repeating dreams. I was part of a group, centered around Dennis, that was working to spread enlightenment. There was a sense that I was an apostle of a new revelation that would help heal humanity. Although it seemed to challenge whatever remnants of common sense I may still have enjoyed, the dreams went on for months. I knew I needed to go to Portland and see Dennis and Claire.

Before we left San Francisco, a mescaline deal with the folks in Colorado and a former Antioch student with whom I had reconnected in San Francisco went bad. While my memory of the details is really vague, no one was happy. I mention it because it became a key mental component of the nervous breakdown that was looming on my horizon.

Mary and I traveled on to Portland, Oregon to visit Dennis and Claire. They had moved there after leaving Yellow Springs. Claire had just given birth to a beautiful baby girl named Dioanna (God's grace), who was ten days old when we arrived. Although Claire was being a conscientious nursing mom after a difficult delivery, Dennis' enthusiasm for drugs was uninterrupted by domestic tranquility. We embarked on a week-long acid/speed run together. Dennis suggested that shooting the acid by-passed the anxiety of waiting for it to come on, so I tried that, mixing it with speed and flying high. I remember looking into the bowl of a pipe and seeing a perfect M. C. Escher-style scene. I tried to draw it in his style, but learned that perception is not technique.

This visit included a blindingly accurate telepathic communication with Dennis that we confirmed in conversation six months later. He had company in the dining room. I was sitting in the living room. I mentally perceived him communicating with me, precisely along the lines of my series of dreams. He explained that there was a group of people charged with altering consciousness and that I was one of them. He informed me that he was the most advanced of our group and needed help in projecting the message. For my part, my task was to help accumulate books and make myself available as necessary. There had been talk of establishing a commune on a piece of land owned by another friend from Antioch. I was blown away by the confirmation of my dream cycle and barged into the next room, interrupting his meeting. We went into the bathroom, the closest private space available. I blurted out: "Have you been talking to me in my head?" He replied: "Yes." I answered: "I cannot do it yet." I would do what I could, but I had other commitments that prevented me from remaining in Portland, including Mary.

Things were not going well with her. We were under a lot of stress. She rejected my messianic calling, among other things, and we were bickering. She threatened to leave. I had warned her that if she made that particular threat one more time, we would be finished. While we stood on the threshold of Dennis and Claire's apartment, the psychic form of Dennis enveloped my own and I held firm to my position. We split up then and there, but I accompanied her home.

* * *

CHAPTER 3

ON THE MEND

WINTER 1968–1969 (CONTINUED)

Mᴀʀʏ ᴀɴᴅ I ᴡᴇɴᴛ ʙᴀᴄᴋ ᴛᴏ Nᴇᴡ Jᴇʀsᴇʏ and I returned her to her parents. A really embarrassing incident occurred at the picnic table with her father and his new wife and family. I repeated something that had already been said, thereby revealing my damaged mental state. Mary and I were quite a pair. We both had bleeding sores and she had anemia. I made haste for my parents' home to hide out and began working the midnight-to-8 ᴀ.ᴍ. shift at my father's factory.

I underwent a complete mental breakdown. I was seized with paranoia. Beginning on the plane ride to New Jersey from either Boulder or San Francisco, I was either seeing or hallucinating federal agents following me because of the mescaline deal gone bad. I was suffering guilt over Mary's condition and reeling from the drug excesses, the psychic events with Dennis, and the abrupt and inept transition to the vegetarian diet of the past year. I spent two weeks crawling on the floor in front of the windows of the house during the day when my parents were at work, ultimately making a failed suicide attempt. My parents were rightly irritated by that, but solicitous. They did not want to commit me to a mental hospital, but allowed me to heal at home. I was a little put out by that decision but, in the long run, it was a blessing. My worst thought today is of my father or mother being forced to find me dead. What was I thinking? I took a trip to Kent State to visit my brother. It would be the scene of the National Guard shooting of the students the following year.

SPRING 1969

Working in my father's factory, I began getting better. I decided to take a remedial math class in an effort to regain my cognitive powers. I visited Dennis and Claire in New Rochelle at Claire's parents' house. They both gave a verbal confirmation of the entire psychic conversation that Dennis and I had had in Portland, the subject of the previous months of dreams. Dennis asked me to buy a copy of Crowley's *Liber 777* from Weiser's Bookstore. I passed on a first edition after Donald Weiser explained some of the nuances of the rare book market and informed me that Weiser's was in the process of preparing a more affordable reprint. I believe I got my copy of the Dove Press edition of *Diary of a Drug Fiend* at this time. It inspired me for many more years to seek fruitlessly to master drugs—as the real-life Crowley apparently never did either. (Bibliographies list the Dove Press reprint as published in 1970, but my memory is of getting it earlier. I could be wrong. The book itself does not carry a publication date.)

I saw Tim Buckley play in a small venue in Philadelphia. He was in real bad shape—stoned, frustrated, and angry. When he died some years later at age twenty-eight, I was saddened but not surprised. I went up to New York to visit a girlfriend and see The Band play at the Fillmore East. I took so much mescaline that I perceived Garth Hudson as God, sitting at the drums with his long beard and illuminated by the stage lights.

SUMMER 1969

I read Crowley's *Magick in Theory and Practice* for the first time. I had little intellectual familiarity with occult literature or the language of Qabalah. I read it cover to cover, most aware that I had understood very little, but that it contained extraordinary value nonetheless. I immediately reread it cover to cover. Although I had been a voracious reader since earliest childhood, this was the first time I had done that.

The book seemed ever-so-slightly more comprehensible the second time. Crowley makes a statement on page 23 about Hé Final being "the Throne of the Spirit, of the Shin of Pentagrammaton." I seized on that for some reason, completely baffled by the term "Pentagrammaton." I spent hours and hours one night reading, drawing, trying to understand it. I had taken amphetamines, making my quest that much more obsessive. Finally, I grokked the formula of YHShVH. Exulted by the discovery, I made an interior demand that Crowley appear to me, as I had "earned" the right to meet him by the intensity of my efforts and the success I achieved. And He appeared to me. I was so stunned. I was breathless and speechless. And the Master's laughter rang through my psyche, good-naturedly mocking and simultaneously inviting. Though amphetamines were involved, my experience was as real as the keyboard on which I now soberly type these reminiscences.

I took a class on Shakespeare at Glassboro State College, meeting the beautiful and seductive Almuth. I had a dream in which I learned of Crowley's Tarot book, *The Book of Thoth*. I drove up to New York to Weiser's and discovered that the elegant Weiser reprint had just arrived from the printer the day before. I also bought *The Equinox of the Gods*. Samuel Weiser had worked with Karl Germer in the late 1950s to bind up the remaining press sheets of Crowley's 1936 publication. My car was towed that day—an entry fee of some sort perhaps.

I drove up to the Woodstock rock festival for a day with my friend Claus. He had been an exchange student from Denmark in our senior year of high school. Although we have somehow lost touch, I still consider him one of my oldest friends. His girlfriend came with us, and, apparently, so did Mary. After our painful breakup, she had enrolled in the University of Colorado and had come back East for the summer. I went to see The Band, hoping Bob Dylan might show up. When the crowd started rudely calling for Dylan to appear, I knew that would never happen. I remember Joe Cocker playing in the rain—surrounded by masses of wires, cords, and cables—just blasting out his songs in a stoned state of ecstasy that must have driven a host of his more practical-minded managers crazy. For my part, I got so high circulating among the crowd of psychedelic revelers that I did not remember Mary having been there with me until she told me when we met up again some twenty years later.

FALL/WINTER 1969–1970

I visited Youngstown, Ohio to see my friend Danny. (My family had moved to Youngstown for my senior year of high school and Danny and I met at my after-school job.) A young woman named Karen was visiting Danny's wife. The four of us took a powerful acid trip together. I was shocked to learn that Karen was pregnant. An article had come out recently warning against taking LSD during pregnancy. But I felt we called a spirit to her baby. (Crowley believed the soul came in around the sixth month of pregnancy and the timing was close.) I offered to help her through the birth. She accompanied me back to New Jersey and we rented an apartment. My parents were horrified.

At the time, I had this beautiful 1962 MGA 1600 MK II, the last and best of the A series. It was painted British racing green. It had a hand crank for emergency starts. The night the baby was born, the car refused to start, with or without the crank, and we borrowed a neighbor's more sensible VW Bug. I felt the car had a spirit and did not like the competition. I named the baby Daemon Rainer, inspired by Rainer Maria Rilke's *Letters to a Young Poet*. Brian visited us. He and Karen enjoyed a natural warmth that somehow eluded Karen and me. We were woefully unsuited to each other and there were a lot of confused feelings between us. The baby was a distraction from our problems, but a problem of his own. However, I had fulfilled my promise to help her through the birth.

I began to keep a regular Magical Diary at this time.

SPRING 1970

I worked a second job at Arby's fast-food restaurant to earn the extra money to travel. (I had worked for them in high school.) My typical day's routine began with a midnight-to-8 A.M. shift at my father's plastics factory, a very dirty job. I would leave work and head to a country-and-western bar for a few drinks, then home to shower and do a hit of speed, then off to Arby's. The restaurant offered to make me assistant manager—which, under the circumstances, is rather funny. But we were westward bound.

SUMMER 1970

On my birthday, I took a powerful psilocybin trip with an intense invocation of Adonai. In July, I saw Leonard Cohen perform in Forest Hills, New York. He played *Joan of Arc* before it was released on *Songs of Love and Hate* the next spring. It was an outdoor concert and the sky was overcast, threatening rain. Cohen came out on the stage and began the evening with a Hebrew benediction. The sky cleared and was absolutely gorgeous for the remainder of his extraordinary performance.

Chapter 4

Portland and the "Abbey of Thelema"

Summer/Fall 1970

Karen, the baby, and I went on to Antioch at the beginning of September, visiting Brian and Mark Tranum. Mark was another school friend, a handsome psychonaut from the Virgin Islands with a curiously flat affect. He later died too young, a casualty of his battle with drugs. Karen and I were absolutely crashing and burning as a couple. We split up, and she and Brian got together for a time.

We were all staying on a farm just outside Yellow Springs. I met Marianne there. She was a deeply intelligent, spiritually aware woman and I was completely taken with her. I read *The Book of the Law* in *The Equinox of the Gods* for the first time. I had taken acid and sat in a field reading. A huge hawk swooped down close to my head at the verse: "I am Ra-Hoor-Khuit; and I am powerful to protect my servant" (AL III:42). I discussed Crowley at length with Marianne.

We met a local couple named Steve and Linda who owned a very rare, full set of *The Equinox*. They were a real inspiration as older and more knowledgeable Thelemites. Kind and generous, they allowed me to make extensive copies for Dennis. I explained to Marianne that Dennis was a qualified teacher and a suitable guide for the next stage of what was now our mutual spiritual journey.

We visited New Jersey so Marianne could meet my parents before we got married. We also made a stop at Weiser's, buying a first edition of the Germer/Motta printing of *Liber Aleph,* which I treasured and carried all over the U.S. I also bought a copy of the newly released Weiser reprint of *Liber 777,* the Dove Press edition of *Moonchild,* and a number of other magical texts, intending to share them with Dennis.

Marianne and I were married in Yellow Springs on the fifth of October. My rambunctious MGA played another prank on me. We were staying at a professor's house where the ceremony was scheduled. There was a fence around the property with a gate. I parked the car to open the gate and it started rolling toward me. I jumped out of the way and laughed. A sports car, to be a real sports car, must either have, or be capable of being imbued with, a soul.

A week later we began our drive to Portland, having been given a huge ball of opium as a wedding gift. We met "The Rifleman" in Utah after pulling off the highway because the mescaline we had taken was making the bugs smashing against the windshield too unpleasant. The Rifleman was hitchhiking east with his 7mm Mauser. He would hide the rifle in the bushes and grab it when a car stopped to pick him up. I made a fabulous shot with it and began to be concerned that our new buddy was off his rocker and might be angered by my good fortune in marksmanship. But he bested the shot, to my relief, and, after several hours in his questionable company, we left.

We drove on to Portland and joined Dennis and Claire. While it was a joy to see them again, there was a growing sense of disappointment. Dennis had assumed a drunken-blues-musician persona, replacing his earlier guru-yogi persona. What we found there was far removed from the expectations that had brought us to Portland. After some weeks living together in their apartment, we all moved to a nice large house on Prescott Street, where we attempted to establish an Abbey of Thelema. Marianne shot drugs for the first time.

Saint Martin the Black

Marty Black lived with us at Prescott Street. He was a friend of Dennis and Claire's and was soon to become one of the people I would care for most in my life. He was a visionary poet and an artistic soul, in whom an inner light balanced a ferocious hunger for drugs. I knew his parents and brother and they were all good people. Marty was unique, and his drug-related death in the mid-1990s saddened me. We never had the chance to renew our friendship across the 3,000-mile barrier that would separate us after 1971.

Marianne and I started doing the Solar Adorations of *Liber Resh vel Helios,* the Lesser Banishing Ritual of the Pentagram, Asana, Pranayama, and other practices, including extensive intellectual work with the Tree of Life and Qabalistic correspondences. I sought for a magical motto and came up with: "Let Shine the Light." I was pleased with its similarity to the formula of LAShTAL that I was studying in *Magick in Theory and Practice.* I took acid to "test" the motto. I became very paranoid and decided it was too weak to be effective. I remembered Brother John's words to Leo back on 7th Street and Avenue D: "Drive on in, Brother, drive on in." I took the magical motto: "Drive On In."

I shaved my head and awoke with a cold. At this point, the whole drug issue was becoming ugly enough to cause real conflict. One night when our car was not working, we wanted amphetamines. We made one of those famous agreements that we would walk to a certain spot on the road in an attempt to hitchhike to the score scene some miles away. If we had gotten a ride by that point, we would accept it as "God's will" that we get high. If not, we would turn back and assume the Universe did not want us to do so. Naturally, what followed was that a complete stranger not only stopped to pick us up, he drove us to the score scene, waited, and then drove us back to the house.

Marty disappeared for several days on an amphetamine odyssey and returned with bloody bare feet, filthy and incoherent. I gave him a barbiturate and prayed that he be able to sleep. This is the first time I remember praying for another person. Thankfully, he slept.

The local grocer refused to cash an out-of-town check, leaving us without food for Dioanna. He cut off one of his fingers in a slicing machine the next day.

John and Merrie

John and Merrie Hodges were two talented and troubled junky artists, into Anton LaVey and the Church of Satan. I don't recall exactly how we met, but we enjoyed a friendship with them. Our relationship allowed some escape from the pressure cooker that was Prescott Street. We also did heroin together. Their primary dealer was an old black junky named Three-Fingered Sam. We were at his house one day when the Portland police showed up to collect their regular graft payment. It was a very dark scene.

Winter 1970–1971

Marianne's birthday was March 1 and March 5 was our six-month wedding anniversary. We embarked on a five-day celebration that occasioned Marianne's famous line, "Let's put this head on another body and continue," just before we collapsed into sleep.

Steve and Linda arrived from Yellow Springs, shocked by the degenerate scene they found at Prescott Street. Between the drugs, alcohol, food stamps, and unemployment, we were living a lifestyle perhaps less than appropriate for the spiritual luminaries we were trying to become. I am ashamed to admit that I was shoplifting during this period, exploring my value system. I soon came to realize that "Thou shalt not steal" was as true in my life as it was for Moses.

We drove to San Francisco to visit Marianne's family and see Claire's brother, Louis. On the way back to Portland, we stopped at Mount Shasta in Northern California, the Holy Mountain. We did a ritual there, left an offering of pot, and performed the Sunset Adoration from *Liber Resh* and a banishing ritual. We experienced the awesome archetypal power of the mountain.

Spring 1971

Dennis and Marty's friend, Tony Williams, was released from prison, where we had sent him an LSD-soaked drawing some months earlier. (One can only imagine what it would be like to take acid in prison.) Tony was a case study in contradiction. A talented poet and artist, he was dark and dishonest. Many years later, in 1985, when I had become Grand Secretary General of the O.T.O., he wrote me from prison, where he was again incarcerated. He excused his drug and crime-ridden life with comparisons to Crowley. I never answered him. I learned some years later of his premature drug-related death.

The domestic scene began to wear Marianne and me down. The Prescott Street "Abbey" disbanded and we took an apartment in downtown Portland. Some inheritance money came to Marianne and we bought a Jeep—an unfortunate move, as it began to bleed us of money for repairs and was not nearly as much fun to drive as I had anticipated. Dennis, Claire, and Dioanna moved to a farm owned by Claire's boss at a music school. Their duties were to do repairs and cleaning. It was a gorgeous property with no electricity or running water. Steve and Linda split up. Steve went off with his new girlfriend and Linda and Marty rented an apartment together.

The Death of John and Merrie

John and Merrie got themselves into deep trouble. John was arrested while shoplifting a flashlight for his grandmother and faced jail time for violating his probation on a high school pot-possession charge. They decided to commit suicide. They gave us their unfinished Winged Disk, a beautiful work of art done in chalk on a painted white board some four feet in width. (The visionary artist Linda Gardner restored and completed the Winged Disk, circa 1993, using the egg tempera technique she learned from Viennese artist Ernst Fuchs. It is displayed on the back cover of this book and has hung over the mantle in the many places I've lived since they gave it to me.)

We "helped" John and Merrie in an effort to gain time to talk them out of killing themselves. I even drove John to his parents' house to get a pistol. They were staying at our apartment. We worked frantically to find and suggest alternative plans to suicide. We phoned Louis and arranged with him to drive them to San Francisco so they could safely leave town, but they refused.

Finally, they wanted to be taken to the Oregon coast after a visit to Three-Fingered Sam. They would go to a motel, do "one last hit," then kill themselves. We dropped them off and were sorely tempted to call the police to arrest them and prevent their suicide. But we decided they were free to do what they chose, even if we disagreed. We realized that if we did call the police to "save" them, John would be put in prison—exactly what they were seeking to avoid. We were fully aware that we would live with the consequences of our decision for the rest of our lives.

Days later, John and Merrie returned to Portland very much alive and spent the night. We awoke to find they had stolen Marianne's cameras and my leather jacket. We hurried to the pawn shop and found them on the street. This was getting tedious. Steve called a day or two later to announce that he had heard a radio report of their deaths. The next morning's newspaper reported that they had been found dead in our apartment building basement by our eighty-year-old super. We were angry at them for violating our trust and bringing down heat, let alone traumatizing the old man. I went down to the basement and discovered a very tiny piece of flesh left by the police forensic team. I ate it without even thinking, incorporating them within myself and acknowledging my magical responsibility in the affair.

We went to the police station to explain what had happened. We spoke to both sets of their parents. They were a very depressing group of adults. John's father was a cop. He had insisted that John get the book thrown at him for the pot charge, and that meant the shoplifting arrest would definitely have landed him in prison just as he feared. Merrie's parents had actually moved while she was in the hospital after a car accident and neglected to pass on their new address. But they were all very hurt by what had happened. We went to the funeral—an evil, Muzak-ridden, impersonal cover-up that just crushed us. We later visited their grave alone several times. They were buried together as they had so dearly hoped.

We found a job through the classified section of the newspaper as live-in babysitters for what seemed, at first, like a hip couple living in the country. We soon learned they were into a predatory open marriage and found ourselves as busy fending off their unwanted sexual advances as we were taking care of their two kids, who were also a drag. But we were in no position to turn down the opportunity to leave the apartment building where John and Merrie had killed themselves. We lasted less than two weeks before moving to the farm with Dennis and Claire and helping with the property reclamation task. Eventually, that arrangement fell through with the owner and we all went our separate ways.

Mount Shasta

Trying to escape Portland, we sold the Jeep and arranged to drive east in the MGA. Stopping what had become regular use of heroin resulted in some withdrawal sickness. In Idaho, Marianne was driving poorly. I panicked and grabbed the wheel and we went off the road, striking a sand bank. I got out of the car and furiously bent out the front fender by hand. We did an *I Ching* reading at Marianne's grandmother's house in Pocatello and were told in no uncertain terms not to proceed farther east, and not to ask again. We turned around. However, we decided to go to Mount Shasta rather than Portland. On the trip to California, we spent the night in a motel, where I listed my occupation on the registration card as a representative of the Abbey of Thelema.

In Mount Shasta, we saw a headline from the local newspaper: "Spirit Fails to Return to Body after Trance." A spiritualist group had protected the body of one of their members for something like a month, until they realized the medium had actually died. No charges were filed against them, it being understood by the local authorities that the spirit world can be complex.

The clipping was hung in the lobby of a motel called the Lemuria Lodge. There we met Jim Michael's (as in "property of" the Archangel Michael), another beautiful psychonaut, and his wife, Judy. We also met a very dreamy mystic we called Beloved Bill. I believe Jim recommended that we see Sister Thedra. We did a consecration ritual of a hand-drawn Tarot deck on Mount Shasta, then went to a restaurant and asked directions to her house. The waitress looked at the address and said: "Oh, you're going to see Sister Thedra. She's the channel." Then she explained how to get there.

Sister Thedra was a woman of immense power and aura, in her seventies and very small. She sat on a raised dais, and was quite warm to us until we mentioned Aleister Crowley. That made her uncomfortable. She told us she had found a copy of *The Equinox of Gods* and wanted to burn it, but the Masters of the Mountain told her not to. She cautioned us of the danger Crowley presented, but agreed that if we retained pure hearts we would be okay. Describing the spiritual work at one point, she pounded her fist on the desk repeating: "Discipline, discipline, discipline." We spent two magnificent hours with her and would see her again.

We bounced back up to Portland for a couple of days, then returned to take jobs at the Lemuria Lodge. Beloved Bill gave me the print of *The Virgin of the Sacred Coat* (which I call the "Virgin of the Sacred Goat"), later published in two of my books, *The Mystery Traditions* and *The Temple of Solomon*. I began working on perfecting the technique for drawing the Magical Circle illustrated in *The Lesser Key of Solomon*, the *Goetia*.

The owners of the lodge were—on the plus side—visionaries, imagining a healing center, bookstore/library, and natural-foods restaurant at the base of Mount Shasta. On the negative side, they were pretentious New Agers, members of a group called the I AM Foundation, which was centered around the Saint Germain communications received by Guy W. Ballard during the 1930s. A psychotic old woman, a member of the I AM, screamed at Marianne one day for wearing a red dress, a color prohibited by the cult. We were given the apartment that had been used by Ballard and his wife during his trance workings, which she transcribed and they later published as *The "I AM" Discourses*. We shot a small amount of speed there. All hell began to break loose. Jim Michael's, in a drunken rant, predicted disaster. He and Judy split up.

SUMMER 1971

We headed up to Portland for a week-long birthday visit. Dennis and I shared the same birthdate, two years apart. He and Claire were enamored of the Jim Kweskin Jug Band. I was not too familiar with them and was initially uninterested in going to hear them play on my birthday. But they were extraordinary and I particularly enjoyed Jim Kweskin. He gave an impassioned talk about the controversial Boston mystic, philosopher, and musician Mel Lyman, of whom Kweskin was a devoted follower.

Upon returning to Mount Shasta, I bought a large reference Bible from a traveling salesman by trading my custom-made gold Bar Mitzvah ring. Although, in retrospect, it was a very lopsided trade, I never really liked the ring and that Bible has proven immensely useful over the decades. It was clear, however, that the magical tide had turned, as Jim Michael's had predicted. We awoke one morning lying next to the body of our beloved kitten, Nuit, who had died suddenly of distemper. Her brother, Palamedes, came down with it as well and we rushed him to the vet. We then took acid and, at 4 A.M., met a huge St. Bernard in the road set to attack. We were saved by his owner, who had been awakened by the dog's ferocious barking. Then two dogs, one black and one white (like the kittens), followed us back to the apartment. It seemed as if they were spirit dogs—circling shades of Nuit and Palamedes. We loaded them into the car and drove them back to where they had joined us so they wouldn't be lost. Palamedes died at the vet's.

Saint Martin the Black came to visit with Ingrid and we escaped with them back to Portland. We stayed with Ingrid, and sometimes Tony, in Portland. He was getting deeper and deeper into trouble. I committed an act of which I remain truly ashamed. At the instigation of Dennis and Tony, I cashed a check that was not mine at a local store near the farm where we had stayed months before. Tony had gotten it and somehow assured me the store owners would not lose any money. They cashed it because we had developed a nice relationship. I have long forgotten where it was or who they were, but it was a great sin that still troubles me.

FALL 1971

I sold the MGA to buy a 1956 International Harvester laundry-style van better suited to the nomadic lifestyle we were living. We started to fix it up while staying with Elona, another girlfriend of Tony's. I installed a really nice black-and-white 1929 Vulcan gas stove that we refitted to operate with propane. We created a fully carpeted interior—a colorful remnant patchwork—and added wooden bookshelves, a food preparation counter with storage shelves, a closet, an 8-track stereo, and a Coleman icebox. John and Merrie's Winged Disk hung at the head of the bed.

Dennis and Claire split up and I realized how close I had become with Claire. While readying the truck and trying to raise money for our departure, we formed the Good Karma Dealing Crew with Marty and Claire, selling Minnesota Green, an unbelievably potent homegrown grass. Our theme song, sung to the tune of *The Good Ship Lollipop,* was "We're the Good Karma Dealing Crew/And we do our dealing just for you/Come along, get stoned; I'm sure you'll find/It's the starting of a life divine." We quickly raised the money to leave Portland. Marianne and I each read *Saint Francis* by Nikos Kazantzakis, a beautiful and influential book.

* * *

CHAPTER 5

ON THE ROAD AGAIN

FALL 1971 (CONTINUED)

MARIANNE, MARTY, CLAIRE, AND I LEFT PORTLAND. We visited Mount Shasta, and then went on to San Francisco, where Dennis was living with his new girlfriend. In Morro Bay, California, along with a crowd of at least twenty others, we saw a UFO hovering over the water. We drove on to Arizona, then New Mexico, where we swam outside Taos. The journey continued up to Boulder, where we visited with Mary and her husband and newborn baby. Claire had to fly back to Portland and Dioanna at this point.

In Boulder, I met an extremely sensitive psychic who claimed to be a granddaughter of Aleister Crowley. As I recall, her grandmother had enjoyed a short romance with Crowley while he was visiting Frater Achad (Charles Stansfeld Jones) in Detroit. I had a very warm interaction with her and attended a lecture she did on parapsychology at the university. I remain absolutely convinced she was telling the truth about her lineage. She was an honest and unassuming woman with no reason to lie. She suffered from the intensity of her psychism, with which she courageously wrestled for mastery. It was so strong, she told me, that she sometimes picked up on police radio transmissions! If I recall correctly, her father had been killed by being struck by lightning, something that Crowley had survived. She encouraged me to strengthen my faith. She introduced us to a local Qabalist who did an important Tarot reading. We continued on to Illinois to visit Marianne's family, then stopped at Antioch.

Finally, we arrived with Marty in New Jersey, happy to see my parents. Soon after, Marianne and I went to a park in Maryland for a three-day retreat of meditation and fasting modeled on *Saint*

Francis. We stopped at my cousin Pete's along the way. He and I have been friends since birth. The retreat was not quite what we expected. Filled with Kazantzakis' moving portrait of Saint Francis' renunciation and holiness, Marianne and I pitched two tents well outside visual or auditory range of each other. The plan was to spend three days alone, then meet up at the truck. It was really cold (in retrospect, not unexpected weather for mid-November). Then a freezing rain began and continued with no let-up. After a miserable night spent braving the elements, I retreated to the van, where I found Marianne. We attempted to continue our self-mortification under less trying circumstances, but the extreme cold soon encouraged us to break our fasts. In sum, there was a lot of meditation and spiritual study for the remainder of our time there, despite the failure to persevere through the original program.

Marty, meanwhile, had stayed quite comfortably at my parent's house. After returning from Maryland, we all drove up to New York City. There, we somehow wound up with Nikos, a German shepherd puppy who had belonged to a bartender at the White Horse Tavern. The idea was to have him be our travel dog, but he had no sense of cars and soon got hit by one. After cousin Pete, a veterinarian, fixed him up, we gave him to a family that owned a farm. Then Marty returned to Portland, this being the last time we ever saw each other.

In early December, I bought the newly published *Thoth Tarot Deck* from Weiser's and fell in love with it.

Undeniable stress began building within our marriage. The "one-year rule" of youthful relationships was in full play. If we hadn't been legally married, with all the intentions that implies, we would have separated.

WINTER 1971–1972

At the end of December, Claire and Dioanna moved to New York. Marianne and I worked at my father's factory, living in our van parked in the factory parking lot. I removed the engine for a rebuild. Although it was never quite successful, it improved things.

Marianne met a yoga teacher named Lorraine, from whom she took classes, encouraging me to do the same. Just after my first class, my talismanic silver "stash box" mysteriously disappeared. Lorraine introduced us to Guru Bawa in Philadelphia. He was said to be 150 years old, drank only water, ate no food, and had facial skin as smooth as a baby's. I liked him. A playful and very funny man, he showed spiritual wisdom and power beyond anything I had ever encountered.

SPRING 1972

We did an Easter-day ritual at the ocean for John and Merrie, a year after their deaths, burning their Tarot cards in a fire on the beach. As we finished, a bird began to sing.

Adano Ley and the All-Faith Fellowship

Lorraine introduced us to Adano Ley who came to give a lecture in New Jersey. I was very impressed with him and took initiation into his All-Faith Fellowship, which involved a special diet, drug- and alcohol-free lifestyle, and extensive meditation. I gave our remaining drugs to a friend who worked at my father's factory. Days later, the van was searched by a local cop in a traffic stop. We were building up to meditating two and a half hours each day as part of Adano's program. I read Manly P. Hall's *The Secret Teaching of All Ages*. At the end of May, we left for a retreat at Adano's center in Tyler, Texas.

We stopped along the way to see Pete near Philadelphia, then went on to Miami to see my uncle (Pete's father) and my grandmother. Uncle Sonny was a prankster and appeared in Chasidic dress. I momentarily thought he was displaying symbols of secret wisdom. As we continued on to Texas, the truck broke down in the Florida Panhandle. A nice fellow towed us to a mechanic named Ed Fellers, who allowed us to leave the truck while we hitchhiked to Texas. We got one ride from a Klan fighter who had risked life and limb in his battle with the group. Another ride came from a nice cop, who escorted us to the edge of town. We met three fellow hitchhikers who were members of the Children of God cult and enjoyed our interaction with them.

At last, we arrived at Adano's center in Tyler—a house in town where he and his wife, Margaret, lived and gave lectures. It had a large group kitchen and a meditation chapel. They also owned a 92-acre plot of undeveloped land in the countryside. Adano invited us to stay on the property and help the group after we rescued the truck. At the conclusion of the retreat, two members drove us back to Florida on their way to Virginia Beach. Ed and his lovely wife helped me get a job digging ditches for a neighbor to pay for repairing the truck.

SUMMER 1972

When the truck was finally fixed, we returned to Tyler and lived in the van on the retreat property. There was a small group of other nomadic students, among whom were two really upbeat women who told us about a New Mexico commune called Synergia, run by a fellow named John Allen. They strongly encouraged us to visit the group when we were in the area.

Adano was struggling with ego issues. One day, he dramatically announced he was going on a liquid fast that made him progressively more ill, until he was forced to abandon it somewhat sheepishly. But I was sympathetic to him. He was a very powerful adept. I remember sitting in meditation in the chapel one day. I was focused on listening for the sound of the universal energy in a posture with my fingers in my ears. When the sound grew uncharacteristically louder, I opened my eyes to see that Adano had just silently entered the room. I blamed his disciples for encouraging him to think of himself as a Perfect Living Master.

Charan Singh, the "Perfect Living Master"

The Perfect Living Master concept is similar to the Christian notion of Christ. The idea is that an advanced being assumes incarnation for the purpose of leading seekers to the Light. The Master is believed to be without flaws or karma, essentially an incarnation of the Light itself. It is very common in Indian mysticism and is a universal archetype. There are some obvious similarities to the Thelemic idea of the Holy Guardian Angel (HGA).

Charan Singh was recognized as such a Master by the Radha Swami Satsang group in India, of whom Adano considered himself an external gateway. However, Margaret was more committed to the Sant Mat teaching than was Adano. I sensed he felt himself in competition with the guru. His disciples certainly believed there was competition, and that added a level of tension and division within the Fellowship.

Marianne had applied to Charan Singh for initiation a few years earlier, but he told her she wasn't ready. She felt increasingly lost after the disappointing experience with Dennis and the trauma of Portland.

I liked Adano, but caught him in an untruth. His disciples set him up by asking him to rattle off Qabalistic correspondences from memory. He fell into their trap and, after a period of reeling off answers to their inane questions, he gave them a false answer. I was the only one who knew enough Qabalah to catch it, but I knew the lie was a conscious effort on his part not to say: "Hey, I don't recall all these details off the top of my head. I can look it up in my references and give you the answer later."

FALL 1972

Brian had come to visit us in Tyler, so we took off with him to San Diego. We expected to return, but this was not to be. We were joined by Brian's friend Soane, a Tongan. We all got a day's work through Manpower, the temporary employment agency, so we could buy a tire in New Mexico. We explored the Carlsbad Caverns, then continued on to Santa Fe and Taos (one of my favorite places on Earth, a magical artistic town in the enchanted mountains of New Mexico). We visited the Lama Foundation in the San Cristobel Mountains outside Taos. Funded in part from the proceeds of Ram Dass' book *Be Here Now,* it was a beautiful, well-organized, and nicely apportioned spiritual community. We found the group was composed of hip young people, more culturally attuned to our energies than the older, more middle-class crowd in Tyler.

Brian and Soane went on to Albuquerque. Marianne and I continued back toward Santa Fe. We picked up a hitchhiker who introduced us to Los Cerillos, an abandoned Old West mining town that had become a popular hippie center. There were several communes in the area and numerous artisans living in town. Walking out on a mesa one morning, we came upon a woman meditating. She called herself Gentle Wind. We met her husband, Bodhi, a talented painter who worked with American Indian themes. Gentle was deeply into Crowley and we struck an immediate rapport. She had never seen a copy of *Liber Aleph*. I trusted her with my copy and told her I'd be back to pick it up. I mention this, because, aside from the fact that this was one cool couple, I began to get the idea of living off the grid and creating products that could be sold to people who lived in more densely populated areas.

We traveled on to the Synergia Ranch near Santa Fe and were most impressed with their techno-Gurdjieffian spiritual energy. They had assembled an auto shop, carpentry shop, machine shop, organic farming laboratory, a large dining room, and a theater. John Allen had a piercing gaze and was friendly and encouraging. This was an amazing place—self-sufficient, yet modern and scientifically sophisticated.

We met up with Brian and Soane in Albuquerque and continued on to the Grand Canyon. We hiked to the bottom. The two of them were acting silly and not conserving energy. They had been mercilessly mocking Marianne and me for being vegetarian and not getting high. On the climb up, she and I reached the top of the Canyon an hour before they did and began to prepare the group dinner. When they arrived, they were nearly in tears from the exertion. It was a funny "gotcha" moment and I still enjoy teasing Brian about it. Then I realized I had forgotten my jacket at the bottom of the canyon and went down to get it. That did it for them!

We continued on to San Diego, where we stayed with Brian's parents for a while. We all worked for Manpower until we got a placement with a highway construction-equipment cleaning crew called Continental Cleaning. The four of us worked there for some months; then Brian and Soane went on to Tonga.

Marianne and I attended a series of lectures by Manly P. Hall at the Philosophical Research Society in Los Angeles. He was the most incredible speaker I've ever heard. He lectured with no notes, with never a pause or hesitation, and went on in a perfectly coherent and disciplined manner for precisely his allotted sixty to ninety minutes. It was uncanny. (Some five years later, I was honored to meet him and shake his hand while visiting the Society on a trip for Weiser's. I was introduced by Dr. Henry L. Drake, the Society's vice-president, with whom I would do some sales work.) We also saw R.D. Laing, a hip psychiatrist and acidhead mystic, who gave a brilliant talk in Los Angeles. I remember thinking that only a psychologically troubled society could establish a psychiatrist as one of its cultural heroes.

Meanwhile, Marianne made contact with the Radha Soami group in Los Angeles. She was desperate to take initiation. I was far less interested, but went along with it. I was especially turned off when I met Charan Singh's American representative, who struck me as weak and passive. I was disturbed with myself for having accepted an appointment for initiation. I found the Perfect Living Master concept troubling, because it seemed to strip away power from the individual, much like the Christian model of vicarious atonement. (I tend to follow the Patti Smith model of salvation as expressed in her song *Gloria:* "Jesus died for somebody's sins but not mine.") Sant Mat seemed to me to place salvation in the hands of the guru. Marianne, having been raised Catholic, found it more natural.

My diary reports a terrible ambivalence to the whole process and an intellectual distaste for the Indian spiritual exemplar. I favored the Crowley-style prankster guru with literary eloquence. Yet, by this time, I had been clean from drugs and alcohol for six months thanks to following the group's teaching. Much good could be said for that. There was also a series of *cledons* associated with Charan Singh. (*Cledon* is an ancient Greek term for the phenomenon in which an unsuspecting person is used by the gods to convey messages to the inquirer—an omen or augury.) In one incident, I was eating alone near the window of a spiritual restaurant in Los Angeles, mulling over the whole problem. A woman I had never seen passed by on the street and we smiled. Then I heard a voice say: "Well, how do you like it?" I turned to see that she had entered the restaurant and was showing me a photo of Charan Singh that she had just had framed.

WINTER 1972–1973

After much wavering and vacillation, I took initiation into Sant Mat, coincidentally on the national day of prayer that President Nixon had declared for the end of the Vietnam War. It was a simple ceremony. We were given a meditation technique that involved listening for the sound current (*Shabd*) that sustains the Universe, widely known in the West as the vibratory AUM. We were taught to meditate on the Ajna Chakra or Third Eye and given a set of names to use as a mantra. According to the teaching, we were also spiritually wired to the guru. That was what would haunt me for some years to come, as discussed in greater detail throughout these pages. I am not sure what percentage of my decision to accept initiation was spiritual, how much of it was part of my attempt to preserve my marriage, and how much was due to the influence of the extensive literature on Indian mysticism I had been reading.

SPRING 1973

We left California and returned to Los Cerillos to reclaim *Liber Aleph*. Then we traveled up to Taos en route to Illinois, where we visited Marianne's family again. They were quite pleased with our new drug-free lifestyle. We made the obligatory stop at Antioch, where I turned down some excellent pot offered by a true connoisseur of the drug.

Around Harrisburg, Pennsylvania, the engine in the van began to struggle again. I nursed it back to my parents' home in New Jersey, but decided I was through being dependent on cars that didn't work. It was simply too much. We would move to New York and travel by subway. I would get a job at Weiser's Bookstore.

We moved to New York and rented an apartment on 6th Street between 1st Avenue and Avenue A. I applied to Weiser's and was told I would be the second person on the list to be hired. I got a cab license and drove for three and a half months while waiting for the position to open up. It might be worth considering making a stint as a cab driver a mandatory part of the curriculum for budding psychologists. One finds an unexpected intimacy in the relationship between driver and passenger, with no shortage of heart-wrenching drama.

PART TWO

1973 TO 1977

✦

* * *

CHAPTER 6

NEW YORK CITY AND WEISER'S BOOKSTORE

"The trouble with Chip is that he is trying to run a military organization with an army of draft dodgers." —Peggy Fitzgerald, General Manager of Samuel Weiser, Inc. (ca. 1973) discussing Chip Suzuki, then the assistant manager of the bookstore

IN THE VERY LATE SPRING OF 1973, I began working at Samuel Weiser's Bookstore—the largest and most famous English language occult bookstore in the world for some seven decades until it closed its doors in the late 1990s. My plan was to work there for four years—exactly as if it were a college course—and to learn how to be a bookseller. I had the intention of setting up a bookstore with an attached coffee shop serving light food. I had never seen one, but it seemed like an excellent idea—a place where people could read, drink coffee, and discuss ideas. Several years later, I entered such a store in California and was turned off by the smell of food and books together. The modern Barnes & Noble/Starbucks phenomenon is a far more isolated version of my four-decades-old vision of a vibrant group of readers interacting with one another in a comfortable social and intellectual center.

Weiser's Bookstore was a crossroads for the world, with visitors from every nation in which an occultist could read English. I met a whole litany of people there. Many of them are my friends today, including Bill Breeze, Dan Gunther, Brian Cotnoir, Tom Schurr, Thaedra Mabrakhan, Ehud Sperling, and David Young.

Several were among the most important and transformative people of my life, including Richard Gernon, Angus MacLise, Harry Smith, Alejandro Jodorowsky, and Ed James. Others were occult luminaries who brightened many lives, including Ophiel, Fritz Peters, and Jimmy Page. I also met some of the contemporary players in the Thelemic movement of the day, including Janice Ayers and David Smith, who represented Kenneth Grant in the U.S. I found them both to be knowledgeable and friendly people and enjoyed our brief contact. I was less impressed with James Lee Musick, who announced himself as an A∴A∴ representative and claimed to have Regardie's support. He seemed to be making a psychic power play with me when we spoke and I found him tedious. I enjoyed the rare book dealer Eric Stevens, who specialized in Crowleyana.

On coming to Weiser's and refamiliarizing myself with Crowley's writings, I realized how intellectually barren the past year had been. Once more, I became taken with Crowley. This caused more strain in my marriage, as Marianne became as inextricably bound to the teachings of her guru as I was to mine. In July 1973, Mark Tranum came by for a visit and I smoked pot with him for the first time in thirteen and a half months. Pot would again become a regular part of my life until 1989.

Summer 1973/Fall 1974

I spent six months working "on the floor" in the bookstore. It was a transformative period. Unfortunately, the volume of my diary for the period from July 1973 to November 1974 was lost at the time. While loading a truck to move to a larger apartment a couple of blocks away, I turned my back for a moment and the notebook was stolen out of an open carton by a passerby.

This notebook would have chronicled an intense period of oscillation between Sant Mat and Thelema. While I was moving toward a re-embrace of Thelema, some obstacles crossed my path. I befriended a bright but irritating customer from Canada. He embodied many of the annoying ego tendencies we might call the "qliphoth of Thelema"—an arrogance and false pride predicated on a misunderstanding of *The Book of the Law.* By way of contrast, I believe humility to be one of the most critical attributes of a spiritual person. My ambiguity, however, appears to have been resolved during this period. My November 1974 diary begins by revealing someone committed to the practices and doctrines of A∴A∴ as outlined in *Book IV,* Parts 1–3.

The missing diary included the primary period of my relationship with Alejandro Jodorowsky, of whom more will be said. It also marked the beginning of my correspondence with Marcelo Motta, who will be discussed in detail in the next chapter.

One of the important career realities I soon discovered was that retail sales was not my interest. Things moved too slowly and I resented the oft-repeated advisory: "This is a bookstore not a library and you are an employee not a customer." Six months later, an incompetent employee in the order-fulfillment area of Weiser's publishing department was fired, leaving a big mess behind— a backlog of orders that required emergency attention. The call came from upstairs for help. I was happy to try something different. After ten days of working with Donald Weiser, I had found the home in the book business I had long known awaited me.

Angus MacLise

Some of the most memorable experiences from my six months on the floor include meeting Angus MacLise. He came into the shop one day while I was at the register. He was trying to sell a copy of Crowley's *Olla.* We got to talking and struck up a fast friendship. He was some kind of archetypical hermetic force, introducing me to a whole group of people and scenes that would resonate for the rest of my life.

Angus was an amazing figure. The quintessential medieval troubadour, he was also a hipster. He was the original drummer of the Velvet Underground. When the band began its meteoric rise to fame, Angus became irritated at the thought that he would have to show up on time for performances, and especially that he would have to stop playing before he was finished. He simply walked out.

Lou Reed hymned him in a 2011 exhibit of Angus' work at the Boo-Hooray Gallery in New York.

Angus spent years living in Kathmandu, operating a small publishing company that produced limited editions of poetry printed on hand-made paper. He was associated with a group of New York artists, musicians, and vagabonds who brought creativity and inspiration to American culture. Ira Cohen, Don Snyder, Sheldon Rochlin, Gerard Malanga, and Mikki Maher are just a few of those luminaries. Angus and his wife, Hettie, had a son named Ossian, who was recognized as a *Tulku* (the reincarnation of a spiritual teacher) by a group of Tibetan Buddhist exiles living in Nepal. Ossian went to live with them at the age of three or four, and was raised as a monk. This was a source of both joy and sorrow for Angus.

Angus had a quiet intensity, combined with the most endearing humility and gentleness of anyone I've ever met. His self-effacing sense of humor underpinned a self-destructive drug addiction that was heartbreaking. How many mornings we later spent on the pier on the Hudson River across from my Greenwich Street loft, greeting the dawn with a hit of speed.

Thaedra Mabrakhan

An exotic-looking woman with Egyptian-style dress and make-up came into the store regularly to sit in the art section and read expensive books into a tape recorder. I was impressed by her seriousness. We eventually struck up a conversation. One day, I came home to find her visiting my apartment with Angus. Thaedra and I have remained friends since. Several of her magnificent pieces of art have appeared in my books and on book covers created by Studio 31.

Thaedra encouraged me to appreciate the spirituality of Voodoo. I spent at least twenty minutes one evening staring at an image in William Seabrook's book *The Magic Island*. It was a temple painting of the Voodoo god Legba and the goddess Ayida Oueddo (Aida Wedo). I was incomprehensibly fixated on it until, in a flash of clarity, I jumped up and grabbed one of Budge's books on Egypt. I recognized the Haitian image as part of a symbol set whose roots were inextricably bound in ancient Egyptian iconography. Legba and Ayida Oueddo are depicted precisely as Osiris and Isis are in *The Egyptian Book of the Dead.* (See the photo insert following page 112.) It was a deep-level understanding for me of an important truth about "the obeah and the wanga" (AL I:37) and the migration of the Mysteries. I would later have a lot of contact with Afro-Caribbean magic (to be discussed), and was prepared to accept, in advance, that what I observed in their rituals would potentially hold many clues for my practice of Thelemic Magick.

Alejandro Jodorowsky

During our travels out West, Marianne and I had been told of a movie by Alejandro Jodorowsky called *El Topo.* When we got to New York, it was playing at a theater on 2nd Avenue near St. Mark's Place. We went to see it one day in the spring of 1973 and were blown away. We saw it again that day and three more times that weekend. It was the most enlightening film I'd ever seen. I remember buying a pack of cigarettes at the nearby Gem Spa and feeling as if I were tripping.

In the fall of 1973, Alejandro came in to Weiser's. I couldn't believe it. It felt as if I had summoned him to visible appearance. He ordered a rare book, *Finger Pointing to the Moon* by Wei Wu Wei. Following standard procedure, I wrote down his address and phone number on an index card awaiting the arrival of the book in the store. I wrote him a long letter that evening, expressing my admiration for his movie and my desire to meet and speak with him. I apologized profusely for using the store as the medium for the communication, but asked him to forgive that breach of professionalism. I didn't get a reply and was saddened.

Six months later, the book came in stock. I phoned him to notify him of its arrival, also normal procedure. He asked if I was the person who had written the beautiful letter. I said I was. He apologized for not having answered it and invited me to come see him. I asked when and he suggested right then. I got off the phone and caught my breath. I wanted to bring a gift and wondered what I had that could possibly convey the intensity of my admiration. I had drawn the Circle of Solomon that Crowley published in *The Goetia* during the Mount Shasta period. It is an intense diagram. Each of the first nine Sephiroth has its Hebrew name, God name, Archangel, Angel, Heaven of Assiah, and Zodiacal attribute written within the body of a snake coiled around the edge of the Circle. This was the finest piece of art I had ever executed, done with the exacting drafting techniques I had learned from Dennis. I had colored it with inks according to the instructions in the book. Then I framed it. It remained covered in a treasured place, as I thought it was just too intense to display openly. I decided it was a fitting gift for one I considered a Master. When I gave it to him, he beamed and hung it in the center of his living room/library. That just knocked me out.

We had a magnificent visit and would see each other many more times during the next year. He was in the final editing phase of his new film, *The Holy Mountain*. My future friend, Ira Cohen (through Angus) had done an interview book with Alejandro on *El Topo*. In time, I would suggest that Alejandro and I do a similar book for *The Holy Mountain*. I wrote up a careful series of questions. When Alejandro reviewed them, he was delighted by my disciplined approach and agreed. We began to record several reel-to-reel interview tapes. I enlisted the help of Bob Skutelsky, my friend and fellow employee at Weiser's. Bob was a·student of Eastern mysticism. I felt Alejandro's knowledge was so vast that Bob's input could enrich the interview process. That may or may not have been the best decision, as Bob introduced a wandering quality to our discussions, well outside the tightly organized queries I had prepared. We never published the book, although the tapes were digitized.

Alejandro later made one of those life-changing offers that represented a fork in the road for me—a life choice that would allow for one or another future, but not both. He asked Marianne and me if we would like to accompany him and his family to France. He was traveling to an estate there and offered us a cottage where we could live and work for him. I felt absolutely committed to publishing and knew the course with Alejandro would lead me away from that field. On the other hand, the thought of being so close to him and his work was hugely tempting. But we decided to pass. I do know my life would have been very different had we gone off with them to Europe. I am happy I didn't—yet I can't help wondering about it.

SPRING 1974

Marianne and I had long talked about going to India to visit the ashram of Charan Singh. Our applications were approved. I decided not to go. It was no longer important to me. Marianne left for six weeks. I was happy she did, because I knew how much it meant to her. It was clear that our relationship was falling apart. During her trip, Alejandro and I went to see *The Exorcist*. I had long feared the concept of possession. While he experienced the film as a professional filmmaker, I was scared. When I came home that night to my darkened apartment, I remember thinking that I would never be able to take LSD again. Not uncharacteristically, I took some that night to confront my fear directly.

                                    * * *

                                 CHAPTER 7

                         WEISER PUBLISHING AND
                         The Commentaries of AL

                              SUMMER 1974

THIS PERIOD BROUGHT SAD NEWS of the death of Mary's baby son
in Boulder. I went into the privacy of the sub-basement and cried
for her. It was the first time I remember crying for another person's
sorrow.

    One of my duties in the publishing office was to direct the daily
mail to the appropriate channels so I could maintain an accurate
overview of the operation. In June, a letter addressed to Donald
Weiser came in from a Brazilian man named Marcelo Motta. He
was inquiring about a manuscript he had sent to Weiser's some six
months before and about which he had heard no response. (At the
time, Weiser was just breaking into the publishing business and had
neither the experience nor the manpower to deal with the responsibilities of that expansion.) When I read the letter, my heart leapt.
He was inquiring about his edited version of Crowley's commentaries on *The Book of the Law.* At this time, Llewellyn and 93 Publishing had both announced their editions of commentaries, edited
by Israel Regardie and Kenneth Grant, respectively. I was very anxious to see what Crowley had written about the book I had puzzled
over—alternately attracted and repelled—since first reading it at
the farm outside Yellow Springs in 1970.

    When I discussed the letter with Donald, he remembered receiv-
ing the manuscript. He offered me the opportunity to find it in
exchange for cleaning the manuscript pile in his office after hours.
He recalled that Motta was a student of Karl Germer and had been
involved with the publication of *Liber Aleph*, and that Germer had
mentioned that Motta was headstrong and erratic. But Donald

also expressed a vague interest in my looking for the manuscript. I found it that night and wrote to Motta the next day to inform him it was under review. My letter is dated June 26, 1974.

Donald was interested in the possibility of our putting out an edition of the *Commentaries* to compete with the other two versions. Llewellyn's edition had been announced and delayed for years and 93 Publishing was a small house based in Canada. Donald felt that, if Motta's treatment was well done, there was no reason not to publish a third version—the independent views of a previously obscure but long-term credentialed Thelemite. There were no recognized copyrights at the time, the situation having been described as a free-for-all for publishers.

My initial reaction to the commentary was disappointment. Not with Motta but with Crowley. I had pondered a number of mysteries of *Liber AL* for some time that went well beyond the social/political slant of the New Comment. I felt my questions were not answered and that the general tone of the comment was a bit superficial. However, without access to either the full version nor with any idea of Grant or Regardie's editing, I thought Motta added an interesting point of view that helped to expand and personalize Crowley's words. I took exception to some of his tone, but overall, concluded that he done a credible job.

I discussed my thoughts with Donald, including my sense of the limitation of the book in general and some of Motta's comments in particular. Donald made the decision to proceed with a Weiser edition of the *Commentaries,* as edited by Mr. Motta. As the designated representative of the company, I wrote to inform him.

I had mentioned my interest in Crowley in my first letter. When Motta wrote back, he informed me that he was a Master of the Temple of A∴A∴ and wove a series of exciting, romantic, and exotic hints, suggestions, and tales. As time went on, the nature of our communication became increasingly personal. His eloquence and the passion he brought to the spiritual path were entrancing. He was a diligent correspondent. All letters had to be sent registered mail because of the postal controls in Brazil. He believed he was under surveillance, and wrote much about the political oppression of the military government.

A sense of danger and intrigue haunted the exchange. I began to open up with questions about Thelema and my own strivings. He increasingly assumed the role of teacher. I shared our correspondence with my friend Bob Roberts, an artist and magician I had hired at Weiser's. The postman would come into the office with the registered letter, the drama and anticipation increasing as I signed for it and began to read. Before long, I observed that his letters answered questions I had contemplated but not yet posed. It became increasingly uncanny and Bob noticed it too, as we frequently discussed Magick.

As the manuscript of *The Commentaries of AL* continued through production, my intimacy with its content increased. Although my editing was light, no manuscript gets through a publisher without an editor. When the book entered the typesetting stage, it required constant proofreading and correction on my part. (This was long before the days of desktop publishing, PostScript type, and paper proofs.) My work with the text familiarized me with *The Book of the Law* in a profound manner. I am proud to say that the text of *The Book of the Law* in *The Commentaries of AL* was one of the first typeset versions without typographic errors. It was not an easy process. We had worked out a typesetting arrangement with Ken Patton, a friend, customer, and Crowley devotee. He set up an in-house, freelance typesetting operation in the back of the office. Ken was a true Southern gentleman, but quite neurotic, and this book and Motta were driving him crazy. The stress actually led him to a nervous breakdown. I had to complete the index for the book (my first index).

One Saturday morning, I was at home and received a phone call from the bookstore. A disciple of Motta's named Raul Seixas was in town and had asked for me. I came in and joined him for breakfast. Raul was a very popular professional musician in Brazil who had performed a couple of songs that Marcelo had written. He was a bit older than I—an interesting person with an exotic rock-star charisma. But he also had some knowledge of Thelemic literature and had worked the system with Motta.

Raul asked what I thought about *The Book of the Law*. I told him that I was uncertain about concepts like the Equinox of the

Gods. I didn't understand what such cosmic events meant to the rational mind. I told him I didn't understand who Aiwass was, that I didn't really know who wrote *The Book of the Law.* He looked me in the eyes and said: "Jimmy, I will tell you who wrote *The Book of the Law.* You wrote *The Book of the Law.*" I experienced an epiphany that has lasted the rest of my life. (Since I am obviously aware that I am neither Aleister Crowley nor Aiwass, what I mean by this is that Raul's remark sparked an intuitive understanding that the nature of Truth within *The Book of the Law* is so profoundly intimate that I must be willing to take personal responsibility for the book.) I believe Raul was later included in one of Motta's hit lists in one or another of his books. Based on that breakfast, I am happy to be in his company.

Meanwhile, my relationship with Motta became increasingly stormy. He began to unleash a stream of anti-Semitic remarks. I wanted to index the word "chosen" and "chosen people" to demonstrate to him the inanity of his constant assertions that the Jews considered themselves "chosen"—as if Thelemites don't! (I didn't do it.) Motta threatened to sink Israel if the Jews did not acknowledge Horus as the Lord of the Aeon. He proclaimed himself the Gatekeeper of Nu on Earth. It's hard to understand why I didn't simply bolt out of the relationship because of his ill-mannered rants and outbursts, which were occurring with increasing frequency. But the negatives of his escalating irritability were balanced by the positives of the psychic nature of his correspondence and the depth of understanding he seemed to bring to a young seeker. In addition, he was a contracted author and I was an employee of the publishing company that was making his book. After a couple of months of this, things began to calm down again between us.

WINTER 1974–1975

Motta mentioned the possibility of his visiting New York and our driving to California together to visit Karl Germer's widow, Sascha. I looked forward to meeting him and getting a sense of what an adept of the Thelemic Path would have developed into after twenty years of practice. But he became ill with phlebitis and was unable to travel. He also mentioned financial difficulties.

My friends at the time included David, a customer at the store who had come to work in the wholesale department. He was an avid book collector and amazingly knowledgeable about rock 'n roll. He had been a radio disk jockey and was friends with many members of the burgeoning New York punk-rock scene. They respected his encyclopedic knowledge and appreciation for their art. He introduced me to Jerry Nolan of the Heartbreakers, who had earlier been the drummer for the New York Dolls—the world's first punk-rock band. Jerry was a good guy who supplied me with some decent junk on several occasions. I appreciated the fact that he lived the life he sang about.

David took me to see Patti Smith perform at the Bottom Line on West 4th Street. I liked her. But David insisted we sit through two performances. During the first set, she spit on the stage. My mind was totally blown by what I considered to be one of the most outrageous gestures I had ever seen by a performer. Imagine my surprise when she did the same thing at the exact same moment in the second set. (Her 2010 autobiographical book *Just Kids* is an absolute must read. She was a close friend of Harry Smith—no relation—and brings him to life in her text.)

SPRING 1975

Marianne and I moved into a loft in Soho, a block above Canal Street. I began to build a Temple. When complete, it would have soundproof lead sheeting in the walls like a music studio, and a Magical Circle painted on the floor.

On April 9, 1975, I signed the Oath and Task of the Probationer. It would have happened six months earlier, as I had written to Motta in September 1974 requesting the Oath, just before he began his period of anti-Semitic rants. He later told me that my letter was lost in the mail. I was much relieved I had not bound myself to him on a spiritual level. But as things improved between us, I again requested the Oath. As many aspirants will attest, the energies with which I had been wrestling went into overdrive.

I was working on my introduction to *The Commentaries of AL*. Motta had asked me to write it. I struggled mightily, as I felt completely unworthy to be part of a book on Thelema. But he insisted and, after a great deal of effort, I submitted it to him and he approved it in mid-May.

On May 2, I was visiting a neighbor with whom I smoked some powerful grass. We sat and listened to a magnificent album by Ali Akbar Khan. I had been struggling with the introduction all day and was tired and frazzled. The raga was simply dazzling and the cares of the day submerged beneath the sound. I heard a voice above the music say: "It is I, the Voice of the Guru, who has called to you in this music." I was stunned and vividly remember my sense of awe.

Through Marianne's connections with the Radha Swami group, we met a couple who were among the most uncannily accurate astrologers I've known. They were also ballet enthusiasts and introduced us to the Bolshoi Ballet that was visiting New York. We went to a performance of *Ivan the Terrible* danced by Vladimir Vasiliev and Natalia Besmertnova. At the opening of one act, Besmertnova was lying on what looked like a couch or pedestal at the top of a pyramid-shaped set of stairs. As she rose, Vasiliev did as well, revealing himself as the altar on which she had lain. I remember thinking: "God take me now, for I have seen the most beautiful thing I will ever see in my life." I was disappointed by the one or two ballets I went to afterward and stopped going. I had attained the highest state I would ever achieve from that art form and remain grateful for that exquisite performance.

An unforgettable dinner took place thanks to Donald. Carl and Sandra Weschke of Llewellyn Publications were visiting New York. Donald invited Marianne and me to join them at Ballatos, a gourmet Italian restaurant on Houston Street. I found Carl to be one of the most intelligent and charismatic people I've met in the publishing business. He and Sandra were practicing witches and magicians in addition to their business ventures, and we spent the evening in an unending exchange about Magick and the Path of the Wise.

Another pair of periodic visitors to Weiser's were David Young and his father, who owned Thorsons Publishing in the U.K. We did a lot of distribution deals both ways with them, as well as co-publishing several titles. David's father and Donald would huddle in Don's office while David and I would try to see how much trouble we could get ourselves into together. We've enjoyed a long friendship and have a good laugh now and then over our youth.

SUMMER 1975

On my twenty-seventh birthday, I purchased copy #27 of *The Book of Thoth* from Richard Alan Miller, a very high-energy herbalist and author, and the owner of Beltane Books in Seattle. Modern-day Crowley collectors will not believe that I paid $275 for the mint-condition copy. (I was later forced to sell it to the O.T.O. in order to pay an important debt on schedule. That timely repayment allowed for the continued momentum that resulted in the publication of *The Egyptian Book of the Dead* in 1994.)

I read *From the Legend of Biel,* an excellent novel by Mary Staton. It has profound Thelemic overtones and real intimations of the HGA. It also allegorizes LSD as a channel to higher awareness and rapid information processing. The book has since been reprinted and is worth reading.

In September, I almost electrocuted myself in the loft with a floor sander, an hour after completing the index for *The Commentaries of AL*. It was Yom Kippur. I had taken advantage of Donald offering the day off to Jewish employees and rented the sander during the week, as it was difficult to do so on the more crowded weekends. The instant I turned it on and heard the extraordinary noise level, I realized I would be showing disrespect to my genetic heritage by continuing. In the hospital, I found my consciousness easily detached from my physical body, a real goal of my magical work at this time. But I knew my duty was to remain—to protect and heal my body. I have fasted on Yom Kippur since, turning it into a day of personal magical power and spiritual contemplation.

FALL 1975

Richard Gernon

Donald introduced me to a fellow my age named Richard Gernon (Gurney), a serious student of Crowley who had written to Donald for books and thanked him for his publishing efforts. Donald enjoyed their communication and asked me to meet Richard and get to know him when he came up to visit the store from Philadelphia. My diary does not mention the exact date we met. My initial reaction was a slight discomfort. He was short and had oily skin. He camouflaged his brilliant and accomplished mind with an almost aggressive disdain for cultural conventions. By way of example, he called himself "Gurney Thundersnatch Bulkrubbish."

Gurney's self-presentation was way out of my personal comfort zone. I've always been a bit effete, with a set of middle-class values about politeness, bearing, etc. He also had an odd way of cocking his head to one side that, in the future, would become one of his most lovable mannerisms. But, at first meeting, it was disconcerting. He had a broad range of learning, however, and we cautiously became friendly. We would ultimately share one of the deepest friendships of my life.

Dan Gunther

In August of 1975, Weiser received an announcement from one Frater K.N., J. Daniel Gunther, announcing himself as an A∴A∴ contact point in Nashville, Tennessee. I passed his information along to Gurney in hopes that we might learn more about this previously unknown individual and broaden our collective database, as it were. As soon as Dan learned of Motta through Gurney, he contacted him. Motta forwarded the letter he received from Gunther and his reply. Frater K.N. informed Motta that he had been authorized by the Secret Chiefs to establish an "American chapter of A∴A∴" and wished to cooperate.

Motta wrote back to him in a surprisingly friendly manner on August 12, 1975. He declared that, as one of the Secret Chiefs himself, he didn't remember authorizing anything, that there were no "chapters" or other organizational bodies of A∴A∴, and that Gunther had miscapitalized "Do what thou wilt," etc. in violation of the very commands of *The Book of the Law* itself. (Motta clubbed us all into conforming to the proper orthography for quoting Class A material.) Assured of Motta's spiritual stature, Daniel immediately submitted himself to his Superior.

Gurney meanwhile was very impressed with Dan and swore the Oath of Probationer. He began to do some studies with Dan and, before long, moved to Nashville so they could work together more closely. I met Dan for the first time when he came to New York at the end of October 1975. We hit it off immediately and have remained close friends for decades. We share many of the same cultural and social-class habits mentioned earlier, so we were a more natural fit than Gurney and I were at first. As I got to know Dan better, I was impressed by his spiritual nature. In fact, some three and a half decades later, I still am. We were in regular touch by phone after that visit. One conversation was particularly painful, as we spoke on the first day of my practicing the speech section of *Liber Jugorum* using the word "I." The excitement of our lively conversation resulted in a number of lapses!

Bill Breeze

Another person who came into my life at this time was Bill Breeze. He was a brilliant young occultist who had a flair for archival and editorial work. A student at Friends World College in Long Island, he later enrolled as an Extension student at Harvard. Bill was prone, however, to long periods of independent study and he lived a nomadic lifestyle.

Bill visited the publishing offices at 625 Broadway one day in 1975, date not recorded. Tall, painfully skinny, and some seven years younger than I, he was an enigmatic and intriguing character, projecting both a youthful discomfort and a profound sense of rebelliousness. He signed the Oath of Probationer during Dan's visit in late October. But he cut contact with Dan in 1976 when he read *The Commentaries of AL.* He felt he was acting in conformity with the Class A Comment regarding people like Motta. "Those who discuss the contents of this Book are to be shunned by all, as centres of pestilence." Bill and I remained in contact whenever he was in New York. Our friendship would blossom and grow strong.

The Commentaries of AL *Goes to Press*

In November of 1975, I turned over *The Commentaries of AL* to the printer after a solid year of work. I began to become restless at Weiser's. There was a sense of completion, a feeling that my mission may have been fulfilled. This can be attributed to several career successes all coming into focus at the same time. Our edition of *The Golden Verses of Pythagoras,* in the deluxe buckram binding with Ehud Sperling's excellent introduction, was published. The full-size, color, deluxe edition of *The Secret Teachings of All Ages* had also just come out. I had played a small part in this. I had suggested to Donald some time earlier that Weiser republish it. He authorized me to contact the Philosophical Research Society. They confided that they were in production of the Golden Anniversary Edition of the book. They were going to reproduce half the original color plates in black and white to save money. I made an impassioned plea that they do all the plates in color and pledged Weiser's help in distribution. Dr. Henry Drake wrote a beautiful letter in reply thanking me for my input and explaining that they had decided to do all the plates in color.

CHAPTER 8

MEETING MARCELO MOTTA IN BRAZIL

WINTER 1975–1976

THE FIRST COPIES OF *The Commentaries of AL* arrived in early January. Even the printer was part of the ordeal. He put the hard-cover boards on with the grain running in the wrong direction and they were warping in the moisture. We stopped the run after seeing samples. I brought some of these copies to Motta in Brazil later that month, explaining that the bulk of the books were being bound properly.

I was responsible for putting Marcelo's comment on AL III:26 on the back of the dustjacket. I wanted to introduce him in a dramatic way to our readers and convey a sense of the depth of his commentary.

"These slay, naming your enemies; & they shall fall before you."
Perhaps the following apologue will be of help: A profane slew a beetle before Ra-Hoor-Khuit, naming a person he considered his enemy; and soon after, the profane went mad. An Initiate slew a beetle before Ra-Hoor-Khuit, naming a person he considered his enemy; and soon after, this person fell before him. An Exempt Adept slew a beetle before Ra-Hoor-Khuit, naming the person he considered his worst enemy, that is himself; and soon after, he became a Master of the Temple.

I was preparing to go to Brazil to meet Motta in person, hand-deliver copies of the *Commentaries*, and work together on his new manuscript, *LXV Commented*, a commentary on *Liber LXV: The Book of the Heart Girt with a Serpent*. There was a flurry of activity—working on my Robe, organizing my correspondence, and beginning a careful review of his new manuscript. I was also reading Liz Greene's excellent manuscript for *Saturn: A New Look at an Old Devil,* while in the throes of my own first Saturn return.

Peter Macfarlane of 93 Publishing came to visit Weiser's and we had a most cordial exchange. My record shows another phone conversation with Dan while I was working on avoiding the word "and." (When Motta read my record, he pointed out that I had missed the clue provided in the *Book IV,* Part 2 discussion of *Liber III,* where Crowley adds that the practice should be limited to periods of the day, like an hour here and an hour there. That is not written in the text of *Liber III* itself and I was making a mess of myself. I would add that smoking grass on a daily basis and practicing *Liber Jugorum* are contraindicated!) Dan and I discussed the possibility of my moving to Nashville. We also discussed Peter Macfarlane's self-admitted use of ritual magick to hinder the publication of *The Commentaries of AL* as a breach of magical chastity.

An example of my state of mind just before the trip to Brazil may be instructive. Motta wrote or asked by phone that I bring him a pistol, a .380 Walther PPK. At this time, I might have been characterized as a garden-variety liberal, appropriately horrified by guns despite the fact that I had enjoyed shooting them numerous times. But I researched gun stores and learned that one didn't just buy a gun and take it on a plane to Brazil. I couldn't imagine how I could do it, even if it were possible to do so without going to prison. I tried to reason through the consequences of his request.

At one point, I accepted the possibility that the work of A∴A∴ might require me to carry the Law of Thelema into prison. I contacted him and explained the problem. To my relief, he was very calm and told me to forget it. The idea from his point of view had simply been to avoid Brazil's high import tariffs. I raise this embarrassing story in support of my statements to come about Motta's undue influence on certain disciples. There is a tendency at the beginning of the spiritual path to ignore reality and common sense when confronted with the demands of a teacher. I tell a story in *The Templars and the Assassins* of an Assassin master commanding two disciples to leap from a cliff to their deaths on the rocks below that he might demonstrate the allegiance of his followers to a visiting Crusader king. Supposedly a legend, I know from personal experience that it is not as implausible as it sounds.

I began learning the ritual of the Star Ruby. Gurney helped by transliterating the Greek into English by phone.

On January 30, Marianne and I were rushing to prepare for the flight to Brazil when Alejandro called. He had just flown into New York. We got together for lunch on that hectic day and he helped me to appreciate the importance of the Marseilles Tarot as a crucial point in the development of Tarot symbolism, and as a coherent resume of Truth in its own light.

Rio de Janeiro

Marianne and I flew to Rio to visit Marcelo. We stayed in his home for eighteen days. He was a most gracious and personable host. His physical appearance was so different from what I had imagined that it is comical to reflect on my fantasy. I had pictured him in my mind's eye as a tall, swarthy, handsome hero like Zorro, or even his fellow South American Jodorowsky. Instead, he was short, somewhat stout, fair-haired, fair-skinned, with acne scars, and he wore glasses.

Soon after our arrival, I had a powerful dream/nightmare in which Motta, my father, and Dennis assembled in a frightening parade of teacher archetypes. I yelled out in the dream: "No! No! No!" On awakening, I discussed it with Marcelo, who explained that A∴A∴ teachings do not seek to make one secure in one's beliefs. The only security is to be found within. This concept would be fully tested as I read his diaries and was able to observe first hand his own failings and weaknesses. This sparked a great deal of conflict in me, because I was immature enough to expect my teacher to be more free of human flaws. I will remain forever grateful to him, not only for his humility in allowing me to read those diaries, but for his determination to break me of my delusional fantasies.

I was honest in discussing my fears and doubts and he encouraged me to do so. He pointed out that I had a tendency to avoid responsibility by embracing doubt and not taking action. This was most perceptive, as will be illustrated again during an incident in 1981. "We are not trying to teach virtue. We are teaching the development of the Will."

The visit clarified many spiritual issues that were in the forefront of my consciousness at this time. The most important perhaps was the ongoing conflict between the image of Charan Singh and the aspiration to the Holy Guardian Angel. My diaries show that I was able to verbalize the conflict clearly and openly in writing for the first time.

Marcelo taught me the pronunciation of the Greek words of the Star Ruby, which I still perform with a slight Brazilian accent. I did my first full run-through of the ritual in Rio. I asked him about the meaning of Crowley's footnote in *Liber XXV*: "The secret sense of these words is to be sought in the numeration thereof." He didn't know the answer. The question puzzled me for decades, until 2011, when Angel Lorenz finally clarified the matter. He pointed out that the footnote occurs after the words "O PhALLE." Brother Lorenz went on: "It is my opinion that it specifically refers only to that phrase and not to all the Greek words of the ritual. The value for 'O PhALLE' [*Gr.*, Ω ΦΑΛΛΕ = 800 + 566] is 1366. 1366 is mentioned in *The Canon* as the value of the sum of *phallos* [*Gr.* φαλλός = 831] plus *kteis* [*Gr.*, κτείς = 535]." The doctrinal elegance of this revelation is one of the reasons Aleister Crowley has held my rapt attention throughout my spiritual life.

Motta taught me that the Adorations of *Liber Resh* are invocations of Adonai. As I was working diligently with the memorization of my chapter of *Liber LXV* during the visit, I was very conscious of Adonai. Marcelo gave me instruction in the Secret Adoration mentioned in *Liber Resh* that I continue to use. Finally, the various strands of sexual magick with which I had been experimenting began to come together to form a unified and coherent whole for the first time as I began to understand the alchemical fusion of ecstacy and intention. This forced the final conflict with Marianne. We decided we would live separately on our return to New York.

Motta gave me what I still believe is the correct symbol for the Mark of the Beast, as used during *Liber V vel Reguli*. I publish it here because its geometrical elegance convinces me of its ultimate utility. (I am aware that it contradicts some notes by Crowley on the subject that remained unpublished during his lifetime.)

Motta, Marianne, and I attended a powerful Umbanda ritual together. He believed the Afro-Caribbean magical systems had embraced the Law of Thelema, because they had recently added a new god to their pantheon whom he identified with Horus. (Unfortunately, I do not remember the name of the specific deity and did not write it down.) He told me that he stayed in Brazil because his country needed him. It was a tyranny and his role was to balance that against the Law of Freedom. I was troubled by his treatment of his girlfriend, Claudia Canuto de Menezes. He sternly said that, if she became pregnant, he would cast her away from him with no further thought. He also told me that A∴A∴ initiates do not reveal their mottos without risk. (Gurney, Gunther, and I had all been calling each other "Frater This" and "Frater That," and he felt we were entirely too casual with our magical mottos.)

I was hoping to be elevated to Neophyte as he had suggested I would be after memorizing my chapter of *Liber LXV*. He teased me with the Neophyte issue, ultimately refusing me. I had the distinct sense that he was playing a control game.

On the other hand, he allowed me to read all his diaries and his correspondence with his Instructor, Karl Germer. This was an act of great courage. His diary contained much embarrassing material. (If one keeps an honest diary, whose does not?) His correspondence with Germer opened me to Germer's spiritual stature. He is often overlooked in Thelemic history, treated as a placeholder between Crowley and later generations. We do ourselves a disservice in not understanding him as the critical figure he was. Germer may have been a poor example of an O.T.O. leader—being an essentially isolated personality—but I observed a luminous spirituality in his correspondence. He deserves a competent biographer.

Reading Motta's diaries and his correspondence with Germer helped me to understand that the Path of Thelema is not about pretensions. I had so many years of contact with so many people of so many different traditions—spiritual systems that encouraged people to act as if they were better, more pure, more gentle, more

THE MARK OF THE BEAST
AS TAUGHT BY MARCELO MOTTA

The Mark of the Beast

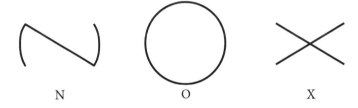

The Mark of the Beast conceals the letters
of the formula of "NOX"

The Invoking Hexagram
of the Beast
The Unicursal Hexagram

Composite symbol traced
in the Second Gesture,
points 19 and 20

K. J. GERMER

METAL WORKING MACHINERY

WISCONSIN 7-5681

**152 WEST 42ND STREET
NEW YORK CITY**

Karl Germer's business card from the 1950s.

open, less flawed, less selfish as a result of their position as spiritual teachers or devotees of spiritual teachers. What I had found instead were people who were manipulating themselves and others through a malignant form of dishonesty and denial. Hadit's exclamation in *The Book of the Law*, "veil not your vices in virtuous words" (AL II:52) is a rallying cry for the healing of the human soul. At the same time, it was frightening to consider that my elders and leaders shared some of my own imperfections. When I raised my doubts about Crowley in the face of his drug addiction, Marcelo told me: "When certain qualities are not assumed to be present in the savior, they are not capable of assimilation in the Highest."

I did note the same occasional bellicosity he had exhibited with me in his correspondence with Germer, whom he idolized. Germer showed a genuine affection for Marcelo in return. There was an increasingly erratic quality in Motta's diaries after Germer's death. Germer had provided an external check and psychological safety valve for his young disciple, and his absence was palpable in Motta's subsequent record.

At lunch one day with Marianne and Claudia, Marcelo made a statement that rocked me. He proclaimed that he had been responsible for the death of Fred Mendel, Donald's brother-in-law and partner in Weiser's, my mentor in the publishing and production field, and my friend. I first met Freddie in 1968. Soon after, I came into the store while he was working at the register. I asked him to recommend a good book on Qabalah. He immediately suggested *Major Trends in Jewish Mysticism* by Gershom Scholem. I asked if he'd read it. He replied: "I don't read." Totally taken by the mythic aura of Weiser's Bookstore as a central hub of the Mystery Traditions, I thought: "Wow, these guys are so heavy they don't even need to read!" Years later, I attended Freddie's funeral and placed a shovel full of dirt on his coffin in conformance with Jewish custom—the first time I had done that. Motta stated that, unless Weiser knuckled under to the publishing program he demanded, more deaths would follow.

I left Brazil troubled by the visit, to say the least. My conflict-of-interest dilemma had now gone into overdrive. I decided I would have to leave Weiser's. On the other hand, I believed I was spiritually on the right path as far as Thelema was concerned—although there had been some conversation about my continuing my A∴A∴ work with Gunther because of concerns raised by Motta's record and the visit. Marcelo and I were much alike in some ways, both being hyper-sensitive Cancerians. It was difficult for me to see many of my own tendencies reflected back in his early diaries. I got under his skin for exactly the same reason. I know I hurt his feelings and am saddened by that, although he certainly returned the compliment manyfold—both before and after.

Back in America

When Marianne and I returned to New York, the pressure of our deviating spiritual paths turned into open warfare. She mistook Motta for my HGA and I had to explain that whatever failings he exhibited were merely the human foibles of any spiritual teacher. I compared Motta to the representative of Charan Singh that I had found so disappointing. I pointed out that this did not mean her guru was a phony. Motta's problems were, likewise, not an indictment of the Law of Thelema.

I began typing my Probationer Record at Marcelo's request (he had eye trouble and did not want to be forced to decipher my handwriting). I had a two-hour phone conversation with Dan and Gurney about the trip. The impingement of the numerous social interactions and domestic concerns needing attention after so long an absence was frustrating, in addition to the backlog at work. But the wind seemed to be at my back in terms of my magical practices. The Mother of All Distractions popped in the door when my neighbor Stephen invited us downstairs for dinner with William Burroughs, Allen Ginsberg, and Chogyam Trungpa Rinpoche. At our wits' end, Marianne and I decided to pass. I spent the evening typing my diary and performing a series of exercises and divinations—sensing the most responsible, if not the most attractive, choice had been made.

Dan and Gurney visited soon after. Dan provided much guidance. I asked him to read my record—an indication of the high regard in which I held him. I also had a very personal conversation with Donald about the problems in my marriage, my hatred of the model of Sant Mat as a spiritual path, and my embrace of Thelema. He was a trusted friend and advisor. (Motta later read about this conversation in my diary and was angry at me for my intimacy with Donald.)

SPRING 1976

I was in the final stages of memorizing my chapter of *Liber LXV* and working on Motta's manuscript of *LXV Commented*. I had just finished typing my record and was deep into the Temple construction while looking for an apartment. (Marianne and I had made an agreement that I would keep the Temple space after I moved out.) We sent a set of *The Equinox* to Marcelo as a thank-you for our stay there.

I sent him the typed record, which he soon returned with a series of perceptive comments. He was disturbed by reading the doubts I expressed about him, and worried about my friendship with Dan. He gave me a condition that I either align myself with Gunther or work with him alone, with no further contact with Gunther on matters of personal magical work. I chose to stay with Motta. I had written that, on returning to New York, I had had a liaison with a prostitute, and later that night had cried over leaving Marianne. He explained that I was undergoing the ordeal of the Vampire and offered me three alternatives: leave Thelema and accept Marianne's spiritual path; leave Marianne and have no contact with even her possessions; or "conquer her ... and bend her to Our purposes." He also stated: "Understand this: a Thelemite must either be married to a Thelemite or must be single. You cannot allow a traitor in the circle. If you are in a boat, and want to go in one direction, and someone wants to go in another direction, you will go nowhere."

I began an inspiring period of magical work with Sally. Marianne and I removed our wedding rings and I rented an apartment on East 3rd Street. I read the *Illuminatus* trilogy by Robert Anton Wilson and Robert Shea, an excellent series of novels.

Copyright Research

On April 26, I submitted a fairly extensive legal brief I had compiled on the issue of the copyright status of Crowley's literary estate. Marcelo, Donald, and I were trying to determine if Marcelo had a legal claim to copyright and how strong it might be if he did. A childhood friend of my father was a successful New York attorney. He offered me his assistance by generously allowing one of his staff lawyers who specialized in copyright law to look over Motta's claims, in particular his claim to title through the "Follower" letter. (Sascha Germer had written to Marcelo in Brazil on October 30, 1962 informing him of Germer's death. She wrote: "You are the Follower. Take it from me, as he died in my Arms and it was [sic] his last Words. Who the Heir of the Library is I do not know up to now.") Donald allowed me to pursue this research at work, because there was no charge to the company beyond my time, and the possibility of establishing copyright was a worthwhile outcome if it could be accomplished. The attorney believed that, based on the evidence he saw, Motta had some chance to establish a claim after a very long, serious, extensive, and expensive international legal campaign. During this investigation, we secured a copy of Crowley's will and learned he had left his copyrights to the O.T.O.

Mrs. Germer's Death

On April 28, 1976, Motta was contacted by Phyllis Seckler, who informed him of Sascha Germer's death. (Phyllis had written him a week earlier, after reading *The Commentaries of AL*.) Phyllis was a longtime member of Agape Lodge. (Officially founded by Wilfred T. Smith in 1935 in Southern California, Agape Lodge functioned in one form or another until 1949, when it ceased holding regular meetings.) Phyllis had met Motta when he visited the Germers in the 1950s. She had later been married to Grady McMurtry, another Agape member, but they were now separated. Sascha had died in April 1975 and the O.T.O. had just learned of it a year later.

Karl Germer had been the head of Thelema, acknowledged by the entire membership as Crowley's successor as Outer Head of O.T.O. after the latter's death in 1947. A Germanic personality, Germer was reclusive and easily angered by the behavior of O.T.O. initiates. He identified himself with Saturn, the devourer of his children; his magical motto was Saturnus. The younger people chafed at his oppressive, humorless, and strict demeanor. Germer died in 1962.

Sascha Germer was difficult as well, and eschewed the help offered by O.T.O. members. She lived in isolation after her husband's death and went into a progressive mental decline. In 1967, she endured a robbery in which she reported that she had been brutalized. No one knew who had done it, but she accused one of Phyllis Seckler's children in a letter to Motta and others. This was untrue. Ed Sanders, in early editions of *The Family*, took the research Grady McMurtry had compiled during his investigation of the robbery, which pointed to members of Jean Brayton's Solar Lodge. (Sanders freely added his own mix of rumor, falsehood, and fantasy to Grady's factual evidence. Sanders politely removed the Solar Lodge chapter from later editions of the book after Bill Breeze pointed out to him that the Solar Lodge was not O.T.O.)

Jean Brayton was "initiated" by Ray and Mildred Burlingame into the Minerval degree in late October of 1962, just days after Karl Germer's death. The Burlingames had also been members of Agape Lodge. While Ray had been recognized as a IX°, he had never been chartered to initiate. Thus, Jean Brayton's initiation and subsequent organizing activities in the name of O.T.O. were as invalid as her group's behavior was corrupt.

The robbery seems to have been the last straw for Mrs. Germer's sanity. She had written to Motta that the robbers had thrown acid in her face, which does not appear to have happened. Her mental state was apparently so fragile that the investigating officers did not believe there had even been a robbery, and felt that the chaos in the house had been of her own making.

In 2007, a founding member of the Solar Lodge, who calls himself Frater Shiva, published *Inside Solar Lodge: Outside the Law*, a book worth reading. He acknowledged the accuracy of Grady's conclusions, admitting that members of the group committed the robbery. Although he says he did not personally participate, one of the thieves told him he had drugged Mrs. Germer, but that he had treated her gently during the robbery. Most of the important treasures from that theft, including Crowley's Golden Dawn Robes, perished in the 1969 fire that destroyed the Solar Lodge ranch. The author expressed acceptance of the fact that Jean Brayton was neither a properly initiated member nor a properly chartered representative of Ordo Templi Orientis.

On learning of Sascha's death, Motta blamed the surviving Agape Lodge members for not having helped her despite herself. He was angry with them for her poor living situation and her lonely death. It is understandable that he was concerned about the widow of his beloved teacher, but there is no record of his having helped her either. He was also well aware of how difficult she could be, she having alienated him as well.

ON MAY 11, I had a phone conversation with Helen Parsons Smith. She was the third early member of Agape Lodge in this story. Helen had been married to two Thelemic legends, Jack Parsons and Wilfred T. Smith. (Parsons succeeded Smith as Agape Lodgemaster and Smith succeeded Parsons as Helen's husband.) During our most cordial conversation, Helen made the first mention of the possibility of my coming to California to help her sort through and organize what was left of the Germer Library.

On May 21, I took acid at my apartment. This was my first trip in some years. I began with a ritual bath, LBRP, Star Ruby, LBRH, ritual consecration of the acid, Sunset Adoration from the roof of my building, and Hatha Yoga. It was hot. But the noise from the street was bothering me, so I closed the windows. Then I closed the door to the room in which I sat, trying to ward off the sounds from the building. I eventually stuffed my ears with cotton trying to achieve more quiet.

I was sitting in asana staring into a full-size mirror after I was too high to continue reading *The Questions of King Milinda,* as I had been doing earlier in the evening. A series of disturbing hallucinations began swirling in the mirror. I was experiencing fears of obsession, possession, and madness. I sat there for over an hour. At last, I realized I was sitting alone, naked, in a New York apartment, in front of a mirror, on acid, on a hot night, with all the doors and windows closed and cotton stuffed in my ears. Going mad was the least of my problems! I burst out laughing.

In early June, I began working with *Liber V vel Reguli* physically for the first time. I discovered the trick of turning *Magick in Theory and Practice* upside down to find the direction for the averse invoking pentagrams. The typography is brilliantly designed for doing exactly that. This may not be so interesting to people used to the later edition of *Magick* published by the O.T.O. in 1994, but it is an enormously cool aspect of Crowley's 1929 edition.

In mid-June, Dan Gunther and I had our first conversation about forming the Order of Thelema Publishing Company.

SUMMER 1976

Marianne rented half the loft to our friend Jane, who had had a construction problem in her apartment. This arrangement resolved Jane's difficulty and helped Marianne and me with the expense of maintaining the loft and my apartment on East 3rd Street. The idea was to sell the loft to Jane, as Marianne was planning to move to Washington State. Jane later did purchase Marianne's half.

I traveled to Nashville to discuss the publishing company idea with Dan and Gurney. I was delighted by the scene and began to consider moving there. I later learned that Motta expressed suspicion to Dan about my involvement in a business venture, which—at this stage of our relationship—was puzzling, to say the least.

Marianne and I spoke to Donald about leaving the company. He was especially saddened by our dissolving our marriage. I remained troubled by my sense that Motta posed a danger to people in the company and that I was somehow a channel for him. Curiously, my diary does not mention Motta's statement about Freddie in Brazil and the subsequent conflict it created with my remaining at Weiser's. It was as if the sheer outrage silenced me. However, I described it in detail during my 1983 deposition before the Maine trial.

I note in my diary that I expressed my first interest in exploring *Liber Israfel*. I had read Migene González-Wippler's book *Santería: African Magic in Latin America* and was intrigued by her discussion of Eleggua and his role as the gateway of Magick. *Liber Israfel* was later to become a monumental component of my life.

California Here I Come

The developing situation called for me to travel to California as Motta's representative in the matter of securing his rights to the O.T.O. property. While we knew the 1967 robbery and subsequent chaos had caused much damage, part of the Library had survived. What remained and how could it be protected?

Coincident to the matter of the disposition of the O.T.O. Library was my planned sales trip to California. Donald and I had decided that our active California bookstore customers would be better served by a visit from the "home office," rather than relying on our commissioned sales reps. These folks were understandably more anxious to get orders than to serve the needs of our customers. The theory was that I could do better by assessing each individual store against our title list. It was a brilliant plan and I would make three such trips.

I did some fancy footwork that allowed me to devote several days to gaining an understanding of the Germer estate situation, meeting the three surviving members of Agape Lodge, and promoting

Motta's interests. Donald agreed to my taking the time in hopes that Motta could secure the copyrights and establish Weiser as his publisher of record, particularly with the possibility of unpublished material being uncovered in the Library.

This entire situation was like walking on a tightrope in a hurricane. On the one hand, here was a psychopath taking credit for a magical murder. On the other, a credentialed authority was suggesting a very profitable partnership with the world's largest Crowley publisher. (I did not tell Donald about Motta's statement about Freddie until some years later.)

I was in touch with Mr. Adolph Gualdoni, the Calaveras County Coroner who was overseeing the disposition of the Germer estate. He was a classically overworked bureaucrat who had been overwhelmed by a series of recent events, including a multi-vehicle accident that had claimed numerous lives and blocked off several roads. He was uncertain about how his time would work, but completely amenable to recognizing Motta's rights as part of the group of claimants to the portion of Germer's property that was held in trust for O.T.O. I sensed that the very last thing he wanted to hear about was a problem between those to whom he was talking. He was far too busy. It suited him just fine to know that we were all united in our desire to protect O.T.O. property.

As the trip neared, Motta warned me that I would be walking into the very headquarters of the Black Lodge. I was impressionable enough to be in a state of great fear and anticipation at the thought of meeting with Grady McMurtry, Phyllis Seckler, and Helen Parsons Smith. Motta painted the picture that I would be fascinated and manipulated, that I needed to be extremely cautious and self-aware, prepared to do battle for my very life and sanity, and that I would be under constant magical attack. I was filled with dread and anxiety as the trip approached. I made several incomplete phone calls to him in Brazil and waited daily for a detailed letter of instruction as to precisely what I should do.

On the other hand, it was not until July 10 that my magical diary makes the very first mention of the California trip as a certainty, and only the second time it was mentioned at all. I had spoken to Helen again. After this entry, scheduling and preparation are lightly mentioned. But my diary at this time is almost entirely focused on a steady stream of sexual partners, including Marianne. There is great sorrow expressed at the loss of our marriage. The record's catalog of drug use includes acid, pot, hashish, cocaine, amphetamines, and alcohol. And, of course, there is the continuing obsession with magical ritual and meditation, along with other spiritual practices, including divination—but not one mention of a question on the upcoming California excursion.

I do know from voluminous letters that I was in regular correspondence with Motta, Helen, Phyllis, and Mr. Gualdoni. These letters refer to numerous phone calls as well, and my handwritten notes of these calls were preserved as part of the discovery process for the legal battles of the 1980s, to be discussed. But with that said, it is astounding to observe how little mention of the upcoming trip passed into the pages of my diary. It is as if that were my day job and the diary recorded only my spiritual life.

I flew out of New York on July 14, 1976, the anniversary of the day the French mob stormed the Bastille in 1789.

* * *

CHAPTER 9

CALIFORNIA AND GRADY MCMURTRY

SUMMER 1976 (CONTINUED)

Having "banished my brains out," I landed in California, and Helen and Phyllis met me at the airport. I was stunned. They seemed the walking embodiments of Jan and Dean's 1960s hit *The Little Old Lady from Pasadena*. As best I remember, they may even have been wearing tennis shoes. My suspicions began to melt and I began to question Motta's sanity. There was clearly a disconnect between what I had been led to expect and what I actually encountered. Both women were entirely pleasant and cordial. (In view of what was to happen with Phyllis, it would have been more accurate for Motta to calmly warn me about walking into a viper's nest rather than frantically projecting me into some Dennis Wheatley-style outpost of the Black Lodge.)

My first reaction to Phyllis was actually one of great warmth and a sense of familiarity. I had been in much closer touch with Helen by letter and phone, and I confused the two of them at first. Curiously, Phyllis had a similar effect on Gurney when he first met her. (Was this a case of magical fascination?) Phyllis could be charming. We three went to her home in Dublin and had a long conversation. Grady was unavailable and would come in two days.

Phyllis, Helen, and I spoke for hours about their experience of the Order in Agape Lodge from the 1930s on. Their views of Karl and Sascha Germer were far different from Motta's—based on their long acquaintance with the couple rather than the youthful fantasies of a young and lonely college student from a foreign country. They recognized Germer's assets and shortcomings. He was close to Phyllis and had acknowledged her in a letter as an Adeptus

Minor (5°=6$^\square$). Phyllis kindly allowed me to cut an almond Wand from the tree she cultivated for that purpose in her back yard.

Helen was a flighty one, but quite brilliant. Her editions of previously unpublished Crowley material were nicely produced. But I learned that she thought her A∴A∴ membership was over because her Instructor, Wilfred Smith, had died. Helen may have had some odd ideas, but she and I remained friendly until the day she died.

Helen and Phyllis were both angry about Motta's announced intention to publish their names in his upcoming O.T.O. Manifesto scheduled for *LXV Commented*. They said it violated the Order's tradition of not naming women members. They also felt that the Agape Lodge members had done the best job they could in protecting the Order. They interpreted the copyright situation and publishing activities of the day as acceptable, even a good thing. They explained that the Order had been moribund under Germer's leadership and that they had expected the Thelemic movement would simply die out. Instead, the publication of the *Thoth Tarot* in 1971 had rekindled interest in the O.T.O. and there had been a flurry of activity since.

I understood their point of view, as I had felt the same way when Motta first raised the issue of controlling publication of the Crowley literary corpus by asserting copyright ownership. I thought the looseness of the situation in the early 1970s had allowed for the most creativity in spreading Crowley's writings. So much was coming into print; I didn't want to see it inhibited by a monolithic controlling authority.

Then C. W. Daniel Publishing in the U.K. released *Crowley on Christ* in late 1974. I read it with great interest and thought it would be a perfect book to give to my father, who was a voracious reader. But the publisher had added *De Arte Magica* as an appendix. So much for sending it to Dad! I spoke to Ian Miller, president of the company, and asked him why they had done it. He said, "Oh, we accidently left it out of *The Secret Rituals of the O.T.O.* and this was our first opportunity to fix that omission." After that conversation, I began to support Motta's position—which is that of the O.T.O. today. In order to have doctrinal coherence, we needed to have control of the message. It's not very complicated either to explain or understand. What religion or school of thought is not in a position to issue authorized editions of its own teaching?

The surviving generation of Agape Lodge members had lived for so long in a spiritual underground, in conditions of scarcity, that they had come to accept "living like a refugee" as normal. *The Book of the Law* is right: "All must be done well and with business way" (AL III:41).

The Library

The next day, July 15, Helen, Phyllis, and I went to the Germer estate. We arrived before Mr. Gualdoni and I climbed in the window to make a quick survey of the place. It was a disaster. Papers, books, and paintings were strewn all over the floor in a most distressing manner. I came back out and, when Mr. Gualdoni arrived, we all went in. Mr. Gualdoni was much at ease as the three of us presented ourselves as a united group. Grady had earlier established himself as a man of good character and presented the requisite documentation to be recognized legally as the legitimate representative of O.T.O. I had informed Mr. Gualdoni from New York that I represented Marcelo Motta, another Thelemite with an interest in the Library. He left us in the house to attend to other duties.

We found a treasure trove in the midst of complete chaos. There was more material than anyone expected to find after the Brayton robbery and repeated vandalizing of the house. We cleaned up as best we could. We found boxes and file cabinets of papers, some paintings by Crowley, and some books. There was a collection of letters from the major players of Thelema. Karl Germer had preserved letters between Crowley and various disciples—including Germer himself, Frater Achad, Gerald Yorke, and others. The Library was a window into Thelemic history. Helen asked me— in front of Phyllis—to consider moving out to California to help her catalog the materials, as she had accepted the role of sorting through and organizing them for the Order. I told her I would seriously think about it. This was later to become a flashpoint between Phyllis and me, especially after she seized the Library. We were in a hurry to go through things, because Mr. Gualdoni was coming back to lock up.

HERE IS HOW I understood the situation. We had found a collection of papers and other effects that belonged to O.T.O. It was in danger of being confiscated by local authorities because of outstanding property liabilities related to Mrs. Germer's death. Mr. Gualdoni knew Grady was a rightful representative of the Order. He accepted my statement that Marcelo was a rightful representative as well. He was willing to separate O.T.O. property from the Germers' personal property. There was no need to overcomplicate anything. Mr. Gualdoni could properly hand over the Order material to us. The county could then proceed to liquidate the personal assets of the Germers to satisfy their unpaid back taxes as a separate matter. It would be up to O.T.O. to sort through any remaining issues within the bonds of the Order.

Meeting Grady

The following day, July 16, Grady came in from Berkeley, where he lived with his girlfriend Shirene and her son Eric. Grady was a trip. I liked him at once. We went to a bar, had a few drinks together, and discussed many things. I found him to have an active mind and a great sense of humor. He seemed entirely comfortable in his own skin, quite different in that regard from the impression Marcelo conveyed in Brazil. He also seemed willing to negotiate—a character trait he would continue to exhibit for the nine remaining years of our friendship.

Grady enlisted in the Army in World War II, having joined O.T.O. at Agape Lodge in April 1941 (according to his testimony in the 1985 San Francisco trial). He was initiated to his Minerval and I° by Wilfred T. Smith. He visited Crowley in 1943 while on leave in England. He held the rank of Lieutenant, and was later promoted to Captain. He and Crowley played chess and discussed life and Magick. Crowley personally gave Grady the IX° and attested to that fact in multiple documents. There was a great deal of turmoil in Agape Lodge, the sole official O.T.O. lodge in the world at this time. Agape had come under the leadership of Jack Parsons, who was engaged in various mysterious magical operations and had been writing cryptic letters to Crowley. Crowley was confused and irritated about not knowing the facts. He appointed Grady as a Sovereign Grand Inspector General of the Order and asked him to collect information about Parsons and the Agape situation for him.

The Caliphate Letters

Grady and I went back to Phyllis' house and he showed me the documents he had received from Crowley known as the "Caliphate Letters." (The title "Caliph" is familiar enough from Islam, where it denotes the political and spiritual leader of the community after the death of the Prophet. In my mind, it is perfectly analogous to our term "Outer Head of the Order," and Crowley used the appellations interchangably.) Crowley's letters to Grady were written on beautiful stationary with wax seals made by Crowley's seal ring and signed by him. Motta had told me that he believed Crowley was pulling Grady's leg with these documents of authorization, that the papers were more a joke on a young American disciple than anything else. I beg to differ.

These letters were the key elements of Grady's legal claim and far outweighed any documentation Motta had. I realized Marcelo's complete misunderstanding of his own legal position. Yes, perhaps he could qualify as one of the "Heads of the Order," a term Germer used in his will. But no, he was neither the Outer Head of O.T.O. nor in any position to "pull rank" on Grady. *Au contraire.*

There were two letters of direct authorization from Crowley. The first, dated March 22, 1946, gave Grady emergency authorization "to take charge of the whole work of the Order in California." The second, dated April 11, 1946, appointed Grady as "Our representative in the United States of America, and his authority is to be considered Ours." Both warrants were subject to the approval or veto of Karl Germer. Whatever Motta later claimed about Germer not having authorized McMurtry's status, Germer also never challenged it. Furthermore, several letters from Germer to Grady in the 1940s and 1950s confirm Germer's full knowledge of Crowley's authorizations, and Germer's acceptance of Grady's position as the pre-eminent leader of the Order in California. Further evidence of Germer's full awareness of Grady's position is contained in a letter Crowley wrote to Germer on June 19, 1946 (copy to Grady). "Frater H.A. [Grady] has an authority which enables him to supersede Frater 210 [Jack Parsons] whenever he pleases. The only limitation on his power in California is that any decision which he takes is subject to revision or veto by yourself."

There were two additional letters, written several years apart, stating that Crowley eyed Grady as the potential Caliph to follow Germer. The first, dated November 21, 1944, describes Germer as the natural Caliph to follow Crowley; however, because of Germer's age, Crowley needed to look for *his* successor. "One of the (startling few) commands given to me was this: 'Trust not a stranger; fail not an heir.'" He wrote that Grady's "actual life or 'blooding' is the sort of initiation I regard as essential for the Caliph."

The second letter, dated June 17, 1947, chided Grady for not keeping in closer touch. Crowley explained that, while Germer was his natural successor, "after *his* death, the terrible burden of responsibility might very easily fall on your shoulders." (A number of other letters from Crowley are considered part of the "Caliphate Letters" collection, including one in which Crowley certifies Grady as a fully paid-up member of the IX° and another assigning Grady rights in *Magick without Tears* and *The Book of Thoth*. All of Crowley's letters to Grady demonstrate a warmth and high regard for this young warrior.)

Motta could not have been more wrong when he wrote to me that Grady interpreted the title of Caliph to mean he could establish a personal dynasty with his children as his successors. Grady explained his idea that his successor as Caliph would be approved by an election of IX° members. This is exactly what happened after his death in 1985, and it produced some creative and unexpected results.

GRADY SERVED IN THE ARMY again during the Korean War and was promoted to the rank of Major. When he returned to California in 1953, he earned his Master's Degree in Political Science. He taught

American government at the University of California, Berkeley
for two years. During the following years, he had some disagreements with Germer. He determined that further discussion would
either be fruitless, or would result in open conflict that might harm
his membership status. He moved to Washington, D.C. in 1961,
taught as an associate professor at George Washington University,
and later worked for the federal government. He was unaware of
Germer's death in 1962, which was kept secret for security reasons.

Toward the end of 1968, Phyllis wrote to inform Grady of the
1967 robbery and he returned to California soon after. He conducted a full investigation and shared his conclusions with the
police and FBI. It was from this investigation that Ed Sanders drew
for his Solar Lodge chapter in *The Family*. Grady and Phyllis were
later married. He then invoked his emergency authorization from
Crowley, informing both Israel Regardie and Gerald Yorke that he
was reactivating the O.T.O.

Now What?

My escalating awareness of the disconnect between Motta's perceptions and objective reality was playing some havoc with me.
What was my responsibility in the face of the fact that everything I
thought I had known appeared to be wrong?

Later that night, after having spent time with Grady, I went
back to my hotel room. We had arranged to visit the Germer house
again the next day. I was studying *Liber O* in *Magick in Theory and
Practice* when I realized I had actually been doing the Pentagram
ritual incorrectly for many years. I was not vibrating the names as
described in Section III of the instruction. Book in hand, I tried to
do the vibration properly, inhaling the name, letting it descend to
my feet, extending myself forward in the Sign of the Enterer as the
Name came rushing forth, uttering the Name, then returning in the
Sign of Silence. Although awkward and confusing at first, it felt
right and I spent some time that night practicing it.

The next day, July 17, Grady, Phyllis, Helen, and I went back to
the house. The dark aura hanging over the interior was oppressive.
Karl Germer's painful death, Mrs. Germer's years of insanity and

isolation, the violence of the 1967 robbery, the vandalism, and the unattended magical energies of the Library had attracted powerful qliphotic energies. It was the most haunted and disturbing place I have ever been in. Helen and Phyllis went outside and Grady and I went upstairs to the bedroom, carefully checking corners and closets with a flashlight. Grady did the Lesser Banishing Ritual of the Pentagram while I sat in the corner. I was overjoyed to see that he used the technique of vibrating the divine names that I had just discovered the night before. He was the first person, other than Marianne, I had ever seen do the ritual. A golden light began to suffuse the room. I couldn't believe my astral eyes. The burdensome atmosphere began to glow with a beautiful radiance. That is how I "met" Grady McMurtry. We went downstairs after he finished. The ladies said that they had seen a golden light coming out of the upstairs window and asked what we had been doing.

Grady told me he was entirely committed to the idea of sharing the Germer finds with Motta in a fraternal manner. He made it clear that he did not claim A∴A∴ leadership and was happy to accept Motta's claims to A∴A∴ authority. He expected the same courtesy from Motta regarding his position in O.T.O. This seemed to me a sensible arrangement between co-religionists who should have been on the same side. I felt there was no need to challenge a unified O.T.O. claim. Had Grady not been so reasonable in recognizing Motta's rights in the matter, I would have been faced with a different situation. But I believed that Grady and Marcelo could work things out between themselves. Grady's legal claims were rock solid. Motta's were certainly far less so on paper. But since Grady was willing to recognize Motta as a Brother, I believed a gentleman's agreement was in place that could satisfy all concerned—without the need to tie things up in an unnecessary legal mess that would drain the non-existent resources of all involved.

By this stage, it should be remembered, I was an educated observer. I now knew the legal positions of *both* men. I had consulted a copyright attorney on Motta's entire legal case. I could now weigh that against Grady's claim. I knew that if I tried to challenge Grady's claim—as Motta either may have, or apparently, expected me to do—it would fail on legal grounds. The preponderance of evidence and documentation were entirely in Grady's favor. Motta certainly had "the Follower" statement from the letter announcing Germer's death by his grief-stricken widow (who was likely not a member of O.T.O.). There was also mention in an earlier letter from Germer himself, dated April 20, 1962, in which he stated: "I am prepared to give you a Charter for a Lodge to work only the first Three Degrees. I gave you many of the Rituals at one time or another. Please state exactly which Rituals you have copies of. Are they complete?" That Charter, if it was sent, never arrived. In 1967, Sascha misinterpreted Germer's letter to mean that he had actually mailed the Charter.

Motta testified in his deposition of December 21, 1982 that he had never been formally initiated into O.T.O. He stated that Germer gave him the IX° directly. I would not dispute that and do not bring up this issue to criticize either Motta or Germer. I was later "raised by my bootstraps" to a couple of degrees in O.T.O. by Grady based on "the situation and the terrain." However, in a court of law, as battling adversaries, it was my informed opinion, as I stated in my 1983 deposition, that Motta did not "stand a snowball's chance in hell" of prevailing against Grady. (I was proved right in 1985, when Motta actually did challenge Grady and lost decisively.) I made the decision in 1976 that, under the circumstances, Motta's best option was to cooperate with the man with the better paperwork, especially since that man was willing to work with him.

As things wound down, Grady and I each agreed to write a letter to Marcelo before I left for Los Angeles. The plan was for Grady to mail them both in one envelope. Grady's letter was a cordial outreach, offering friendship, respect, and an acknowledgement of Motta's A∴A∴ work and position. He referred to A∴A∴ as "the flaming heart" of O.T.O. His letter made no secret of Grady's strong position regarding copyrights through O.T.O. and the will, but he offered to share materials with Motta.

Motta's reply made future cooperation between himself and Grady impossible.

On July 18, after writing my letter, I flew off to start my business trip in Southern California with the intention of working my way back North and taking initiation with Grady on July 27. I wanted to prove to Motta my willingness to put my soul on the line regarding the decision to cooperate with the O.T.O. I wrote Motta a separate handwritten letter on July 19 from my motel in Los Angeles. I tried to explain myself further, acknowledging my suspicions of Phyllis, criticizing Germer's handling of the disposition of the Library (which really angered Motta), and telling him that I was planning to leave Weiser's and return to California to make copies for him and help archive the Library for the O.T.O. (I made the mistake of referring to Germer as "Karl" in my letter, because I had just spent so much time with Phyllis, Helen, and Grady, who all referred to him that by that name. This angered Motta more than anything.)

Dan and Gurney Arrive

Daniel, Gurney, and I had been in close touch before I left New York, and they were aware of my legal researches and the nature of the task ahead of me in California. When I actually surveyed the situation and arrived at a series of conclusions that differed so greatly from Marcelo's expectations, I was desperate to have some confirmation—or at least an outside point of view—while there was still time to rearrange anything in the event I was mistaken. Dan located me at my motel in Los Angeles. During a long phone call, we discussed the possibility of him and Gurney coming out to meet Grady, et al. I begged them to do so and give me feedback and an independent assessment of the O.T.O.

Dan and Gurney both responded to the call of duty and I picked them up at the San Francisco airport on July 25. We three went to Phyllis' house. Dan has a vivid memory of Gurney entering the house, sitting down on the couch, and letting out a huge fart! While my memory is less vivid on that specific incident, it rings true for two reasons. The first is that it is quite characteristic of our old friend, Richard. The second is that it would have been a totally appropriate magical commentary on what was soon to follow with Phyllis.

Grady arrived shortly after we did, and Helen came to say hello and help Phyllis with the preparation of the meal. Dan and Richard discussed their magical practices with Phyllis. They were on an active course of creative magical work in Nashville. The trouble began when Gurney mentioned he was an aspirant to A∴A∴. Phyllis whirled around: "How dare you mention the A∴A∴ in public! It is so sacred that to refer to it openly is blasphemy." We were shocked. Gurney replied: "I signed the Oath of the Probationer. On the Task it says, 'He shall everywhere proclaim openly his association with the A∴A∴ and speak of It and Its principles, even so little as he understandeth, for that mystery is the enemy of Truth.'" She left the room.

Grady was uninterested in this particular drama, and apparently quite tired. At one point, he dozed off in his chair. Phyllis' outburst had him rolling his eyes. Soon after, however, he became animated as he regaled us with Crowley stories that we soaked up like young sponges. He showed us a pocket-sized portable chess set Crowley had given him as a gift, and told us a story of a young Kenneth Grant coming to the door and asking to see the Master. Crowley coyly turned, looked into the room and said, "What Master?" We were just delighted to be able to hear Grady share his memories.

Later, Gurney demonstrated the Star Ruby. He was the most powerful dramatic ritualist I have known. This was the first time I had seen the Star Ruby performed by anyone other than my own fledgling efforts. Gurney had mastered the ritual. I sensed fear coming from Phyllis. Despite her long association with Thelemic magick, I am not surprised. Gurney was a professionally trained stage actor and able to project his voice and enhance his motions in an extraordinary way. Under Dan's tutelage, he was also tuning in to the energies of the New Aeon in a profound manner that, I believe, exceeded anything in her long experience.

Later still, we told her we were each learning *Liber V vel Reguli*, the Ritual of the Mark of the Beast. Phyllis raised her eyebrows. She walked into the bedroom off the living room, a private place where her better books were kept and which, I believe, she used as a Temple. After perhaps ten minutes absence, she emerged with an all-knowing look on her face. She explained to the three of us that she had just consulted her Holy Guardian Angel and he had told her that we were all too young and not of sufficient Grade to work on that ritual!

We locked eyes with each other, dumbfounded. We may have been "kids," but we all knew Crowley described the ritual as "adapted for the daily use of the Magician of whatever grade." We also knew that a Thelemite would never presume to make a statement like "My Angel tells me you should ..." A Thelemite knows it is the duty of each of us to meet our own Angel and that "Each mistake is the combing-out of some tangle in the hair of the bride as she is being coiffed for marriage" (*Magick in Theory and Practice*, p. 171). We silently wrote her off as either delusional or a fraud—a gate to be passed. Shakespeare's dictum that even a fool would be considered wise if he remained silent is quite true. Her inappropriate assertion was so uncalled for that it forever colored our perceptions of her. Everything she said after that was simply irrelevant.

On July 27, 1976, I joined O.T.O. with Grady as my initiator, assisted by Helen Parsons Smith. Gunther and Gurney joined with me. While Motta had told Dan to take initiation if it were offered—presumably to gain credentials for Motta's future Society Ordo Templi Orientis (SOTO) efforts in the U.S. (commenced in May 1977 under Dan's leadership)—Dan and Gurney requested initiation as enthusiastically as I did. We three agreed that Grady was a legitimate spiritual leader. (We were all to have our ears pinned back accordingly when Motta learned of our actions and conclusions.)

Helen surprised us by giving me a joint after the ritual. She was opposed to drug use, but someone had given it to her and she passed it along to us as an act of kindness. I thought it demonstrated a great breadth of soul on her part. I guess I did something similar by eating the first chicken I'd eaten for years during a little banquet we had later. My diary mentions that Grady was openly encouraging me that evening—in front of Phyllis, obviously—to return to California to help Helen with the Library.

Some Thoughts on the Motta Mission

Many readers will doubtless be aware of Motta's displeasure with me over the California/Germer Library episode. To make a long story short, the situation blew up after the events described above, which resulted in years of animosity and legal battles, to be further chronicled in the pages to follow. The case went as far as the Supreme Court of the United States, which declined to retry it.

Motta blamed me for my part in it and repeatedly expressed his hatred of me. However, in my opinion, he bore a far greater responsibility for his disappointment than I did. To paraphrase Harry Truman: "The buck stopped there."

To begin with, Motta simply had no concept of diplomacy. He was singularly unable to "play nice with the other children." He tried to bully a group of older, more experienced O.T.O. people in California who had, frankly, very little regard for him. They had met him as a twenty-three-year-old in 1955–56, and he was now trying to order them around after so many years of no contact.

Motta strutted his "Follower" letter from the grief-stricken and desperate Sascha, while spitting on Grady's direct authorizations from Aleister Crowley. Sitting alone in his apartment in Rio with a typewriter and a bottle of liquor, he acted as if he were the Lord of the Aeon Himself. There is no question in my mind that he considered himself the "Inner Head of the Order," with authority over Grady and everyone else in O.T.O. In fact, in the Maine trial in 1984, he finally openly claimed to have become the Outer Head of the Order upon Germer's death in 1962. Although the transcripts of both trials are laden with typographical errors, both he and his attorney repeated this statement several times, despite the fact that he had previously abjured the position of Outer Head in countless letters and published manifestos. It was a shocking turnaround. He firmly reasserted this claim at length in the 1985 San Francisco trial, both in his own testimony and in his attorney's opening and closing statements.

IN OUR CORRESPONDENCE and memoed phone conversations prior to my going to California, Motta advised me to express to Grady,

Helen, and Phyllis that he was willing to share the Library with them—a position he had also expressed in his letters to Phyllis and Helen that spring (the not-so-subtle point was that he believed he was in control of it). Motta stated that all Heads of Lodge should work together and have copies of everything. (Motta's use of the term "Heads of Lodge" was a paraphrase from Germer's will, which referred to "Heads of the Order" as those entitled to inherit O.T.O. property. Remember, Motta believed Germer had made him a Head of Lodge.) He told me to say that the Library should remain in the United States, and even that he was willing to share his royalties on the Crowley portion of *The Commentaries of AL*—on condition that they legally establish O.T.O. in the United States. He wanted me to excuse his lack of contact with them by explaining that he had "just come out of the desert."

This all seemed quite reasonable. I explained to him that I intended a diplomatic approach. I wrote on June 30 that I had just spoken to Mr. Gualdoni and that he was finally ready for me to come. "I just got off the phone with him and feel quite excited that we may be closing in on the home stretch with this, if I can just keep Helen, Phyllis, and him in a nice balance. I think, with my natural diplomacy, that I can pull it off."

Then Motta turned on a pivot—just days before I left New York. Now what was I supposed to do? (All capitalization is transcribed from his original letters. Any comments in brackets [...] are my own.)

July 7, 1976
For your information, neither Helen Parsons Smith nor Phyllis McMurtry have ANY legal right to the Thelemic Library: Helen has NEVER had an O.T.O. patent, and Smith [Wilfred T. Smith] was not empowered to nominate her a Head of anything—only Germer had this authority. I stated otherwise in my Manifesto for my own purposes, and I will not attack Helen if she affirms herself a Head, on the contrary, I will support her—but NOT Phyllis. Phyllis has no right whatsoever unless she can show a Power of Attorney from her husband Grady—if he IS her husband—he has been strangely silent throughout. Grady never had

any authority to nominate Heads of Lodges—again, only Germer had this authority—and again, I quote him as Lodge Head for my own purposes. Therefore, understand that I will not accept Phyllis McMurtry as either an equal (as Head, I mean) or as an heir. Her children robbed Mrs. Germer, and she has still not explained to my satisfaction how the Book of Thoth plates ended up in Grady's hands. They were originally in the Thelemic Library, and furthermore, anyone who says that copies had been made is a thief and a liar. [Motta confused the black-and-white line-art plates of the various Trees of Life et al., as published in *The Book of Thoth*, with the color paintings of the cards by Lady Harris. The former were in the Germer Library. The latter are in the Warburg Institute.]

The real kicker was his letter of July 10. Because he had waited so long to reveal this change of (or true) strategy, the July 10 letter arrived *after* I left New York. He was obviously aware of this probability, as he sent a copy to Donald and asked him to forward it to me in California. The letter came in a packet of correspondence that met me on July 21, *after* I arrived in Los Angeles. Thus I received this letter *after* all the events with Grady and Mr. Gualdoni of the week before.

Here are a series of extracts from that crucial letter. As the reader will note at the end, Motta was quite aware I would not see it before I left New York. I believe this lengthy extract (for which I ask the reader's forgiveness in advance) demonstrates that there was simply no way to win under General Motta's command. (Remember there is no evidence that Sascha Germer was a duly initiated member of O.T.O.)

July 10, 1976

As I stated in my previous letter, I do not think that either Helen Parsons Smith or Grady McMurtry EVER had a Charter from Germer, and I do not think that Germer EVER acknowledged Grady's ridiculous claims to a Caliphate or whatever. Also, I am now convinced that they all participated indirectly in, and profited indirectly from, the robbery at Headquarters. Further, being

Mrs. Germer's next door neighbors, so to speak, and obligated towards her in every possible way, they allowed the woman to starve to death. Now, like the vultures of Phyllis' first letters to me (!...) [in original], they are gathering over the remains.

The situation is very simple, here. I have two letters from Mrs. Germer (you have copies of them both, I trust) textually affirming that I have a Patent from Mr. Germer, dating of 1962, e.v., (some months before his death). I also have a letter from her stating that in his death bed He found time to confirm his trust in me by stating that I was "the Follower", whatever He may have meant by it.

I will accept as CO-HEIR in the Thelemic Library anybody who can fulfill these two inalienable points:

1. Show letter from Mr. Germer acknowledging him or her Head of an O.T.O. Lodge AND letters from him, in the six months prior to his demease [sic], proving that the person was still considered in good standing with him.

2. Show letters from Mrs. Germer, after Mr. Germer's death, proving that she considered them as Brethren of the O.T.O. in good standing with Mr. Germer.

[. . .]

I want you to go to West Point and retain a local lawyer to defend my rights, Mr. Germer's rights, and Mrs. Germer's rights. A local lawyer is best in a small town—he will be trusted. Ask anybody for money that you can—Weiser, if he will help as he says, or K.N.—if you need it for expenses.

IF anybody else can prove himself or herself on the points I stated above, they can have my share of any rare books, or value of them: I demand only xeroxes OF ALL PAPERS AND UNPRINTED DOCUMENTS in the Library. These should be sent to K.N.'s custody, with the understanding that they belong to me (IN WRITING, PLEASE!).

If no one else can satisfy the local authorities on this point, I claim the entire Library, and equally I want it sent to K.N.'s headquarters provisorily.

Now, re the Swiss Metzger: You read Mr. Germer's letters to me about that man. If he can present letters written to him by Mr.

Germer, six months prior to Mr. Germer's death, acknowledging him as a friend and ally, I will recognize him as a CO-HEIR, or if he can present letters written to him by Mrs. Germer in the first three months following Mr. Germer's death containing instructions from Mr. Germer, in his death-bed, I will recognize him as CO-HEIR. Not otherwise.

But even if I am compelled to recognize him as a co-heir from a purely legal point of view, I do not recognize his magickal right to represent THELEMA or the O.T.O. in any way. I hope I make myself clear.

Also, hence forth, I do not recognize the right of Helen Parsons Smith to speak in Name of O.T.O. I never, of course, recognized the right of Phyllis McMurtry to do so, but I now add that I do not recognize the right of Phyllis McMurtry to speak in name of the A∴A∴ either.

As for Grady McMurtry, I shall wait until such time as he be willing to speak for himself, if he can, to decide one way or another.

[. . .]

Try to keep your mental balance. You are going to go against people with years of experience at establishing psychological dominance over untrained auras. Keep up your Banishings and Invocations, for this war.

Understand, I want no conciliation whatsoever. Those people must not be allowed to get anything that they can't prove clearly that they have a legitimate right to get, and I WANT THE LIBRARY or, failing this, I WANT COPIES OF ALL UNPUBLISHED MATTER.

As you know, I have a list of the printed contents of the Library here, that Mr. Germer ordered me to make when I was there, and of which he ordered me to keep a copy. If you need this, ask for it. [Note: This list was compiled over a decade before the Brayton robbery of 1967.]

I am sending this letter care of Mr. Weiser, against the possibility that you may already be in California when it reaches the U.S.A.

During my 1983 deposition for the 1984 Maine trial, Robert Mittel, Motta's lawyer, bore down with a vengeance on the July 10 letter. He challenged me: "So you did not attempt to communicate with anybody on July 25th or 26th, or whenever you got that letter from Motta, to the effect that, 'Wait a minute, the deal is off'?" I told him I hadn't. He continued with this line of questioning. I answered that, despite Motta's letter, I purposely did not "call the deal off" with Grady or appear in court to fight the Calaveras County recognition of Grady as the legitimate representative of the Order. "I was working for one thing, and by that point, I knew more about the situation than Motta. I was not about to go into court with his ridiculous and asinine claims and try to defend them. I was powerless by the weight of reality."

During the Maine trial itself, Weiser attorney James Erwin asked me in some detail whether either Gunther or Gernon attended the hearing on Motta's behalf. In fact, they too were in California, and knew it was taking place and that I was working. They also chose not to attend.

MOTTA WAS AN INCOMPREHENSIBLY INEPT strategist and tactician. His failure to provide me with an itemized list of instructions that would allow him to succeed is inexcusable—if success had been his goal. Giving me his power of attorney was like handing an electric clock to an aborigine and expecting him to plug it in and set the alarm. I have long felt he "sent a boy to do a man's job."

I did not understand the task with which I was being charged, nor did he explain it. Quite frankly, I do not believe he either knew what he wanted or what he expected me to do. If he had, he would have told me before I left. For example, there was never one word about the funds required to hire a lawyer (before his rather haphazard mention of asking "anybody for money" in a letter received a week after my completing my task). Nor did he ever provide written confirmation or verbal direction that hiring a lawyer is precisely what he expected me to do (except when it was too late for me to do so). His July 10 letter is so filled with irrational conditions that, had I received it prior to my "mission," it *might* have been enough to jolt me to my senses.

The situation, as I understood it, was totally amorphous. I therefore used my own judgment. I still believe I made the right decision. Had Motta worked within the agreements with Grady that I made on his behalf, the entire history of Thelema would have been far different. We would have experienced a Golden Age at that time, saving thirty-five years of effort to reach the place we are in now, and the unimaginable legal expenses and personal sacrifice imposed on us to get here.

THE ALTERNATIVE TO MOTTA setting me up to use my best judgment would have been for him to give me a list of specific tasks. If he wanted to hire a lawyer and was short of funds, he could have negotiated with Donald Weiser. Donald could have advanced him the fees for an attorney against Motta's future royalties for *The Commentaries of AL* and *LXV Commented*. I have earlier pointed out Donald's awareness of the financial benefits of Motta securing the copyrights. It would have been unlikely that the company would not have helped finance a portion of his legal quest.

In my 1983 deposition, I testified that—because of Motta's statement about Fred Mendel—I no longer believed it was in Donald's best interests to get more deeply involved with him. However, at the time of Motta's letter, I had not yet said anything to Donald. Motta could have spoken directly to Donald about hiring a lawyer. Or, he could have asked me to speak to him. If Motta had approached me, I would have raised my concern about his Freddie comment and perhaps the two of us could have talked it through and moved on. In 1985, in the San Francisco courtroom, he would clarify his remark to me, as will be mentioned in chapter 16.

Motta should also have consulted Donald on his strategy. The three of us could have discussed, modified, and executed it in a coherent manner as allies. The simplest example of what I mean is that he could have asked Donald to check with one of Weiser's attorneys to suggest a West Coast attorney with whom I should work. The only lawyer who had been involved at this point was my father's childhood friend, who was giving Motta a "freebie." In retrospect, the whole thing seems like a farce. Motta never "bellied up to the bar," and he resented me for the rest of his life because of it.

"IF YOU WANT SOMETHING DONE RIGHT, do it yourself." There is absolutely no reason Motta should not have flown to California himself. He was an English teacher, fluent in the language. He had gone to college in the United States. He knew Grady, Phyllis, and Helen. If he had financial problems that prevented him from buying a ticket, he could have raised the funds from his loyal students—me included—who would have been only too happy to help bring him to the U.S. to resolve this.

Instead, he chose what I suggest to have been the most irresponsible, even cowardly, path. He left the entire weight of the decision in my hands. And after I made my best decision, he pounced on me like a leopard because he did not like what I did.

In 1984, Motta forced the issue of having my Magical Record submitted in evidence in the lawsuit—seeking to learn of a conspiracy between either me and Grady, or Weiser and Grady, to deprive him of his rights. He wrote that I had betrayed him. I did nothing of the sort. I am sorry if I did anything wrong and wish things could have turned out better for him. But I did the best I could. For those of us who believe in the Weighing of the Heart and the Judgment of the Soul in the Afterlife, that's my story and I'm sticking with it.

HERE ARE SOME OF THE PROFESSIONAL FACTORS with which I was wrestling at the time. I was on an extremely complex business trip that involved weeks of diligent preparation. I had made sixty to seventy appointments—three and four per day—with bookstores from San Diego to San Francisco. Each appointment was dated, timed, and confirmed. I pored over street maps, phone directories, customer lists, and order patterns to arrange the most coherent strategy for setting up my itinerary. I personally made many of the phone calls scheduling my visits—often with reluctant store owners who thought I was a commissioned sales rep trying to profit from meeting them. I had to explain patiently, over and over, that I was not working on commission—that we were offering a service to go over our line of books in detail, making suggestions for our mutual advantage. There were also matters of food, car rentals, airlines, and motel reservations to be arranged.

On a personal level, Motta knew I was in a very unsettled stage of my life, having read my diaries. Marianne and I literally watched a large plant in our loft wither and die from the painful energies we were generating. In addition to the sadness and mutual sorrow, there was the standard menu of anger and recriminations, accompanied by the litany of false starts and stops in the process of dissolving our relationship. There were practical matters of splitting up books and records, and debts and assets to be sorted out. To complicate things, Marianne worked as Weiser's bookkeeper, so I was responsible for replacing her at work in the midst of leaving town for a three-week trip.

MY BIGGEST ERROR IN THE MOTTA DRAMA was that I was guilty of "mixing the planes," which resulted in a series of divided loyalties. The first mention of my awareness of this possibility is a diary entry dated April 11, 1975—two days after signing the Oath of Probationer, more than a full year before my trip. I firmly believe I maintained an overall commitment to what I still perceive to be the Truth. However, I wound up serving a variety of masters, all of whom seem to have had disparate agendas. An employee of a company has an obligation to his employer. A disciple has an obligation to his Master. A seeker of Truth has an obligation to the Truth. The holder of a power of attorney has an obligation to his client. While it is impossible to change the past, the one thing I would do differently is to have "recused" myself from the case—like a lawyer or judge—knowing that an objective assessment would be impossible for me.

This is not to excuse Motta from the slipshod management of his campaign. But neither do I seek to excuse my three most obvious mistakes:

1) My inability to place firm limitations on the expectations of others;

2) My not having demanded a complete and clear written list of the precise responsibilities with which I was being either entrusted

or saddled—along with a full accounting of the required financial resources to accomplish these goals;

3) Most especially, not understanding that the right course of action for me, under the circumstances, was to simply stand up and say: "No, do it yourself."

Dénouement of the California Trip

I made firm plans with Grady, Phyllis, and Helen to return to California to help Helen archive the Library and copy materials for Motta. I arranged with a bookstore called the Philosopher's Stone for a part-time job in San Francisco based on my knowledge of esoteric literature and the cordial relationship we formed during my sales trip. I had fallen in love with a woman named Miriam, whom I met through Grady at a pagan festival on Lammas. Organized by Aidan Kelly of the New Reformed Orthodox Order of the Golden Dawn (NROOGD), this was a joyful, impressive, and elaborate gathering of many local Northern California covens. I met Robert Anton Wilson and Isaac Bonewitz there.

When I returned to New York, my friend and co-worker Bob Skutelsky offered me his San Francisco apartment a few blocks away from Miriam. It seemed my destiny was fixed.

Grady had given me a copy of the 1936 pamphlet of *The Book of the Law* published by the O.T.O. in London. There were multiple copies in the Library. I used it to produce the Weiser edition of *The Book of the Law*, correcting some errors, and adding the facsimile of the handwritten manuscript. This was the first popular edition in history that included the manuscript as specified in the book itself. It remains in print to this day.

***

CHAPTER 10

HARRY SMITH AND THE GAME CHANGES

I ARRIVED BACK IN NEW YORK ON AUGUST 4, 1976 and gave Donald notice that I was leaving Weiser's. I planned to take a couple of months to help with the transition. I was in contact with Miriam and packing my belongings. Marianne left to go west after selling her share of the loft to Jane, who allowed me free access to continue packing and arranging my possessions.

And then along came Harry Smith. I had heard of him for years and wanted to meet him. Most of the store staff didn't particularly like him, because he would come in near closing time and somehow Donald would be called and insist they stay open. Harry was often drunk and surrounded by a boisterous crew. On the other hand, when I had first asked Donald about him three years earlier, he said, "Harry Smith is the most knowledgeable occultist I have ever known"—this coming from a man who literally grew up in his father's store, and who had a pretty worldly and cynical attitude to the poseurs and self-important magi and gurus of the day. I was startled by his respect for Harry.

But Harry was elusive and hadn't been to Weiser's for some years. Finally, he came by the publishing office to say hello to Donald and I was introduced to him. Some time later, I saw him at a concert by his friend Percy Heath at the Village Vanguard. Harry had lived at the musician's home for a time. Marianne and I greeted him cordially. He slipped out the back door. Finally, soon after Marianne left in late August, Harry came by the office again. After speaking privately with Donald, he emerged and asked if I'd like to join him. And we were off on a whirlwind, thirty-hour visit that has transformed my life to this day. He told me that Donald had assigned him the task of curing me of sex magick, a charge he subsequently repeated to everyone to whom he introduced me.

TOP ROW: My father and mother.

LEFT: My maternal uncle, Sonny, was a close friend and mentor.

ABOVE: Brother Bob, ca. 1987.

TOP: Claire in Portland 1970.

Dennis Deem on a visit to New York.

MIDDLE: Mary before we left for Denver, 1968.

Brian Crawford, psychedelic superman and lifelong friend.

RIGHT: My 1962 MGA 1600 MK II, ca. 1969.

TOP: Marty Black in Portland in 1970. Marianne and me, ca. 1970.

MIDDLE: This was our "hippie van."

John and Merrie in happier times on a day we all shared in the woods some months before their suicide.

LEFT: Guru Bawa was my first contact with a bona fide Holy Man, 1972.

OPPOSITE: Donald Weiser had his hands full with staff like me, ca. 1976.

Photo of Legba and Ayida Oueddo from Seabrook's *The Magic Island*. Compare to Osiris and Isis from the Papyrus of Ani.

ABOVE: Angus, Hettie, and Ossian.

Weiser's Bookstore at 734 Broadway. The publishing department was upstairs.

RIGHT: Ed James and Ehud Sperling at the 1976 Weiser Christmas Party.

Marcelo Motta some years after we met in Brazil in 1976.

Gurney at his desk in Nashville, ca. 1976. He and Dan Gunther pursued an active course of magical work and study together.

Gurney is seated at left. His wife Deborah O'Melia passed away some years ago. Dan and I rounded out the crew above in 1977.

This photo by Sherri Lane captures the essence of Grady.

Bill Breeze at Harvard Divinity School in 1977 soon after we met at Weiser's.

Harry Smith visiting in Park Slope.

Jane and I shared many adventures.

The net result of our excursion into the Infinite was that I perceived Harry as the living embodiment of Crowley's dictum: "Always tell the truth but lead so improbable a life that no one will believe you." The things that went on in our first thirty hours are beyond description. Zany, cosmic, initiated, fearsome, loving, and profound. I was swept off my feet. Harry knew what I wanted to learn. I remember internally verbalizing my thought with as much clarity as if it were yesterday: "Who wants to sit around reading a bunch of dead people's correspondence when I am in touch with the living Flame here in New York?"

Another turn simultaneously appeared on the road before me. In the beginning of September, Jane and I became lovers. There was an unexpected depth to our relationship. I was still in love with Miriam and had been chomping at the bit to move out to California. Then Claire came for dinner at the loft one evening. She adored Jane and helped open my eyes to my new reality.

I rescinded my resignation to Donald on the morning of September 27. Later that day, when the mail arrived at the office, I received an unctuous and self-serving letter from Phyllis Seckler denying any agreement that I could catalog and archive the Library. At the risk of speaking ill of the dead, I moved her representative piece on my life's chessboard from the square of qliphotic fantasist to that of lying harpy.

I moved back to the loft with Jane and became a regular companion of Harry's. I introduced him to Bill Breeze, Gurney, and several other friends. But he, Bill, and I drank at the same fountain. Oddly enough, Angus didn't like Harry. He certainly respected him as an artist and filmmaker, but I gather that Harry had acted in an insulting manner to Angus. I should say that, the longer I knew Harry, the less he drank. I do not remember him ever drinking anything stronger than beer in my presence. Angus was not so lucky.

Harry was a multi-faceted genius who made a name for himself in a number of disciplines. He was presented with a Lifetime Achievement Award at the 1991 Grammy Awards for his work in preserving and disseminating the American blues and folk music that inspired such people as Bob Dylan and Jerry Garcia—*The Anthology of American Folk Music,* released by Folkways Records in 1952. He recorded The Fugs' first album. His collections of string figures and Seminole artifacts are in the Smithsonian Museum in Washington, D.C. He recorded peyote ceremonies of the Kiowa Indian tribe, also released as an album by Folkways. Harry's film-making techniques included developing the collage method that was popularized in the 1968 movie *Yellow Submarine* by the Beatles. He was a mentor to Kenneth Anger. Harry's paintings and artwork are beautiful and have been shown in numerous exhibitions and books, including a publication devoted to his work from the Getty Foundation.

The most important area where we touched was the spiritual. Harry was intimately familiar with, and a devotee of, Aleister Crowley. He told Bill and me that he had painted a room red and gold and tied himself to a fixture against powerful Kundalini rushes, while performing the invocation of the Holy Guardian Angel from the Eighth Aethyr as described in *The Vision and the Voice*. Harry was the incarnation of surrender to a greater Truth, of which he intimately understood himself to be the vehicle.

Motta and A∴A∴

Upon my return to New York from California, a letter awaited me from Motta. He cut me off from further correspondence. He told me three times not to contact him again. I got the message. (I naturally disobeyed him some nine years later in a San Francisco courtroom, as will be mentioned later.) In no way, shape, or form did he ever claim to expel or sever me from the Order. To quote his statement from his 1982 deposition: "So what I told him in the letter was that I was cutting contact with him and transferring him. He was not being cut out of A∴A∴."

Dan thus became my Instructor. I sent him my record at the end of August. Although I was disturbed by the whole transition with Motta, I was actually relieved to have a non-confrontational and sane relationship with my Superior—at least for a moment.

Jane and I went down to Nashville in early October and Dan, Gurney, and I resumed our discussion of starting a Thelemic publishing company. Dan's girlfriend and future first wife, Brenda, was a physical therapist. She brought home a bio-feedback machine from the hospital. We all experimented with it and had it humming on both its alpha and theta channels. Brenda told us that achieving theta was far rarer than it appeared to a group of budding magi.

I met David Bersson during that trip. He was a young student of Dan's staying at the house. He had made a long and courageous trek to meet Dan, who has always had a soft spot for strays. I found David to be painfully shy and odd. I heard him performing his rituals in the Temple, and the high pitch and discordance of his magical voice were disconcerting. The fact is, however, that he was practicing the system as diligently as he could. Jelks Cabaniss was also around at the time. One couldn't help but like him. A bit of a spoiled rich kid, he had a pixie-like sense of humor and was a hell-raiser.

Naturally, the moment Motta got word of our intentions to found a publishing company, he went ballistic and forbade Dan and Gurney from associating with me in a business venture.

Mr. Motta forced Dan to write a belligerent letter to Donald Weiser in October 1976, laying out a series of impossible demands regarding publication of his *LXV Commented*. I was embarrassed to hand it to Donald. I called Dan in Nashville and explained that the letter was completely unprofessional and, quite frankly, ridiculous. It would never fly. Dan was reasonable and thoughtful during our call. He later told me that the letter had been dictated and that he had nothing to do with its creation or content, although it bore his signature.

Like clockwork, a letter arrived soon after—long enough after for Dan to explain my reaction to Motta, for Motta to dictate Dan's next move, and for the U.S. Post Office to complete its daily rounds. Dan's new letter cast me out into the Outer Darkness for a change. He explained that he was no longer willing to act as my Instructor because of my demonstration of hierarchical indiscipline regarding my comments about his business letter to Weiser. If I had been a worthy student ... blah, blah, blah. Once again, I was without an Instructor. My diary records a sense of relief that I was finally free of this madness. Dan told me some months later that his disassociation with me was also done on direct orders from Motta.

A Word on Gurney

I did have the option to approach Gurney to continue my A∴A∴ work. He had been elevated to Neophyte. By rights, still being a Probationer, I might have chosen this course. (I even considered it for a moment during a period of despair in February 1977.) But he and I were peers and it would be absurd for me to expect him to "guide" me. Second, within hours, days, weeks, or months, I knew I would be booted again in response to Motta's irritation over something I would either say or do, or not say or not do. I decided to bag the entire thing and work alone.

Phyllis Seizes the Library

The dysfunctionality of the O.T.O. also came into sharp relief at this time. In addition to forbidding me from coming to California to work on the Library with Helen and make copies of documents for Motta, the inestimable Phyllis Seckler decided that she had the right and obligation to sequester the Library from Grady. Their relationship was so convoluted and bizarre that, rather than have her thrown in jail, Grady somehow acquiesced, despite his considerable irritation. Perhaps Motta's words were coming true on a more mundane plane than he had fantasized. One could, I suppose, console oneself by reading Martin Starr's *The Unknown God* if one needed to be reassured about how ill-aspected the Thelemic community had been in the even earlier days of Agape Lodge.

As night follows day, in 1979, the aggrieved Madame Seckler announced that the storage room in which she had put the materials she had stolen from the O.T.O. in 1976 was burgled by an unknown thief. Suspicions have abounded for decades. The most informed speculation places the theft at Phyllis' door, possibly with Helen's collusion. The circumstantial evidence pointing to Helen's involvement is that she advertised some of the missing materials for sale, had knowledge of the location of the storage facility, and possessed a key to the unit. However, as a book dealer, it is conceivable she purchased the goods from a third party and unknowingly offered them for sale. On the other hand, both women had long-held, deep-seated resentments against the financial irresponsibility of many of the Thelemic men in their lives, and it is not a stretch of the imagination for me to assume this provided them with the self-justification for such behavior—if they were in fact responsible.

Phyllis' letter castigating Grady, me, Gunther, and, one imagines, every other male on Earth—as published in a 2011 collection of her writings released by a group of her few remaining disciples—should be proof enough. Phyllis was especially angry that the leadership was considering expelling her for having stolen the Library in 1976 and refusing to return it since. Her deposition for the 1985 San Francisco trial is laced with bitterness. To be fair, she claimed during the trial that the rumor mill in Northern California was well aware that she had placed the Library in storage. It is possible that a determined individual could have called storage facilities in geographic proximity to Dublin, located the proper one, and, making use of an expert with locks, opened the unit while keeping the padlock undamaged. She was forced to read her diary entries for the period of the theft from the witness stand. While one may imagine her creating a false diary account of her reaction to, and efforts after, the theft, it is by no means certain that either she or Helen was the thief.

Working Alone

Angus had moved in with Jane and me in mid-October 1976. In November, he introduced us to a friend from Kathmandu—a highly initiated Western-born Tibetan Buddhist and an inspiring author and translator. He was also addicted to heroin at the moment, and had brought back some exceptionally pure dope from Thailand. He helped me to undertake my life's second excursion into addiction. Jane and I spent nearly two months snorting the finest heroin I have ever experienced. The Karmapa Lama visited New York at this time and we all attended his teaching.

Thanksgiving 1976 found me at the Chelsea Hotel packing Harry's library. It was an unbelievably quiet Zen/Sufi-like experience. He asked me to wrap each book separately before fitting it into a carton. I was at one with my task and with him, at peace with the developments with Gunther, and optimistic about the future of my spiritual Work.

A couple of weeks later, Sibyl Ferguson remarked that my aura showed signs of ill health. (Heroin is like that.) She was a dear friend of Donald's who worked part-time in his private office. She was an author and a psychic whose accuracy was so high that she had been recruited by government intelligence agencies to collect information by remote viewing on foreign UN diplomats. She soon ceased that line of work. She was a close advisor to Donald and would occasionally share insights with me. She confirmed an Egyptian incarnation, mentioning a particular initiation ceremony inside the left front paw of the Sphinx.

December brought some excellent news. I finally got permission from Gerald Yorke and the Warburg Institute to begin the photo work on a second edition of the *Thoth Tarot*. I had spent a year and a half on that particular quest. More details are discussed in the next chapter.

Our Buddhist friend finally left New York around the Winter Solstice, and Jane and I breathed a deep sigh of relief. It was past time to clean up, despite whatever physical discomfort may have awaited us.

Jane and I had a funny social visit the night before New Year's Eve. Several women from a small cult called the Source came to Weiser's to ask for our help in book distribution. They invited me to attend their evening's activities. I knew their health-food restaurant on the Sunset Strip, one of the first in the country. (It may have been the location of my cledon experience with the photo of the Indian guru.)

When Jane and I arrived, they presented a little slide show introducing the group, which was headquartered in both Hawaii and California. They were led by another Perfect Living Master, a Western guy they regarded in an Eastern fashion. The last slide showed him smiling, holding onto a hang glider moments before he plunged to his death on the rocks below! They were devotees of pot, which they called "the sacred herb." You were only allowed one toke, but the Hawaiian grass was superb and I had been working a lot with Pranayama and made the best of it. Jane did not fit their female pattern—the familiar Earth Mother/Aphrodite hip-pie type. Jane was wearing a pair of knee-high leather boots that she refused to remove. In any case, it was clear that our hostesses were far more interested in recruiting a man than an independent woman with attitude.

Another West Coast visitor to Weiser at the time was an attrac-tive representative from the Rajneesh Publishing Company. We did take on their books for distribution. She sat in my chair while we discussed our business arrangements, with me alternately stand-ing or sitting on the edge of my desk. When she left and I sat back down, the seat of my chair was pulsating with heat.

Yana Bragg of Ourobourus Publishing became a friend when she came to seek Weiser's help in distributing the book *Mind Magic*. I was impressed with it. Yana's enthusiasm was infectious. I met Bill Harvey, the author and president of the company, and enjoyed him as well. We later decided to remake the book in a new edition with art by Isaac Abrams, the famous psychedelic artist. *Mind Magic* would become one of my earliest and most interesting projects in Studio 31. We all remain friends. I had the opportunity to help make an updated edition of the book in 2002, retitled as *Freeing Creative Effectiveness*.

WINTER 1976–1977

Back to California

My interpersonal kaleidoscope continued uninterrupted as 1977 dawned. I took a second sales trip to California beginning the third week of January. I stopped first for some vacation time with Mari-anne in Washington, then continued on to San Francisco to begin the sales effort. I spent several days with Claire, who had left New York, moved to Denver, and was visiting California. She accom-panied me on some sales calls, helping me spread occult wisdom as happily as we had pot in the days of the Good Karma Dealing Crew. I continued on to San Diego and saw Brian and Linda. They were married in 1974 and I had visited with them and met Linda on my sales trip the previous July.

During that first trip, I had visited a bookstore in the San Diego area run by a group that called itself the Order of Thelema. The people in the store seemed educated. I was told that their membership included some 150 people, among whom were many professionals. There was just a hint of cult-like insularity and secretiveness, but I was cautiously positive about them. During this second visit, the façade fell away as I found myself in conflict with a disturbing and unwarranted arrogance. By way of example, they refused to extend the standard Thelemic greeting to anyone who was not a member of their Order. I couldn't help but think of Crowley using it with his grocer.

Israel Regardie

I had the honor of meeting Israel Regardie during these trips. He asked me to call him "Regardie." He was an amazingly energetic man. I remember coming to his house on my first trip. He put me on an electric chiropractic massage table that helped soothe some of the road fatigue from my extensive driving. We went to lunch at a local restaurant in Studio City. He drove like a teenage hot-rodder. It was really funny, as he was over seventy. The restaurant was staffed by aspiring actors, all of whom knew and enjoyed him.

Regardie told me he regretted his Christian phase, and that he wanted to rewrite *Twelve Steps to Spiritual Enlightenment* and lose the New Age Christianity. He told me that he had accepted the fact that he was a Thelemite, and that his unfortunate personal relationship with Crowley had long colored his view of Thelema, to his detriment. He was not impressed with Motta. He had written a particularly tongue-in-cheek thank-you letter after I sent him *The Commentaries of AL* back in January 1976.

> I must confess that both your edition and Kenneth Grant's amuse the living hell out of me. . . . [Motta] is very much like Kenneth Grant in constantly pointing out where Crowley was wrong—which is gross impertinence. But then Mr. Motta claims to be a Master of the Temple and has crossed the Abyss! Phooey! . . . All

I can say is: it should be a lot of fun watching in the near future the battle of the giants claiming successorship!

I enjoyed Regardie, finding him honest, cheerful, and sincere. During a later visit, we discussed establishing a publishing company with his agent, Sachlan Linden, and his friend, the astrologer Lynn Palmer. The discussions never got very far.

Back in the City

On my return to New York, a lot of the horror of the last year caught up with me. I was not in a good emotional state. I was especially frustrated by the lapses in my magical practices. I set a minimum number of exercises I would do each day for thirty days or kill myself. I managed to get through this by mid-March and live to tell the tale, but it was not pretty. When I missed a day, I would double the practices the next day to catch up. It caused a lot of stress with Jane. Our relationship was further strained by our multiple partners. With my apologies to Crowley, "open marriage" is not a successful relationship strategy for me, as it diverts attention from the primary partner. Add drugs and alcohol to the mix and one is not left with the recipe for a gourmet delicacy.

The Denderah Zodiac

I began development of what was to become the first Studio 31 publication, *The Denderah Zodiac,* a magnificent color poster. This project was also fraught with some agony. I had found a beautiful piece of art in an old book by the famous English astrologer Raphael. Without doing any preliminary research on the design, it seemed as if it would make a great poster. I approached my friend, the artist Alden Cole, with the suggestion. He did a lot of covers for Weiser's and we made a good team. Donald and I agreed on distribution terms. The project became live. Alden did a fabulous recreation of the art. Meanwhile, I had become friends with a color printer named Larry Barnes, of whom more will be said in the next chapter. Larry did a color separation and made a match print for proofing purposes. Everyone was thrilled.

I sat down to do the research and write the accompanying text. I laid out my various reference books and the match print on a large table. Then the giant Looney Tunes hammer came out of the sky and smacked me right between the eyes. I realized that our friend Raphael had seriously modified the real Denderah Zodiac without having bothered to mention it. The original Egyptian zodiac has four kneeling double figures of Horus and four standing figures of Isis holding the heavenly circle aloft. Raphael had eliminated the figures of Isis. While his design was quite nice if one were unaware of the original, removing the Goddess seemed to me a magical perversion.

I was sickened by the amount of work and money that had been poured into the project so far, and the unhappy result of my carelessness in not having researched it more diligently before committing to it. Despite much advice, and the strong temptation to publish a "modified Denderah Zodiac as interpreted by the astrologer Raphael," I am happy to say I killed the project. Alden graciously executed a tracing of the original zodiac from the drawings of the Napoleonic expedition of 1799, an option suggested by fellow artist Denise Satter. He then did an exquisite coloring based on his research in Egyptian art. Rather than the $800 beating I expected, Larry managed to get my loss down to $400 for the two color separations.

Lann Rubin

I became friendly with Lann Rubin, the owner of Mekaneeses Bookstore on West 4th Street. Lann had been a customer of Weiser's wholesale. He was a very bright, talented, self-disciplined, and powerful magician. Donald suggested we publish a revived *Occult Review*. The original *Occult Review* had been a staple of the early 20th-century British esoteric scene, running for some forty-five years in various formats, and including articles by the leading lights of the day—Aleister Crowley, Dion Fortune, Franz

Hartmann, Arthur Edward Waite, and many others. I proposed Lann as the editor.

While Lann was loathe to get involved with such a time-intensive undertaking, he invited me to participate in a six-week class he was holding after hours on Qabalah, Tarot, and Magick. His reading list was excellent. I decided to give it a try in April. The idea was that, if the class experience was mutually compatible, he would invite people to the more private magical group he ran. The time I shared with Lann was a blessing. It helped to bring some order into the chaos of my personal life, and some healing to the nerves rubbed raw by the Motta/Phyllis magical juggernaut.

The most memorable experience with Lann was a retreat he held at a farm in upstate New York in August 1977. One of the exercises he gave us was to erect a private altar in solitude and pray. I entered a most fervent state, inflaming myself in prayer, overcoming much of the damage from my having taken the "insincere" initiation of Sant Mat years before. I had erected a barrier between myself and God. I believed on some level that I had sold my soul to the Devil—that I had accepted Charan Singh as my quasi-HGA in a moment of spiritual weakness, and that I could not reach out to my true HGA or God without feeding a vampiric link with the demon guru. The agony was so great that I often considered that death would be the only way to solve the error of this incarnation. It was not fun. I thank Lann for helping facilitate the first major breakthrough in that six-year period of torment. His later admission that he used the Thoth Deck and Crowley as an introduction to his mystical Christian inner doctrine caused me to part from him and the group.

I spent the year from summer 1976 to summer 1977 carefully acquiring and refining the magical weapons of a ceremonial magician, finalizing the Temple construction, painting the Circle, and building my Altar.

PART THREE

1977 TO 1979

✦

* * *

CHAPTER 11

THE EARLY DAYS OF STUDIO 31

As I was working late one night at Weiser's in the spring of 1977, I rested my head in my hands for a moment. I had a vision of myself becoming progressively older and grayer, dying and becoming a skeleton sitting at the desk resting its head in its hands, and eventually becoming a pile of dust on the desk. I decided to leave the company and begin my own freelance book production service. I arranged for lunch with a book designer named Peretz Kaminsky who had done Liz Greene's *Saturn* for us. Peretz and I had become friendly during the process and I felt I could turn to him. He said that of course I should leave, and that, since I was a specialist in occult books, I had a ready-made professional identity.

The Necronomicon

My first project began as I was leaving Weiser's. It came through the amazing Larry Barnes, who was obsessed with the universe described in the writings of H. P. Lovecraft. Larry was an artist and a color printer, the head of Barnes Graphics, an adjunct to Barnes Printing, his father's company. He had walked into Herman Slater's Magickal Childe Bookstore in his quest for the mythic *Necronomicon*, the famed grimoire of darkness described in hushed and fearful tones by Lovecraft as the work of the Mad Arab Abdul

Alhazred. He was convinced it was a real book and sought desperately for a copy.

Herman himself seemed to have stepped out of the pages of an occult novel or a Hammer Film production. Bright as they come, Herman was the ultimate social butterfly. He had built the Magickal Childe into a legendary Manhattan occult emporium. He had contacts throughout the world in small publishing houses and among purveyors of esoteric goods, who supported his efforts, despite the fact that he was never one to be overly concerned with the rigors of financial management. His charm and sincerity of purpose won over the hearts of all who knew him, dating back to the store's origin in Brooklyn, when it was known as the Warlock Shop. Herman was a true believer, a practitioner of the magical arts as well as a shopkeeper. The Magickal Childe's motto was "Hard Core New Age" and Herman wasn't kidding.

Herman explained to Larry that he was in possession of the manuscript of the *Necronomicon,* as edited and introduced by a mysterious New York adept named Simon. They were awaiting a publisher. Simon had gotten the manuscript from a pair of renegade priests of dubious Slavonic Orthodox lineage who were involved in stealing rare manuscripts from libraries. He describes this at length in his 2006 book *Dead Names: The Dark History of the Necronomicon.* Somehow, Simon had obtained a copy from the pair before they were arrested. With much time, money, and effort spent in reconstruction, translation, and research, he created a coherent manuscript with the famed sigils in place. Simon had attracted a following of serious students who had been experimenting with the *Necronomicon* system for some time. Deadly encounters and unholy energies had convinced them all that this was the real thing.

Larry was startled. In a frenzy, he arranged with Herman to meet with Simon, acquire the publishing rights, and meet me, the occult world's newest full-service book design and production studio. Larry came to pick me up at Weiser's in his Cadillac and the whirlwind began. A frenetic, brilliant, funny, and tragic soul, he was a connoisseur of cocaine and heroin, and a denizen of his own carefully constructed world of Lovecraftian mythos and Barnesian creativity. He was one of the funniest people I ever met. His

An example of Larry Barnes' creative doodling.

paranoid magical worldview was peopled with extraterrestrials, other-dimensional intelligences, and the continual inspiration of, and interaction with, cledons. (The cledon concept can, of course, apply equally to any other apparently random occurrence, even license plate numbers with qabalistic significance to the initiate.) Larry was also a magnanimous and honest soul who cloaked these attributes beneath his rapid-fire zany persona.

Simon describes himself in the preface to the second edition of the *Necronomicon* (in his first meeting with Larry and myself) as, "attired in a beret, a suit of some dark fibrous material, and an attaché case which contained—besides correspondence from various Balkan embassies and a photograph of the F-104 fighter being crated for shipment to Luxembourg—additional material on the *Necronomicon* which proved his bona fides." We've known each other now for decades and I could not create a better description of this unique individual—seemingly equally at home in the worlds of clandestine intelligence agencies, corporate boardrooms, and candlelit temples.

We three were a perfect fit. I took the manuscript home to read. It had been rumored to be so dark that I was concerned about participating in an unworthy effort. What I found instead was a coherent Sumerian grimoire with an entrancing tale by the Mad Arab. It was only toward the end that the loathsome figures of Lovecraft's legendary warnings emerged. I walked about the street for some time contemplating my involvement. I decided there were essentially three classes of readers who would be exposed to these horrific entities. The first were those dark souls who could invoke those energies with or without the book that I was to help launch into the world. The majority of readers would be either uninterested or unable to do much damage to themselves or others. And the third class was made up of those able to raise such energies because of their magical development, who would either choose not to, or who would do so in a responsible manner that befitted their spiritual stature. I decided to go ahead with the project.

I hired the typesetters who lived downstairs on the second floor of our loft building, and arranged for Khem Set Rising to ink the seals from the manuscript. Simon had drawn them very well using a felt-tip pen. But for proper reproduction, they needed to be redrawn with a Rapidograph pen, the fine graphic mechanical pens that preceded the technology of Adobe Illustrator. Khem was living at our loft and working away. Jane suggested that, since I had all this activity going on at our #21 Soho address, I call my business Studio 21. I immediately made the leap to Studio 31, the qabalistic formula enshrined in the title of *The Book of the Law, Liber AL vel Legis,* Book 31.

What a loony period the *Necro* production would be. For some reason, nearly everyone who entered our loft shed blood. Larry and I were, of course, shooting either heroin or cocaine, so that accounted for our personal bloodletting. But others were constantly cutting themselves in minor accidents. Then one night, I got a frantic call from the typesetters downstairs. Their loft had been overrun with rats bursting through the walls. I repaired the holes in their walls, after inserting broken-glass-laced, extra-coarse steel wool.

The Temple in my own loft had a padlock on the outside of the door so it could be sealed as a private space for my magical work. On July 4, Jane and I returned from dinner and fireworks. I had an uneasy feeling when we walked through the loft door, itself secured by a heavy-duty police lock. I hurried around the corner and flipped on the lights. I discovered that my Temple door was open, that the hasp had been broken, and that this appeared to have occurred from the inside out. Jane and I just looked at each other in bewilderment. Nothing else in the loft was the slightest bit disturbed. To quote one of Larry's characteristic sound effects: "Dun, dun, dun, dunnnnn!"

The *Necro* launch publication party was scheduled for December 1, 1977, the thirtieth anniversary of the death of Aleister Crowley, to whom the book was dedicated. Simon had arranged a huge bash at the Inferno Disco down the street from the Magickal Childe. It involved musical performances by Pierce Turner and Larry Kirwan of the Major Thinkers, a profoundly Thelemic rock band whose driving beat was a staple of the New York Pagan music scene of the day centered around the Bells of Hell nightclub. The O.T.O. band, The Workers, led by Michael Kramer, performed as well. They were a new band and enthusiastically cheered by the frolicking crowd. It was an altogether successful evening presented by Simon's StarGroup One. Several hundred people were there. The only drawback was that the book wouldn't be ready for another three weeks! Larry was obsessively making last minute improvements to the binding die artwork he had designed. But it did arrive on the Winter Solstice and it was beautiful. While, as my first book, it contained several technical layout flaws, I had three more chances to improve it, including the recently published deluxe 31st Anniversary edition from Ibis Press.

The Magickal Childe and the New York Occult Scene

The *Necro* party was a fitting event for the period described by several people as the Occult Renaissance in New York City, which lasted from the mid- to late 1970s through the early 1980s. Many of the various Wiccan, Pagan, and Magical groups then flourishing in the City were socially entwined with the Magickal Childe. Unlike Weiser's, which was a formal bookstore specializing in Eastern and Western mysticism, the Magickal Childe was an occult emporium. With incense, candles, herbs, robes, and bat's wings, it also had a more eclectic, if less comprehensive, supply of books, magazines, and pamphlets. Tarot readers, astrologers, and psychics gave readings, and there were ongoing classes and presentations in the back room. The back room also featured a full working Temple shared by a number of groups.

The Childe threw an annual Samhain/Halloween Party for which Herman would get a permit to block off the street, where people would sing and dance, and eat and drink. Various groups performed rituals in the Temple. These were altogether refreshing gatherings, singularly devoid of competition and intra-group rivalry or hostility. The Internet was far in the future, so instead of the disembodied socialization process of Facebook and/or other e-groups, we actually showed up in person and interacted with each other the old-fashioned way. Wiccans like Ray Buckland and Margot Adler hobnobbed with O.T.O. magicians. Golden Dawn offshoots and Church of Satan members enjoyed whatever elements they shared in common with Santeria adepts, psychics, and diviners. It's hard to imagine the ease with which people interacted during that period, because it does not occur today. Urban shamanism was its own community and Herman Slater was its official ringmaster.

Thoth Deck and Booklet

I had been working on an improved second edition of the *Thoth Tarot Deck* for two years. I had convinced Donald that the original photos (shot by Llee Heflin) and color separations did not do justice to the paintings. Since the Crowley deck was obviously a good seller, why not improve it? Donald put me in touch with his friend in London—Stephen Skinner, the occultist, writer, and publisher. Stephen and I arranged for a professional photographer to shoot 4 x 5 chromes of the paintings at the Warburg Institute, having cleared it with Gerald Yorke. Rights to the first printing had been acquired by Llewellyn Publications from Grady. Because the copyright situation was so chaotic at this time, we felt we were free to proceed on a second edition, co-published with Llewellyn and U.S. Games. It was a complex maze of hurdles, as was usual with magical projects, but we eventually succeeded.

While I had left Weiser's by this time, I was on good terms with everyone. Stuart Kaplan of U.S. Games asked me to write an introductory pamphlet to be included with the deck. I began to compile divinatory attributes of the cards from Crowley's *Book of Thoth* and the Golden Dawn materials. I had been using a modified version of a method of reading that Robert Wang described in his book *An Introduction to the Golden Dawn Tarot,* which accompanied the Golden Dawn deck he had created with Regardie. Bob and I had become friends and he gave me permission to publish the layout. I also mentioned the new booklet to Bill Breeze, who was aware of a catalog compiled by Robert Cecil for an exhibit of the paintings by Frieda Lady Harris. (At the time, we did not know Robert Cecil was the author of the catalog.) Bill had also found a second exhibition catalog prefaced with a short essay by Crowley that he gave to me. So the pamphlet turned out to be a really useful compilation of various sources that could be well-utilized in working with the cards, both for divination and meditation.

The problem was that, when I walked into the Weiser offices one day in early September 1977, I was proudly informed that the first color proofs had arrived and didn't they look great? I almost lost my lunch when I looked at the borders around the cards. Because of the technicalities of print production, a consistent border had to be standardized and placed around each of the images of the seventy-eight paintings so that the cards would be of uniform size with uniform borders. Unfortunately, someone had decided that the border looked better in baby blue rather than the neutral gray that Crowley and Harris had chosen. I pointed this out and was informed that everyone had agreed blue was the most elegant color, and both the staff of Weiser and U.S. Games were unanimous. I was also reminded that, since I no longer worked there, I didn't have a leg to stand on to complain.

I was devastated. The deck was my responsibility and I had no idea how I could possibly fix this. Crowley writes that any act of magick that is not an invocation of the HGA is black magic. I had taken this to heart and have always been somewhat reluctant to perform magical ceremonies whose goal is to get personal results on the physical plane. There is something impolite about it when you think of it. But this was different. I had clearly been appointed to the task of releasing a proper version of the Crowley/Harris deck and, after two years, was on the very verge of success. Non-initiates and people who were less aware were making a power play that would damage the spiritual impact of the deck by changing the vision of its original designers to something they "liked better," while taking advantage of the chance to needle me about having abandoned ship. It was a case in which I felt I had no choice but to perform magick to right the situation.

It worked, but in an interesting and dramatic sequence. Stuart Kaplan is a diligent researcher into Tarot who has since published four large encyclopedias of the cards. I went to his office the next morning to try to convince him personally to use the gray border. My arguments fell flat. I left, despondent, thinking the magick had failed and unable to understand why. Then, on the street, I experienced a sudden illumination. I became aware of an argument that would appeal to his best instincts. I remember calling him from a pay phone and somewhat breathlessly explaining the qabalistic significance of the border colors, and why blue would violate the psychic energies that the color gray would stimulate. He immediately accepted my reasoning and ordered the proper gray borders restored. When I walked into the Weiser office later that day, my former assistant, who had replaced me as manager, was shaking her head. She didn't understand how a dozen people had chosen the blue and it was being returned to Crowley's gray.

Reio Nagle and the House of Hermetic

My next book-production project in Studio 31 was also interesting, if of less mythic proportions than the *Necronomicon*. I returned to California on a freelance basis for my third sales trip for Weiser. The first two had done so well for Donald, and I had enjoyed the work so much myself, that I went again in October 1977. I had met Reio Nagle at the House of Hermetic on Hollywood Boulevard in Los Angeles during my first trip in 1976 and had purchased my Magical Dagger from her—a nicely-made blade in a blank oak wood handle that needed to be sanded and shaped by the purchaser. I also bought some very pure Abramelin Oil that she had personally mixed.

Reio was in her seventies, with a powerful spiritual aura that touched me deeply. She was the daughter of two witch parents. Her sister, Eleanor, with whom she ran the store, had passed away. Reio had such classic dignity. She was an inspiration. I felt that, as a young man with a long life ahead of me, it was easy to be absorbed with occultism and alternate religion. She, on the other hand, was closer to death and had spent a lifetime pursuing a spiritual path very close to my own. Her example encouraged me to think that, if my path seemed correct at twenty-eight, it would also feel right when I was her age if I pursued it with integrity.

Reio's sister had written several pamphlets under her magical motto AIMA, the Great Mother. They were for sale at the shop. Reio wanted me to turn them into a book. Being quite inexperienced in production, I compared it to the *Necronomicon,* set a ridiculously low price, and proceeded to make *The Ancient Wisdom and Rituals.* I wish it had been reprinted (and I had the chance to redesign it), because it is an excellent occult primer. Recently, I took AIMA's article on the Pentagram ritual and included it in the 2009 third edition of Israel Regardie's *Healing Energy, Prayer, and Relaxation* from New Falcon Publishing. AIMA's article is a brilliant analysis of the Qabalistic significance of the Pentagram that demanded preservation.

I made a sales call to a shop in San Francisco called the Mystic Eye Bookstore. It had changed ownership numerous times, but when I was there in October 1977, it was owned by a woman named Ereyn, the most adept oil and incense person I have ever met. She invited me to return to the shop after hours and took me on an astral journey of many planes through her skilled manipulation of fragrances. It was amazing. She had been offered a very high-level position in a French perfume company based on the creativity of her ordering patterns with them. One of her staff was an uncannily accurate astrologer who provided insight into a complex period of my life.

Back in the City

Finita, Jorge, and Susanna—three Argentinean Thelemites—came to New York in 1977. I believe they contacted me through Weiser's. They were working on a Spanish translation of *The Book of the Law*. Jane and I and Bill Breeze all became close friends with them. We referred to them as the Argentinean Adepts. Finita and Jorge joined the O.T.O. and, after a time, established Hoor Camp. Finita was an extremely advanced Tarot reader, and Jane and I began studying the cards with her. They shared a diagram with us that they called the "Black Tree." It is made by connecting all the Sephiroth, which adds sixteen new paths that they associated with the Court Cards. It was discovered by Susanna's boyfriend, Guillermo, and published long ago in *Gnostica News*. Here it is again.

WINTER 1977–1978

At the end of January, Jane and I split up. (We remain lifelong best friends. She is my daughter Rachel's godmother.) I moved to an apartment on Thompson Street (#32, Apartment 11, Rent $220) and tried to make Studio 31 a growing concern. Things were going all right when the latest turn in the road approached.

SPRING 1978

Gandhara Verlag

At the end of March, Bill Breeze approached me with the idea of starting a publishing company called Gandhara Verlag. Gandhara was the name of a kingdom in the Pakistan/Afghanistan region that lasted from the first millennium BC to 1000 AD. It was an ancient crossroads of civilizations, mentioned in the *Ramayana* and *Mahabharata*, and later ruled by the Persians. It became an important Buddhist center, with much Greek influence in its iconography. It is believed to have been the birthplace of Padmasambhava, the great adept who brought Buddhism to Tibet. Its 2000-year history

The "Black Tree"

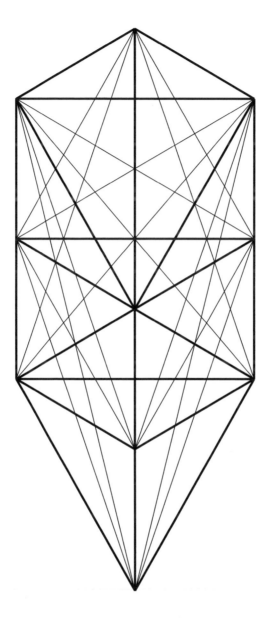

The Black Tree is created by connecting all the Sephiroth on the
Tree of Life. This adds 16 new Paths to the standard 22.
There are 16 Court Cards in the Tarot.

extended well beyond that of our publishing efforts, despite our great visions of things to come.

Our first title was to be Crowley's very rare *Bagh-i-Muattar*. We felt that the growth of the gay movement would open a whole new market to a work that had been virtually destroyed by English customs officials in 1910, only some ten copies having survived. Bill had located one in the Harry Ransom Center at the University of Texas in Austin. We thought we had a potential bestseller on our hands. The plan was for me to leave my Thompson Street apartment and for us to rent two Tribeca lofts. We would warehouse the books ourselves and do order fulfillment for other small publishers, while offering book design through Studio 31, and typesetting through Bill's innovative use of what was then cutting-edge technology. Unfortunately, New York real estate and our rather impractical use of resources combined to make Gandhara a dismal commercial failure.

We rented the two lofts at 393 Greenwich Street from Ben Reeve, the brother of Superman, Christopher Reeve. You couldn't turn on a radio or TV or walk past a billboard without Superman jumping out at you in those days. Bill and I embarked on a massive loft renovation, including sandblasting the walls and ceilings and installing two bathrooms. A friend of Bill's named Franz put up the initial investment and then went off on a year of travel, studying Zen Buddhism in Japan. We had an amazingly high-priced, show-business lawyer who set up the deal wearing cowboy boots, with his feet on his desk. Bill and I had somehow spent all night awake before our appointment and Bill gave me some acid as a stimulant. I'll never forget leaning over and mischievously whispering in his ear, "Billie, I think I took too much!" It was all very funny in its own way, although we would be in debt for years to Franz before managing to pay him off.

SUMMER 1978

On a personal magical level, this was an interesting period. The cover photo of Bill and me was taken by my brother looking out on the fire escape of our fifth-floor loft. There was a great deal of poverty. I remember once finding 25¢ on the street, buying a candy bar, and rushing back to the loft to split it with Bill. As things continued downhill, we decided to sell the third-floor loft and live together on the fifth. Our first buyer was a personable fellow, a musician, who came by with his girlfriend. She had attended the same high school I had. They offered us a substantial deposit.

A friend named Al Brunelle rushed over to warn us not to accept the money. Al, a teacher at the School of Visual Arts, lived with Helen Wheels, a talented punk-rock singer and bandleader. He had done a Tarot reading on our situation and been told to warn us. We reluctantly passed on the offer. It was not easy to refuse the $1500, because we were literally hungry. Later, we learned our potential purchaser was a hustler with a bad reputation for tying people up by giving real-estate deposits, occupying the space on a "good faith" handshake, and never paying the balance of the fixture fee. We finally sold the loft to videographer Wendy Clarke, the daughter of avant-garde filmmaker Shirley Clarke. We paid Franz back a substantial portion of what we owed, and Bill and I lived together upstairs.

Eric Hill and his future wife lived with us for a while. Eric had helped Jimmy Page found the Equinox Bookstore in London. This effort had fallen to the chaos of drug addiction. Eric had been the "Crowley person" at Weiser's before I assumed that mantle some time after he left. Eric was also a very early O.T.O. member under Grady. He was angry at Bill and me for some reason and purposely let Bill's car get towed when we could least afford to redeem it. I found a sigil in my copy of *The Goetia* that Eric had placed between the pages as a curse against me.

Things seemed to be going from bad to worse. One night when I was trying to sleep, I heard Bill making some very weird noises in his sleep from his bed nearby. I remember lying there listening to him, contemplating how broke we were, and how utterly hopeless the situation seemed. I felt a sense of complete desperation. The next morning, Lann Rubin called. We hadn't seen each other in a couple of months, but he offered his help because he had psychically picked up on my mental state the night before. He proposed to come by and ritually cleanse the space. At first, I was grateful and relieved, until I realized that allowing him to come into my space to resolve my problem would magically cripple me forever. I refused his help and made a full break with him that day.

Grady and the First Degree

I decided instead to take the I° O.T.O. initiation from Grady while he was visiting New York in August 1978. I had first been offered the initiation several months after my Minerval when I went back to California. I told Grady then that after the ordeal with Motta and Phyllis, I needed to take a pass on going further with O.T.O. I had started studying with Lann, who told me that, if I took advancement in O.T.O., he and I would have to stop working together. Grady said that I was being tested. I thought smugly that he was probably right and that I was making the right choice.

I was disappointed that Grady had been unwilling or unable to muzzle Phyllis, and was immensely suspicious that he had offered me a leadership position in the New York O.T.O. when I felt so completely unqualified. It was now almost two years later and I realized, in no uncertain terms, that the O.T.O. was my last option. It was the only fraternal organization on the planet that accepted *The Book of the Law*. Whatever failings it may have had, the Order and I were on the same page. Unless I pursued O.T.O. membership, I would have to work as a totally solitary practitioner for the rest of my life.

The I° was a timely initiation indeed. It solidified my break with Lann, helped heal the wounds of my rift with Motta, and deepened my relationship with Grady. On a magical level, I was cleansed of the drug obsession that had reasserted itself during the Gandhara debacle. I have never shot drugs since my I° initiation, save one time in surrender to the needs of a friend.

Some days after the ceremony, I entered an intense Kundalini state. I met my Angel in the guise of a hobo sitting on the stoop next to my loft. He said to me: "If you hunt for me, I will hunt for you three times harder." The experience completely solved the crisis of my six years in psychic hell over the Sant Mat issue. The HGA, Charan Singh, and God all blended together in an absolute harmony. The problem—which had been the worst spiritual crisis of this incarnation—simply dissolved in ecstasy.

On August 8, I traveled to New Jersey, where Grady was staying. I carried years of magical diaries with me and signed the Oath of Neophyte before him. A student had come into my orbit who signed the Oath of Probationer. I commented in my diary that Grady's recognition of Marcelo as my receiving Brother established Grady's integrity as Caliph. It was witness to the truth of his 1976 letter to Marcelo regarding O.T.O./A∴A∴ unity. Grady also made an interesting comment about the Perfect Living Master concept: "Jim, don't expect to find any success stories in human bodies."

This period marked the successful conclusion of my Saturn return.

Angus was living with Bill and me. In conversation about spiritual matters, I learned he had taken the full Bodhisattva Vow before the Karmapa Lama—the Oath I had so longed to take in a fully ritualized manner after reading *Siddhartha* over a decade earlier.

Around this time, while spending the night with a Rajneesh disciple named Judith, I saw an eye looking at me from the Inner Planes. I was aware that it was my child seeking incarnation and that Judith was definitely not the mother.

After some four months of struggling to establish Gandhara Verlag, Bill left to rejoin Peter Macfarlane of 93 Publishing in Canada. Angus expressed his anger at Macfarlane for encouraging Bill to just walk away from me (and split up the band he and Bill had started). Peter certainly was underhanded about it, as he failed to inform me of his offer to Bill. I felt good that Angus cared, but it was the right thing to dissolve the company. Bill and I had started to argue and we weren't making any progress in our publishing efforts.

In August, Bill took his Minerval in Syracuse, New York, where Grady had continued on to visit Mike Ripple and Ra-Hoor-Khuit Lodge.

* * *

CHAPTER 12

THE TREE OF LIFE AND
The Egyptian Book of the Dead

While working at the publishing and wholesale offices of Weiser, I met a charismatic black man named Kanya Kekumbha who ran a bookstore in Harlem called the Tree of Life. He bought immense quantities of a popular metaphysical book called *The Finding of the Third Eye* by Vera Stanley Alder. Kanya sold more of it than anyone else. I couldn't understand how—the common stereotype did not identify his Harlem clientele as the most prolific readers and book buyers, something he and I joked about many times. He bought several cases of the book each time he came, paid cash, and was always cheerful and energetic. He was also interested in titles we had on astrology, vegetarian foods, natural healing, and classical metaphysics. He continually invited me up to the store on 125th Street and Lenox Avenue, the Macdougal and Bleecker Streets of Harlem. When I left Weiser, we remained in touch.

Kanya asked me to come to a meeting of the local Community Planning Board in August 1977, because the Harlem politicians wanted to tear down the Tree of Life building and put a parking lot in its place. I had a healthy curiosity about his operation and wanted to support him, so I went to the meeting. I was amazed to see the number of people there, so many telling heartfelt stories of how much Kanya and the message of the spiritual literature at the Tree of Life Bookstore had helped them. Drug abuse, poverty, ill-health, poor diet, lack of intellectual stimulation—all were left behind to a life-sustaining message of spirituality, hope, self-empowerment, hygienic eating, and clear thinking. People were using healing herbs taught to them by Dr. John Moore, Kanya's partner and friend, and there seemed to be an abundance of love and good energy in the hearing. The Community Board was impressed as well, and voted to deny the request for the demolition of the Tree of Life building.

I noticed a woman in the crowd whose beauty and exotic energies hypnotized me. She stood out magically, the rest of the room dissolving in my perception. When she stood up to speak, the spell was somewhat broken, but she indicated how much the message of the Tree had meant in her life. Some time afterward, I returned to visit the bookstore and was introduced to Wileda. She swept me off my feet. Then we had a date, which was a disaster. She was hostile and morose, and I wrote her off to a kind of fascination and left it alone.

FALL 1978

A number of months after that first date, Wileda contacted me again. At first, I ignored her answering-machine messages, but she reached me one day and asked if we could talk about business. I said yes and she came to my Greenwich Street loft. We had a far more pleasant visit this time.

This was right after the Kundalini/HGA experience mentioned earlier, so my vibratory frequency was still pretty high. Recently, I had taken some acid and was walking in the neighborhood, abuzz with good energy. I saw an attractive woman approaching on the other side of the street. As I walked, I started tapping my foot in an ecstatic rhythmic pattern. I knew she would have to cross the street because the resonance I was emitting was irresistible. Sure enough, she did. We passed each other in that New York City, good-weather, pedestrian politeness, but I smiled at the perfection of the phenomenon. Wileda and I experienced a similar resonance and her aura was really clean. I was puzzled by the difference between our last encounter and this one, but liked her.

Wileda was impressed with my library and asked a lot of questions about myth and symbol. She told me she had a friend, a white artist named Elisa Decker, who was dating a Voodoo drummer from Haiti named Frisner Augustin. (Frisner later taught drumming at Hunter College and opened for a Rolling Stones tour in 1994.)

She said she might be able to arrange an invitation to a ritual. I was eager to explore it. Some time later, we went to a Voodoo ritual in Brooklyn. I took acid. It was an incredible evening; the music and magical energies were overwhelming. A baby reached out his hand to me and I took it and smiled. Someone next to me said: "Baby has spirit, you will have baby." When Wileda mentioned that she had two older children, I began to wonder if she were not the mother I had anticipated. We bought tickets to the King Tut exhibit that was touring the country and coming to the Metropolitan Museum in March. The racial diversity represented in Egyptian art made me think that maybe we were on the edge of a new breakthrough. Wileda and I could help stimulate the racial liberation that would perfectly mirror the spiritual and cultural aspirations of my generation, as well as the promise of freedom inherent in *The Book of the Law*. While we stood on line for the tickets, a beautiful woman with a child of mixed race passed us and seemed a harbinger of the thoughts I was having.

The Halveti Jerrahi

I had been attending a Sufi group in Spring Valley, New York to which I was introduced by Ehud Sperling. Ehud and I had known each other since we worked together on the floor at Weiser's Bookstore. He had gone on to found his own publishing company, Inner Traditions/Destiny Books. I had done some freelance work for him since.

Sheikh Tosun Bayrak, the leader of the group, was the translator and editor of *The Book of Sufi Chivalry*, which Ehud would publish in 1983. Tosun held *Zikr* practices at his home each week. The Zikr is an intense dance, chanting, and breathing ritual. Among the Halveti Jerrahi, it is performed by an inner circle of men in motion while the women form an outer circle and chant. The power raised by this practice was extraordinary. Tosun attracted a serious group of American students, several of whom had converted to Islam and were learning Arabic. One, in particular, was memorizing the Koran. The group also had some outlying members, like myself, who were clearly not on our way to becoming Muslims, but were welcomed nonetheless.

I became so skilled with the Zikr practice that Tosun asked me to fill in at a performance at the United Nations, where I was presented as a robed Dervish.

The Zikr practice and my time with the Sufis were a magnificent learning experience on many levels. I stopped going after about a year, after Tosun's wife asked when I was going to become a Muslim. As an adherent of *The Book of the Law*, it would be impossible for me to accept Muhammad as the last Prophet, a central tenet of their faith. I later incorporated variants of the Zikr practice into numerous O.T.O. rituals with TAHUTI Lodge.

The Middle Pillar as a Group Ritual

I was working at this time with a student named Andrea. She wanted to learn the Middle Pillar ritual. On November 12, while Wileda was visiting, the three of us did the ritual together. I talked them through the visualizations and energy circulations. It was a very creative experience and we repeated it several times. It would later be further modified and remains an important part of the work of TAHUTI Lodge.

Wileda and I were married on December 1, 1978. We were hit with a huge traffic jam on our way to the Justice of the Peace in Queens, so we missed our appointment. We returned to Manhattan, where Kanya performed the spiritual wedding at our loft during the party we had arranged. Meanwhile, the Justice of the Peace called to say that he had filled out all the paperwork already and had to perform the wedding that day. So he came to the party and married us legally. It was typical of the time.

The high cost of the loft became oppressive. A friend of Wileda's was leaving her apartment in the Bronx. I sold the loft to a young New York lawyer, one among the new hoards of Tribeca denizens. Most of the money went to Franz. We moved to the Bronx near Yankee Stadium. It was an absolutely gorgeous apartment in an absolutely abysmal neighborhood.

WINTER 1978–1979

The Denderah Zodiac was finally printed on the Winter Solstice of 1978. It was an absolutely beautiful production. I began working for Kanya at the Tree of Life Bookstore in January 1979. This would be a whole new opportunity to increase my understanding of people, politics, and spirituality. The Tree was a psychic community center. Its mission was optimistic and idealistic. It was an enterprise devoted to the raising of consciousness through an embrace of spirituality. Because it was located in Harlem, Kanya's mission attracted many poor and disadvantaged people. However, there was another stratum of hip, educated, psychically-aware black folks who shared a kind of fluid mobility and independence that was quite different from my primarily white cultural experience. It was as if they functioned with a different sense of time, an intimacy and ease that I admired and enjoyed. I was easily accepted after people felt out my energy.

I found a sense of political mission that I remembered from 1966. The Tree had been established in an abandoned building that Kanya had spent years renovating and improving. However, big money interests had set their sights on the property, and Harlem politicians like Charles Rangel, Carl McCall, and David Dinkins were enlisted in their effort. Part of my work involved publicity and an attempt to get them to back off. They prevailed despite the hypocrisy of their expressed appreciation for the work of the Tree. On the other hand, Kanya was obstinate about retaining that particular location and refused to accept the oft-repeated offer of a free alternate building. Whether that particular promise would ever have materialized is anyone's guess.

I worked long hours and was on the streets of Harlem at all hours of the day and night. After roughly a year without the slightest hint of a problem—just after I quit—I was robbed at gunpoint outside my apartment in Inwood, the neighborhood at the northernmost tip of Manhattan where we had since moved.

The Egyptian Book of the Dead

"And the all night girls, they whisper of escapades out on the D Train." (*Visions of Johanna* by Bob Dylan)

One night in January, while we were still living in the Bronx, I was returning home from the Tree of Life on the D Train at 3:00 or 4:00 in the morning. I found myself alone in a subway car. I was given a vision of *The Egyptian Book of the Dead* that would finally see publication fifteen years later.

When I worked at Weiser's, I had come across a copy of the "elephant folio" edition of *The Papyrus of Ani* that E. A. Wallis-Budge had published with the British Museum in 1890. It was kept deep in the basement, off-limits to all but invited customers and staff like myself, having lunch and obsessively seeking hidden wisdom. I spent hours marveling over the stunning full-color images of the papyrus. These were full-size reproductions in facsimile of the seventy-eight-foot-long scroll that Budge had secured in Egypt in 1888.

Ani's papyrus was painted about 1250 BC. It is the best-preserved, longest, most ornate, and most beautifully executed example of an Egyptian *Book of the Dead* ever found. When Budge returned to London, he cut it into thirty-seven nearly equal lengths for ease of handling. The sheets were glued onto wooden boards to keep them rigid. He immediately commissioned a facsimile to be prepared as an exquisite, limited-edition, bound set of color lithographs. It preserved forever the awesome beauty of the ancient original. Budge's translation took five years. The British Museum published the translation in 1895. (This is the ubiquitous Budge translation published by Dover since the 1960s and all over the Internet today.) The extraordinary nature of the find encouraged the museum to display the papyrus under a large skylight in a central hall. The glue holding the sheets on the boards and the direct sunlight damaged the delicate papyrus.

As I was studying the text of the Budge translation, I began to realize that I was one of the few modern people who even knew about the color images. Budge's Dover reprint was like reading all the balloon text of a comic book without being able to see the illustrations. Moreover, it was loaded with footnotes that completely interrupted the flow of the text if one were trying to read it as an inspirational holy book.

During the train ride that night, I was given a production plan for a modern edition of the papyrus. I leapt up and began pacing the empty subway car, while literally watching what appeared to be an instructional video on how I was to put the papyrus together as a book. The images would run along the top of the page. The translation would appear below. No footnotes or explanatory text would interfere with the flow. For the first time in 3,500 years, word and image would be joined together as the papyrus was origi-

Budge's edition of *The Egyptian Book of the Dead* was one of the most widely encountered but least-read books of the day. It was especially helpful to me when creating my edition of the *Papyrus of Ani* because Budge included a careful hieroglyphic recreation of the text of the papyrus with an interlinear English translation. This allowed me to understand and correct errors he had made when cutting the papyrus five years before it was translated.

nally intended—an illuminated, full-color, sacred text designed to uplift the soul to higher Truth.

I discussed the idea with Donald Weiser. We were all aware that it would be an enormously expensive project. He allowed me to buy the book. I promised that, if he could arrange to publish it before I did, I would let him photograph my copy.

I began to study the book and work within the parameters of the vision I was given of how to lay it out. As I went deeper into it, I began to realize that, since Budge had cut the papyrus before it was translated, he had made some fairly substantial errors that damaged the flow of the scroll. Many cuts were made in the wrong places, chapters were interrupted, vignettes were split, and the hieroglyphic text often appeared on different sheets from its accompanying images. I began to plan ways to present it properly.

Larry Barnes and I discussed doing the book through Barnes Graphics, but we were never able to raise the staggering sums that were required. I would spend a decade and a half attempting to bring it to publication, until Bill Corsa and I managed to do so in 1994 through Chronicle Books, aided by the insight and courage of Caroline Herter. The computer technology that had been developed in the intervening years allowed for exceptional freedom in reattaching and restoring the images of the papyrus in proper sequence for presentation in a book.

PART FOUR

1979 TO 1989

✦

* * *

CHAPTER 13

THE NEW YORK O.T.O.

WHEN I TOOK MY MINERVAL INITIATION in California in 1976, I asked Grady to share some secret O.T.O. techniques—as I am sure many readers can appreciate. He somewhat wryly directed me to Kris Dowling, who ran the Mobius Chapter in New York City. He told me Kris was knowledgeable and that we should speak.

I got in touch with Kris when I returned to the City and we met for lunch. He was a bright and educated fellow, but I felt he was so demonstrably uncomfortable and nervous that I was less than enthusiastic about going much further with him. Nor did I feel he had insights into the information I was seeking. We parted cordially, as he had been very polite and as personable as possible for such a highly strung person.

I was thus completely disconnected from the New York O.T.O. My own struggles with Motta—and the A∴A∴ problems I had been undergoing with Dan and Gurney—occupied my complete attention. When Grady offered me initiation into the I° and I turned it down in January 1977, I was even further dissociated from O.T.O. I might have considered myself a "dormant" member, although my dues were paid and I did maintain Good Report.

I promised Grady that I would respect all Order publishing rights, and would work to ensure that the O.T.O. name would continue to appear on the "Caliph Card" of the new Crowley Tarot deck that Weiser was producing. In a commercially printed deck, there are, necessarily, 80 cards printed—two more than the standard 78 of the Tarot. In the first edition of the deck, Grady had written a short paragraph for one of the extra two cards. It bore his name and title and contained the Order Lamen and contact address. It was known as the Caliph Card. The Order's mailing address was not included on the Caliph Card of the second edition.

Phyllis made the false accusation that I had been responsible for removing the address. Grady had taunted her in a letter, suggesting that, since she had betrayed me about working on the Library, I retaliated by deleting his P.O. Box address from the card. This was not true. I frankly don't remember what happened; however, the problem began when Phyllis attempted to co-opt Grady's leadership by retaining her Dublin address as the contact point for the Order after they separated. Both Bill Breeze and Bill Heidrick recall that Helen asked Donald Weiser to remove the address from the deck because of the squabbling between Phyllis and Grady.

During the research for this book, I asked Donald about it. He doesn't remember the details either, but added that, if there had been a conflict, he would have taken the path of least resistance and dropped the address. I found a letter from Grady to me dated August 15, 1977, in which he asked if the Caliph Card would be included in the new deck and, if so, what address would appear on it. I answered him on August 18, saying the Caliph Card was being typeset at that moment with his Berkeley address as planned. I reminded him that Donald had the last word.

This exchange of letters took place a year *after* Phyllis' betrayal and lends credibility to the idea that Helen must have objected to Donald at the last minute. Helen and Donald knew each other as fellow booksellers and publishers. Her account of the war between Grady in Berkeley and Phyllis in Dublin most likely resulted in Don simply throwing up his hands and telling me to yank the address altogether. I do know that "punishing" Grady for Phyllis' pettiness is simply not in my DNA. The Caliph Card *was* included in the new deck. It displayed the Order Lamen, along with Grady's statement about the deck, and was signed with his name and title as Caliph.

LAShTAL Lodge

When my 1978 understanding about the crucial spiritual importance of the O.T.O. in my life encouraged me to take the I°, Grady
initiated me in New York at the Magickal Childe Temple. By this
time, Mobius Chapter had become LAShTAL Lodge. It was a dys-
functional entity. Kris' insecurity and anxiety had encouraged him
to surround himself with some fairly scurrilous and hostile officers
who treated anyone they perceived as the slightest bit threatening with great rudeness. It was an appalling characteristic of that
group. Tom H. and Steve K. were his two most highly-placed
henchmen. They basked in demonstrating an overt belligerence as
a sign of their superiority. There was a competition between them
as to who could be the most smarmy. One slightly brighter light of
LAShTAL was a fellow from New Jersey. While more intelligent, he
was diffident about asserting his better character.

There was a good deal of personal hostility directed at me. Part
of it, I know, was due to my earlier dismissal of Kris. Had I been
more diplomatic and fraternal, and checked in with him from time
to time, the whole situation might have been different. Hindsight
can be 20-20. On the other hand, I was not in a position of leadership where such concerns would have been my responsibility. Tom
and Steve made no secret of the fact that they considered me a
Motta plant—either a spy or a traitor—and were jealous of my
access in the publishing world. I was less than interested in contact
with them, and their attitude reinforced my disdain. So we were in
a sort of armed truce. I accepted my outsider status and they were
only too happy to oblige.

SPRING 1979

This was all about to change when Grady came back into town and
I took my II° initiation. In *Magick without Tears* and his *Confessions*, Crowley attributes the II° O.T.O. to learning to live in the
world. I remember clearly, during the initiation ceremony, looking
around the candlelit room and realizing that, despite my standoff-
ish attitude, I was once again in a darkened chamber and swearing

great oaths with these same people. I had gone too far to back out. If there was something wrong with them, I had damned well better be a part of fixing it, because, like it or not, I was "a member." It was an enlightening realization.

Grady stayed with Wileda and me for three days during his visit. We believe Wileda became pregnant with our son, Satra, within a day or two of my II°.

Soon after Grady left, baseball season started. I was horrified to observe that the fans left a huge amount of litter in the Yankee Stadium area. Wileda and I moved out immediately and soon secured an apartment in Inwood Park in Manhattan, a beautifully wooded neighborhood.

The Gnostic Mass

I began to become more active in LAShTAL Lodge. Despite the ill will against me, I was seen as someone with knowledge—thus the situation was ambiguous for all of us. I began to attend the Gnostic Mass at Kris' apartment on nearby Dyckman Street and felt a calling to participate.

Finita and I asked Kris if we could begin to work on the Mass. (Neither Jorge nor Wileda was interested in being Priest or Priestess.) Kris enlisted us for the Children role one Sunday. Then he informed us that we had one week to prepare for Priest and Priestess. We accepted his challenge. We spent the week on fire, working every night on the Mass. We accomplished a reasonable first performance on May 19, 1979. Wileda had taken her Minerval by then and was one of the Children. Kris served as our Deacon. He was an excellent teacher. He had studied in a Jesuit college and understood much about the working of the ceremony. He went on to become a Bishop of the Slavonic Orthodox Church and later formed an offshoot branch known as the Celtic Orthodox Church.

Finita and I insisted on observing the first silent communion in New York. This proved to be the beginning of the end for the raucous practice into which the LAShTAL Mass communion had degenerated. People were well-behaved during the Mass itself, but the minute it was time for the communion, they'd start laughing and joking and pushing each other in line. It was insane. Kris made the announcement that we requested silence and the folks were cooperative.

We had become aware that Wileda was pregnant. The idea of the baby was enormously important to me, as was its juxtaposition with my II° initiation and beginning to perform the role of Priest— my "ordination into the Priesthood of the Light," as I called it. I had shaved my head before that first Mass in an effort to get psychically closer to the baby, due in December. It seemed to add something to the Priest role as well, because there was an Egyptian feel to it. (Speaking of Egyptian, Wileda's pregnancy occurred soon after the inspiration for the *The Egyptian Book of the Dead*. As Ogden Goelet, our supervising Egyptologist, later observed, my two children bookended the project. Rachel was born in 1994 as the book was at press.)

I loved the Mass. Within a year, Kris ordained Michael Kramer and me as Priests. It was a meaningful afternoon. He sat us down and began to question us on our ideas of the Priest as far as ministering to the community. He raised hypothetical problems to us and asked us to offer our counsel for someone in the situation he posited. What was so helpful was that Michael and I understood that this was different from an O.T.O. initiation, in which we were supposedly elevated as individuals. Kris made it clear that the role of a Priest was to serve the community. I thank him for that.

SUMMER 1979

On the Summer Solstice, I took some psilocybin and wandered off into the woods of Inwood Park. I had left work early, as planned, and was looking for a place to be alone. As the psilocybin continued coming on, I noticed the litter in the woods and became more and more despondent. I finally found a completely private, clean space to lie down—underneath a large sticker bush that protected me from interference. I became acutely aware of the lack of vitality and life force in the natural surroundings, as if Nature were threatened by an unenlightened humanity. I roused myself to return to the Tree of Life, where I felt I was making a contribution to the purification of the modern soul. Stephen Gaskin of The Farm was supposed to be visiting that day. I felt that perhaps even the energy transfer of shaking hands with him might help in the world healing. As it turned out, he didn't come in that day, but I knew I had done the right thing by returning to the Tree. I closed the store about 8:30 P.M. and went home.

I tried to call Wileda several times to tell her I had gone back to work, but had missed her. She had become anxious at my absence and began looking for me in the woods. She began to develop symptoms of a miscarriage. I worked diligently to calm our unborn baby, feeling like a consummate jerk for having caused her anxiety. Everything settled down. Within the month, I learned that Angus had died that same day in Kathmandu. I have perceived a linkage between him and Satra ever since.

Around my thirty-first birthday, I met Dr. Vasant Ladd, an Ayurvedic physician from India who visited and gave a talk at the Tree of Life. I went to see him several times afterward at the apartment where he was staying. He treated me with energy healing and herbs, cleansing much of the drug-related damage I had created. He also treated Wileda. He told us she was pregnant with a male child, a great sage. We created the name Satra (the truth or essence of Ra or the Sun), a combination of Indian and Egyptian traditions.

One evening, I went to the Bells of Hell nightclub to hear Larry Kirwan and Pierce Turner. Jim Garvey was there, as he was a regular. Alan Cabal was there as well. Alan was an interesting character—brilliant, funny, and creative, with a lively and perceptive mind. He had a pure-hearted aspiration that was striking. But he was also one of the most self-destructive people I've known and could be an obnoxious drunk. He managed to get himself beaten up more than once. A talented writer, he later began crafting articles for *The New York Press* and elsewhere.

On this particular night, he antagonized a fellow patron at the bar and the two of them got into a fight. Cabal needed help. I jumped on top of the other guy from behind and pulled him off Alan. Just at that moment, Bokar walked into the club to see me with my shaved head riding through the air on top of this enraged drunk. It was funny. Bokar is a martial artist. We soon became friends for life.

Alan was involved with Bonnie and her husband, Chris Clare-mont, who also lived in Inwood Park. Chris was a high-level writer at Marvel and was writing *Doctor Strange* at the time. This particular evening was immortalized in Issue #38, December 1979. It features Turner & Kirwan at the Bells of Hell (called Hell's Bells), an Alan Cabal-like figure killed at the bar, a take-off on the bar fight, a Simon-like cleric visiting from the Vatican library to warn Doctor Strange, and a great magical battle in Inwood Park.

Oba Oseijeman Adafunmi I

Kanya hosted an evening with Oba Oseijeman Adafunmi I (born Serge King) at the Tree of Life on July 21. He had founded the Kingdom of Oyotunji in 1970, a Yoruban community near Shel-don, South Carolina that is still functioning. He had spent many years studying African religion in the Schomburg Research Library in Harlem. I was so impressed by his talk that I handed him my personal copy of *The Book of the Law* that Gurney had made up. Smaller in length and width than a pack of cigarettes, Gurney had made one for himself and one for me, having figured out the imposition so that it folded perfectly with the pages in order after he cut and stapled it. We had carried our copies for years. King Adafunmi looked at the book and indicated that he knew it was a very special gift and promised to read it.

On July 27, Simon joined Wileda and me for an Akan ritual in Queens. The group was led by Nana Dinizulu, a powerful magician, who held the ritual in honor of his friend Oba Oseijeman. Akan is the indigenous religion of the Ashanti tribe of the West African country of Ghana. Their technique of calling spirits had a different flavor from the Voodoo tradition. It seemed more subdued—even with the characteristic drumming and dancing—but, if anything, the spirit presence may have been stronger among the African community.

On July 30, Oba Oseijeman returned to the Tree. After his talk, he offered to conduct Ifa divinations for those who wished to participate. Back during my Weiser days, my friend Sally had been heavily involved with Santeria, having left Wicca behind in her quest for more serious magic. She told me of her *padrino* (priest or spiritual advisor) and offered me the opportunity to have him read my shells. But she cautioned that whatever he advised me to do would be mandatory. I discussed it at some length with her and decided to pass. It seemed far too risky to make such an agreement in advance.

After Oba Oseijeman's moving talks some five years later, I felt perfectly comfortable—indeed, honored—to enter into a serious magical relationship with him. He gave me a set of practices from the Yoruban tradition that was way out of my comfort zone at first. We discussed these at some length and worked out a program in which I could substitute Egyptian deities for those of the Yoruban pantheon. We also agreed I could replace the meat offerings he counseled with grains. I have maintained the practice scrupulously ever since.

Oba Oseijeman helped heal another rift in my psyche. Here I was—a Jewish-born guy who had left his birth religion behind at age thirteen, yet studied Qabalah and worked with Hebrew letters, names, and diagrams. It was disconcerting and had long been a source of stress. By following the Yoruban teaching of honoring one's ancestors, I managed to incorporate my genetic predecessors into my spiritual practice and these conflicts were resolved. To no one's surprise, he identified me with Eleggua, or in my symbol set, Tahuti. He gave us advice about the baby as well.

My interaction with African magic convinced me that, when the Egyptian mysteries disappeared from North Africa, initiates traveled south in addition to their missionary activities elsewhere.

SOON AFTER OBA OSEIJEMAN'S VISIT to New York, I left the Tree of Life Bookstore. My semi-volunteer position needed to be sacrificed so that I could earn enough money to allow Wileda to stay home with the baby. I had learned that Bokar was a graphic artist and assistant art director at an ad agency/print brokerage house, and he offered me a job. The place was a complete nuthouse, but I was grateful. Bokar and I enjoyed working together and we would do so several more times in the future.

* * *

CHAPTER 14

THE FOUNDING AND EARLY YEARS OF TAHUTI

ALLYN BRODSKY AND NUMEROUS other New York O.T.O. members had been pressuring me for months to break off from LAShTAL Lodge because of the excesses of Tom and Steve, Kris' poor leadership, and the lack of magical ritual and creativity in the Lodge. They even suggested that we leave the O.T.O. and proposed that I start my own magical group. This was ironic because, as mentioned, Grady had suggested I start an O.T.O. group in New York when I was initiated in 1976 and I had long considered this an indication of his short-sightedness. When the urgency built within the community for me to take a leadership position, I insisted we needed to observe hierarchical discipline and be patient and loyal to the Order.

Meanwhile, James Graeb came in from California to inspect LAShTAL. He was treated with contempt, distrust, and supreme rudeness by the aforementioned dwellers on the LAShTAL threshold. After Graeb returned to California and reported his experience to Grady and Bill Heidrick, he contacted me and asked me to open an O.T.O. body in New York. I had only to accept and announce the name. This time, I leapt at the chance to serve the Order.

FALL 1979

At dawn on the Fall Equinox, John Warner and I performed the Morning Adoration together in Inwood Park and I announced the name, thereby founding TAHUTI Encampment. John was a part-time writer for Marvel Comics. We had become friends earlier that spring. He was working at Weiser's and came up to visit me at the Tree of Life several times. He was also an initiated Gardnerian

TAHUTI LODGE

September 24, 1979 e.v.
Calculated for Sunrise
New York, NY
40N43, 74W00

Placidus Houses

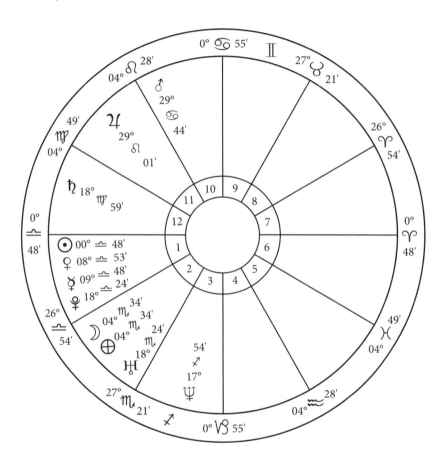

Here is the Lodge birth chart calculated for Dawn, in New York City, at
the Fall Equinox, 1979 E.V.

Our Lodge emblem combines the image of Tahuti from a flyer Crowley produced advertising *The Book of Thoth* with the Order Lamen. It was designed at the founding of the Lodge.

witch, working with High Priestess Bonnie Claremont (later Cabal). Bonnie and John initiated me into the three degrees of Gardnerian Wicca and they both took O.T.O. initiation.

Jim Garvey began to come around the O.T.O. in the fall of 1979, just after TAHUTI was formulated, but before I had been chartered to initiate. So Jim took his Minerval Degree in October from LAShTAL. He was the last person to join TAHUTI before we became a chartered initiating body. (Jim Garvey was one of the most generous, loyal, and hard-working members of the Lodge until his untimely death from cancer in 2009. It would be impossible to enumerate his many contributions to the work of the Lodge and the wider Order, or to express how much he is missed by his many friends, both in and out of the O.T.O.)

We decided to do a ritual to establish the Camp, which we performed on October 22. Brodsky wrote a poetic Oath of Encampment. Garvey made a beautiful calligraphic rendering of the poem and we all signed it. Embarrassingly, I was not attentive enough to have made sure that the parchment included the proper Thelemic form—"Do what thou wilt shall be the whole of the Law" as its opening and "Love is the law, love under will" as its closing. (At our tenth anniversary, we renewed the Oath and corrected the error.) We were flying by the seat of our pants in the effort to develop ourselves into a proper magical body and we did our best. We took out a small ad in *The Village Voice* announcing the establishment of the group in New York.

I took my III° initiation at this time. The effects were extraordinary. I danced alone in a trance ecstasy to a Santeria drumming album for hours after returning home that night.

Ed James

Elisa and her Haitian boyfriend Frisner invited Wileda and me to a Voodoo ritual in the Bronx for an invocation of Ogun, the Lord of War. I felt especially comfortable with this group, as there was a palpable intimacy and warmth among them. I was surprised to see Ed James come into the room, and impressed to observe the reverence with which he was treated by everyone present.

I knew Ed from Weiser's. He was a gifted intellectual and a powerful magician. He had worked at the store in the late 1950s or early 1960s. He had an encyclopedic familiarity with the Western tradition, especially Franz Bardon and Aleister Crowley. He had known Karl Germer. I visited him several times both before and after I was with Wileda. She was particularly impressed with his spiritual stature. While she was pregnant with Satra, he gave her a series of practices to insure the health of the baby and a safe delivery. She followed these scrupulously.

When Ogun came in, he was carrying his characteristic sword. He put the point against his abdomen and began to push. The sword bent. It all looked so real. I was impressed and thought the intensity of these folks was cool, and that perhaps the O.T.O. could make similar use of such dramatic effects in our rituals. Later, when Ogun swung his sword in front of my eyes, I realized it was not a stage prop! I was blown away. I quickly reexamined everything I thought had been going on all evening. A psychic woman who had come into the Tree of Life told me that Satra, our as-yet-unborn child, had a potential problem with his lungs. Later in the ritual, when all members of the congregation went up to receive a personal audience with the Loa, he puffed mightily on his cigar and coughed on Wileda's belly. I immediately understood that he had healed the baby in the womb and was filled with gratitude.

We were invited to return to the same group for an invocation of Ghede, the Lord of Death, near Halloween. This time, we were invited to attend the morning ceremonies when the sacrifices began. Wileda and I were each handed a rooster. Her's was white; mine was black. I began to realize what was going to happen. I tried to calm the rooster and fill it with love. I experienced a series of conflicting emotions, until I realized that this being may have spent countless incarnations preparing for the honor of being sacrificed to the gods. I became completely comfortable and held him for a good two hours. Then he was taken from my hands and killed. After the ritual that night, I participated in the feast despite my vegetarian diet. I appreciated the ecology of blood sacrifice, as everyone ate what had earlier been the divine offerings.

Soho Studio

As is often the case with Magick when the energy builds, it appears the Gods most enjoy playing. The ad agency where I had been working for three months with Bokar made an expensive move to new quarters. There was a hiatus in their work flow. I had incurred the enmity of one of the partners, and was laid off—six weeks before Satra was to be born. A few days later, I found a freelance position at Soho Studio, specialists in book production. (Eventually Bokar and Michael Kramer would work there as well.) It was a great arrangement, as I was able to work my own hours and openly conduct Studio 31 business. I learned how to make a proper book and remained there for five years, thanks in no small part to Gerry Burstein, the owner of the Studio and one of the finest role models of my life. Among many other things, Gerry taught me to appreciate Thanksgiving. This was our one paid holiday of the year. It is the quintessential, non-denominational, universal, American day of unity, centered around home, hearth, family and friends, acknowledging the presence of a God of one's understanding in national affairs—or being free not to, if one is so inclined.

Bodhisattva Vow

Angus had introduced me to another friend from Kathmandu, an initiated Vajrayana Buddhist named John Reynolds. An American-born Ph.D. who eventually joined O.T.O., John was deeply learned in Mahayana Buddhism and Bonpo Shamanism. He was teaching a class on the Tibetan *Book of the Dead* and informed us that the lineage holder of the Nyingma school, Dudjom Rinpoche, was coming to New York to offer initiation.

I took Refuge on November 10. The next day, I finally achieved my long-held goal and took the Bodhisattva Vow before a Master empowered by tradition to enforce the binding nature of the commitment. Kris and Elizabeth took it as well, giving me great hope that the O.T.O. would be strengthened in our work. It was especially gratifying to have accomplished this before the coming of the baby. I perceived the monks in their red and gold robes as partaking of the Rosicrucian current, serving as Guardians of Humanity.

WINTER 1979–1980

The Winter Solstice Ritual

Brodsky wrote a Winter Solstice ritual. It was the first of some forty we did over the next four years. I drew up a Thelemic version of the eight Wiccan festivals, which we interpreted as the "rituals of the elements and feast of the times" (AL II:36). We agreed on a practice in which one person took the responsibility to write a ritual following the broad outline of the cycle. Each rite quoted extensively from *The Holy Books,* giving the very highest interpretation to the ceremony.

We had some great successes, with far fewer duds than might have been expected. The first Solstice ritual was quite funny, in that Wileda was nine months pregnant. About twenty people attended. She played the Goddess about to give birth to the Sun and her sole duty was to waddle across the Circle announcing herself. We had a standby plan in case she started to give birth. We made it through the ceremony and Satra was born a week later.

The Birth of Satra

Satra was born at a birthing center in which a group of midwives handled the event. It was pretty cool, in that there were no sick people around. We were under close supervision throughout the pregnancy. The center was only available to healthy people; doctors monitored Wileda and were available at a nearby hospital for emergencies. Luckily for us, and especially Satra, Wileda never used drugs or alcohol, so, despite my own excesses, we had a healthy child.

The night Satra was born, Margot S. was over at the apartment and we were practicing the Mass. I had had liberal helpings of ritual wine throughout the evening. I was resting on the couch when Wileda announced that her water had broken. Fortunately, Margot had some coke so I revived from my partially-comatose state and was up and at it. When Satra came, I held him. He was like an old friend. I said a couple of times: "Welcome aboard, Son." There was something so familiar about him.

We came home and spent a very isolated period for the first few weeks, protective and careful of overexposing him at first. I was happy. I did the things a Magician might be expected to do when he brings home his first son—bringing him into the Temple, introducing him to the Gods, the Ancestors, and the Magical Weapons.

On New Years Day 1980, we introduced Satra to the Sun, trees, grass, water, and later the Moon and stars.

In February, I led a small group of TAHUTI members in a group Middle Pillar ritual. I was inspired to work with the building of a god form for the first time. It was a powerful experience, repeated very rarely thereafter. It must only be done with the most trusted fellow ritualists.

SPRING 1980

In April, I took my IV° initiation. TAHUTI was elevated to Chapter status (now called Oasis) and I received a Charter to initiate the Minerval Degree. From that point on, TAHUTI was self-sustaining, as, by dint of the hard work of hundreds of people over the decades, it remains to this day.

In May, Wileda, Satra, and I took a Tara initiation from Dudjom Rinpoche. Afterward, I had a vision of a past life with Satra while I was holding him and we looked into each other's eyes. It seemed from the expression on his face that he experienced the vision with me. Of course, this may be attributable to a baby mimicking facial expressions.

In June, I did my first performance of the Mass of the Phoenix (*Liber XLIV*), noting in my magical diary that the Magician stands in the traditional place of the deity.

Gurney Joins TAHUTI

One day, I received a phone call from Richard Gernon. He explained that he had broken with Motta and just moved to New York. He wanted to retake initiation in O.T.O. in full honesty. I was conducting my first Minerval initiations that evening, Father's Day. I was highly suspicious, but told him he could do so. I did not mention that I would be the initiator. And so he took his Minerval again, nearly four years to the day after the first time.

Eventually, I began to trust Richard and we became best friends and allies, building TAHUTI together on the principle of the O.T.O. being an outer court to A∴A∴. Despite whatever problems we had had with Motta, we were both absolutely committed to the highest level of magical work and continued our A∴A∴ practices individually.

Gurney told Bill Breeze a funny story about Motta. After Dan Gunther had been forced out of Motta's SOTO, Gurney became the head of Motta's "Mentu Lodge" in Nashville. He was extensively involved in the production of Motta's self-published books, beginning with *LXV Commented,* which Motta had pulled from Weiser in 1976. In 1979, Motta learned that Bill was publishing Crowley at 93 Publishing with Peter Macfarlane in cooperation with McMurtry, giving O.T.O. its first proper copyright notices. He went nuclear. He told Gurney and Jelks to write to inform Bill that he had not sent in his Probationer Record and was pirating Crowley, therefore contact was being cut—it was not an expulsion letter.

The letter was sent to Bill's old college on Long Island. The school forwarded it to Bill's father, who opened the letter and called the Nashville Police to track Bill down. (Bill had run away from home in his mid-teens and was in only occasional touch with his parents, who did not know where he lived.) The Nashville Police Department sent two detectives to the house/publishing office. Gurney and Jelks were upstairs writing letters and snorting coke when the cops knocked on the door. Jelks was so freaked out that he withdrew his financial support from Motta—which was the beginning of the end for that scene.

Bill told Gurney and me about the premier screening of Kenneth Anger's new film, *Lucifer Rising*, at the Whitney Museum. We went and Kenneth was there. We approached him after the film to purchase two records of the soundtrack and thank him. In conversation, we mentioned that we were members of the O.T.O. Kenneth was very excited and cordial, and we arranged to get together for further discussion. This was the beginning of a friendship with a modern luminary and elder of the Thelemic path. He was especially close with Wileda and we visited together in each other's New York apartments whenever he was in town. Although Bill had met him before, this was the period when they became good friends.

FALL 1980

The Samhain Ritual

Things became more complicated with Kris and the ever-dwindling LAShTAL crew. TAHUTI decided to rent a separate Temple space from Michael Kramer at his apartment in Brooklyn on Marlborough Road. He retained most of the apartment, but we had his closed living room. He also allowed us use of the "War Room," what would have been the dining room. It was a nice spacious apartment and accommodated us for years. Michael painted beautiful murals on the walls of the Temple, which may be partially seen in a video we made of the dress rehearsal for the Samhain ritual of 1980.

The seasonal rituals had different effects on those of us who wrote them. My Samhain 1980 and Beltane 1981 rituals, in particular, were true magical invocations in every sense of the word. Samhain actually began for me during the Spring Equinox ritual of 1980, when Michael invoked Bacchus. I looked at him with the garland of flowers in his hair and his carefully trimmed beard. He seemed to have stepped right off a Roman coin—as if he were Bacchus himself. I thought: "Michael is Bacchus. Who am I?" The answer came: "The Lord of Death." That night after I returned home, I drew a picture of the deity sitting on his throne before an altar with a skull. His hair was very long and streaked with gray;

he wore a high-collared robe and held a Crook and a Flail in his crossed arms.

I "reserved" the Samhain ritual and spent the next seven months writing it and preparing myself. The other participants were Wileda, Gurney, and Bil Padgett. Bil was a close friend and Satra's godfather. He had led a Thelemic group in Atlanta, Georgia, chartered by Kenneth Grant. He tired of the lack of spiritual progress and moved up to New York, where he became a crucial member during the early years of TAHUTI. He eventually moved back to Atlanta and founded Eulis Encampment, later Eulis Lodge. His work lives on today in Dove and Serpent Oasis.

I let my hair grow for the entire seven months preceding the ritual. It was most uncomfortable, even though I characteristically wore it rather long. For the two months prior to the ritual, I was assigned a massive book project at Soho Studio. The author studied the Kennedy assassination from the point of view of the forensic evidence. Thus I was labeling diagrams of Kennedy's wounds and working extensively with autopsy photos. I was also meditating regularly on a skull that Gurney and I had purchased together at the Magickal Childe when it was legal to do so. We named it Zaur Anpin (the Lesser Countenance). I was plunged into the realm of death that I was invoking.

A fellow freelancer at the Studio named Rob Stellboum and I had become friends. He was a film student at the School of Visual Arts and had been given a class project to make a documentary of a cultural phenomenon. We allowed him to film our dress rehearsal for the rite. (The video has recently been digitized and posted on the website for this book. It provides a real window into Gurney's theater skills.) The day after the ritual, I got a haircut! In March 1981, Bil, Gurney, Wileda, and I did a followup on-camera interview at Rob's apartment, while Satra created numerous distractions and Rob's cat looked on.

Meanwhile, Kris Dowling had a real problem with Bill Breeze. Ever the rebel, Bill refused to take a test required to advance to II°, based on his understanding of *Liber LII: The Manifesto of the O.T.O.* It states that "Every man or woman that is of full age, free, and of good report, has an indefeasible right to the III°." Bill neglected to concede that "good report" is up to the Order to determine. He was a devotee of the "free school" ethos of the day, which taught that people cannot be measured by exams. Further, Crowley states in Letters 13 and 71 of *Magick without Tears* that O.T.O. is not a teaching Order like A∴A∴. Bill refused to yield. Frustrated, Kris assigned Gurney to conduct the examination. When Gurney reported that Bill had passed, Kris still refused to give him the degree. He had me conduct the initiation under his Charter. I also gave Finita the II° at the same time.

I drank a lot that night and had a nightmarish incident with a woman named Mary Jablonsky, an unbalanced lover of Michael Kramer. Although not yet a member, she thought she could help Michael by hurting me. She accused me of having burned her with a cigarette on her breast while we were passing in the hallway of the Marlborough Road apartment. She said I did it to warn her away from approaching the Temple. I had no memory of it, but was conscious enough of my responsibility as a leader to make sure that it was investigated thoroughly. I was also aware that drinking to the point where I could not honestly remember my actions had severely compromised my magical integrity, no matter what had actually happened.

Needless to say, we learned that I had done nothing of the kind. Mary finally admitted to making up the whole thing. It was a valuable, if stinging, lesson for me. I had been re-initiated into the very Degree I was administering, that of learning the importance of proper behavior. Kris naturally managed to use the whole incident as ammunition against me with California before Mary's lie was discovered.

Later that same November, I had another incident with drinking that continued to highlight the problem I was having with alcohol. That being said, my drug intake was nowhere near that described in earlier parts of this book.

When John Lennon was killed in December, I experienced the first celebrity grief connection I had felt since the assassination of President Kennedy in 1963. My sense is that it was a similarly double-barreled blow for many of my age group. I was fifteen in 1963—young and inexperienced enough to be taken in by Kennedy's myth. My affection for Lennon, however, was a less delusional admiration. Lennon's murder brought a particular closeness with Gerry Burstein, as I came into work early that morning and Gerry and I were alone for some time discussing our feelings.

WINTER 1980–1981

Grady's Visit

On December 31, 1980, Grady raised me to the apogee of the O.T.O. initiation system. I have always been a stickler about my personal Temple, going in carefully prepared, allowing no one but either my lover or children to enter. But Grady elevated me in the Temple—the first and last "outsider" ever to enter that space. He wore his combat boots, as he always did. Although it was supposed to be secret, Kris' paranoia and Heidrick's obsessive record-keeping outed us some seven weeks later.

I believe Grady was well aware that Kris and LAShTAL were crashing, as TAHUTI was flourishing under my leadership. The New York City initiate population was nearly equal to that of Northern California and needed to be protected. While the "secret of the IX°'" is more widely discussed and written about today than ever, something more than technique is involved. The Constitution and the Open Letter are very clear about the responsibilities of the Degree within the hierarchy of the Order.

Some Order critics have characterized Grady's Sovereign Sanctuary initiates as "political IX°s," as if there were something dishonorable or unmagical about what he did. Well, you could have fooled me. I was thoroughly humbled by his trust in me and am still undergoing the magical repercussions of my elevation. (I might also point out that the primary difference between Grady and his critics is that he actually held the Degree they accuse him of misunderstanding.)

Grady met Jerome Birnbaum on this trip. Jerry was a knowledgeable magician and Qabalist. He had done a lot of work with Simon, experimenting with the manuscript of the *Necronomicon*. He and Grady hit it off well, as they had both served in Korea. The problem was that Jerry was unbalanced with women. He had been involved with Kris' wife, Elizabeth, before their marriage. Jerry had mistreated her. When Kris and Elizabeth learned in February that Grady had instructed me to initiate Birnbaum, they both resigned from the Order. This led to the closing of LAShTAL. What I do not remember is whether Grady ever sat down and discussed it with them. He should have. But he was a Force of Nature in his own way and I believe his behavior was choreographed by the Will of the Order, which often appears to have little regard for personal feelings.

Grady also met Margot Adler of WBAI during this visit. Cabal had arranged for Margot to interview the three of us on the radio. She later joined the Order for a time.

SPRING 1981

The Initiation of the Severed Rooster Heads

The morning of the Spring Equinox ritual of 1981, I got a disturbing call from Alan Cabal at the Temple. The folks at Marlborough Road had been out to a concert at CBGB's rock club featuring Michael Kramer's band, The Workers. They all spent the night in Manhattan. Alan returned alone to Brooklyn to find five bleeding rooster heads nailed to the door in the shape of a pentagram. As I was about to leave my apartment in Inwood to join him, he warned me to carry a weapon. I put a 10-inch crescent wrench in my shoulder bag and realized I had just crossed a line. I would henceforth always be armed.

We had no clue at the time who had done this thing. Brooklyn had a large Santeria presence, of course, so that was definitely one possibility. Years later, we were presented with reliable evidence that Simon had encouraged dissident Lodge members—of whom more will be said—to do it as an act of magical theater. Curiously, that evening, The Workers debuted their new song "Exponential Potential," popularly known as "Horus Avenger." It features a line about "attending a high school in Poland." Martial law had recently been declared in Poland in an attempt to thwart Lech Walesa's growing

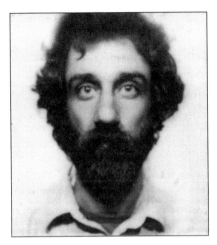

My 1981 NYC Rifle/Shotgun License photo.

Solidarity Movement. That particular night was filled with unrest and violence in Poland, as Michael was singing in Manhattan and the rooster heads were being nailed to our door in Brooklyn. The morning headlines declared: "Panic in Poland—Bloodied Workers Vow Revenge." We appreciated the synchronicity.

I spoke to Al Brunelle about buying a gun. I knew he had many underworld contacts and could undoubtedly arrange this. He questioned me as to why I wanted one and what I intended to use it for. I explained that it was to protect my family. He led me through an understanding that if I had to use a firearm to protect my family—and it was an illegal weapon—I would be imprisoned, even if I acted in self-defense. He asked what I thought would happen to my family if I went to jail. He proposed instead that I get a rifle/shotgun permit, which would legally allow me to own a self-defense shotgun in New York City.

I was stunned. My first thought was that, after all the political rallies and drugs of my earlier life, I could never pass a background check. I also innately rejected the premise that the State should be in a position to "allow" me to have a gun—like the parent of a teenage child. Finally, I felt that applying for a gun license was an indication to the authorities of some kind of madness, paranoia, or evidence of unusual and dangerous life circumstances. I considered it, but dawdled for a while. I ultimately did apply and, to my surprise, received the license. But by then, the horror of the rooster-head incident had receded somewhat and I put the license in a drawer.

In the meantime, however, a curious thing was happening. Because of my intention to buy a weapon, I began to read gun magazines and books, trying to find the best model and learn something of the field. I have mentioned that I was a bit of a "stand-off lib" when it came to guns. I had the common hoplophobic superstition of the New Ager that owning a gun meant one would "attract" violence. I also suffered from the urban arrogance of the sophisticate, looking down on the rough virtues of the "country class." On the other hand, I had shot guns as a kid and enjoyed marksmanship and the concentration it involved.

As I started to read the gun literature, I learned that, far from being a bunch of beer-bellied, toothless rednecks, these folks were serious as a heart attack about retaining the constitutionally protected liberties that animated and distinguished America from every other country on Earth. The most intelligent of them, like Mel Tappan and Jeff Cooper, viewed ownership of firearms as a sacred trust, very much like a Knight Templar would regard his sword and lance.

The Second Amendment is a banner of freedom; that which distinguishes the free man from the slave, the citizen from the subject. It represents autonomy and competence in a world filled with dependency and helplessness.

This was an entirely alternate understanding for me. I remember once walking into a pawn shop in Oregon in 1970 and making some loud-mouthed, rude, East Coast Leftist comment like: "I suppose I could just buy a gun here if I wanted to." The raw need to survive, protect, and defend had awakened me from the hypnotic state of theoretical urban bookworm to an awareness of the instinctual reality of the human condition.

This period of study subsequently led to an entire change in my political philosophy. I understood on a very direct level that freedom depended on individual autonomy—that I had been an unwitting enemy of Liberty by my embrace of the Collectivist state. The idea of a government "caring" for "its" people is an oxymoron. Government has no feeling and people belong to themselves. For nearly a decade and a half—first as some brainwashed little megaphone of youthful innocence skillfully manipulated by adults with a sinister agenda, followed by my drug-soaked mystical quest—I had been a perfectly acceptable subject. I had never voted in my life. It was beneath my spiritual grandeur; such quaint social rituals did not apply to we exalted few. I paid little attention to my political masters, allowing them to forge my chains while I danced around my Magical Circle conceiving of myself as one of the Forces of Light on the Planet. My reflexive interest in self-defense was the beginning of a study of the political organization of human societies that continues to this day. I owe a debt of gratitude, therefore, to those who severed those roosters' heads and nailed them to our Temple door. Their outrageous assault on the O.T.O. helped lift the curtain on a major element of the Trance.

Beltane

The Beltane ritual that year was one of the highest rituals of my life. Looking over the script may or may not convey its intensity. (It is included as an appendix.) I read it today and get goose bumps. It is a dialogue between a Priest and Priestess, artfully composed exclusively from sequential verses of *Liber VII*. Paul G., an ex-Marine and professional truck driver, told me the next day that he was driving home after the ritual and had to pull off to the side of the road. A vision of the Goddess overpowered him. I was not surprised. This ritual helped establish the proximate conditions for that which followed.

Liber Israfel and the Holy Guardian Angel

On May 6, I decided to look at Crowley and Alan Bennett's invocation of Tahuti in *Liber Israfel* on my way to work, with the thought that it could be adapted as a group ritual for TAHUTI Lodge. I had read it in the course of my studies in *The Equinox,* but was hardly intimate with the ritual. I grabbed my copy of *Equinox,* I:7 off the shelf, placed it in my shoulder bag, and walked to the A train station at 207th Street to begin the long journey to Houston Street (essentially, 1st Street).

I opened the book almost idly and had begun to read the first lines of the invocation when I was hit with the most extraordinary experience of my life. A wave of energy surged throughout my body. My consciousness expanded far beyond the boundaries of anything I had ever experienced through drugs, ritual, or meditation. It would be inaccurate to call the experience anything other than "union with God"—and that is hardly a scientific description or comprehensible explication for most. It was, and is, inexpressible. ("No ear can hear Him, nor can eye see Him, nor tongue speak of Him, but [only] mind and heart."—*Thrice Greatest Hermes*) I have no idea how long the initial wave lasted, but when it subsided a bit, I simply wept. I got off at my stop and walked into work. I sat at my drawing table in Soho Studio silently weeping throughout the morning. My friend and fellow initiate Michael Kramer came over gently to make sure I was okay.

After work, I was getting ready to go home. I had worn my denim jacket with the sleeves cut off and a large golden Horus appliqué on the back. I had adopted that regalia as a challenge, a bold statement that, as TAHUTI Lodgemaster, I was not ashamed to identify myself with the message of the New Aeon. As an emblem, it was also a target, indicating I was willing to sacrifice myself for these ideals, much like a Templar knight with his red cross proudly displayed on his white robe. I am a generally understated dresser, and this was a most uncharacteristic article of clothing for me.

An incident had taken place recently in which I had acted in an unusual and despicable manner. I had pressed sexual attention upon a Lodge sister with whom I was practicing the Gnostic Mass and who was not receptive. I crossed a line of unwarranted advance while inebriated with wine from the practice. I stopped, of course, but it was a classic example of the abuse of power we try so hard to avoid in the Order. As bad as I felt about it, I had kept it to myself, neither discussing it with the woman, nor doing anything else to resolve it.

The event loomed large in my mind in my altered state of consciousness. Kundalini had been running continuously up and down my body all day. Although I felt unworthy, I put on the "colors" because it seemed like a necessary act of truth. I wandered around a playground for some hours. I decided I would resign from O.T.O. I would inform Grady that, while I loved the Order, I had shamed it and was morally ineligible to continue in a position of leadership. I would tell him that I hoped we could remain friends.

Grady's face loomed before me and his eyes bored into mine; I felt a shudder of ice run through my body. I realized in no uncertain terms that he had far more important concerns than friendship with a quitter—that, if I could overcome my shame and become a better person, if I could continue doing the work of the Order and be a better leader, I could retain his friendship and reclaim my honor. If I left, however, I would condemn myself to the outer darkness as a weakling and a traitor to the Work.

I got on a subway going home. I began to perceive a rattling sound like that of a rattle snake. I was drawn up before a serpentine energy that was guarding an entryway to the inner sanctum of the Forces behind the O.T.O. and Thelema. I began to feel my heart constricted by invisible hands. I saw in my mind's eye an article in the local section of the newspaper with a story about a subway rider found dead of an apparent heart attack. The rattling and hissing and serpentine energy increased. I understood that, unless I was prepared to confess to my wife and make the proper amends to all involved, I would be killed for having violated the spiritual task of leadership I had been given.

In fact, I explained it to Wileda. My energy level was so high that she accepted what I said. It was clear that she was the Guardian of the Pylon for that which had occurred during the subway ride home, and that I was to live through the experience. I went into my Temple and performed *Liber Israfel* in full for the first time, reading from the book. As I uttered each line of the ritual, it was absolutely true within my consciousness. The Guardians of the Watchtowers attempted to intimidate me and I stood up to them, indicating that I was a human being who, while prone to sin, was entitled to the Kingdom by virtue of my birth and aspiration. I was completely enveloped by the Angel. The interior of my body was suffused with healing energy. I was renewed and reborn, cleansed and energized on a cellular level.

I finished the ritual and came out of the Temple, trying to understand what was going on. For a brief moment, I thought I might be experiencing "the Ordeal x" mentioned in *The Book of the Law* (III:22), but soon laughed at my presumption. This state of mind lasted for over a week, the energies coursing through my body, the mythic state of consciousness opening continuous vistas of understanding.

We held a Lodge meeting in which I revealed some of what had happened to the group, without being specific or burdening anyone with my problems. My state of consciousness revealed a teaching for each individual present and I expressed it. Gurney was sitting next to me and we had a telepathic exchange of information. It began with a beeping sound in my mind, as I felt his consciousness enter the sphere of my own. We turned and nodded to each other, mutually accepting the experience. I explained to the Sister in question that her task would be to overcome her legitimate resentment against me personally and take her next degree in the Order, which she had delayed for some time for unrelated reasons. It was a most unusual Lodge meeting. We all sang the Voodoo-inspired New Orleans jazz classic *When the Saints Come Marching In*. They had.

The members of the Lodge signed an application to Grady for membership in the Guild of Drama and Thaumaturgy, dedicated to the special practice of spiritual magick. Each of us made an advance during that meeting, although some members were lost as a result. Those of us who remained became stronger. The text of the application is included in the appendices.

Visiting Grady in Montreal

New York needed a Bishop of E.G.C. to replace Kris. (The Ecclesiae Gnosticae Catholicae is the liturgical arm of Ordo Templi Orientis. There are many precedents and various lines of succession involved. Caliph Hymenaeus Beta produced a special issue of

Larry Barnes was an intensely creative soul. He is shown above with Dorian visiting one of the earliest incarnations of Studio 31.

Herman Slater and Priestess in the Magickal Childe Temple. Our Gnostic Mass altar and steps are visible behind them.

Simon in a rare publicity shot for the *Necronomicon*.

The brilliant and zany master photographer Don Snyder at Studio 31.

Our VGC stat machine and type processor at left, Linotron 202 at right. The Denderah Zodiac poster is on the wall.

OPPOSITE: John Warner at the annual Weiser Christmas Party, ca 1980.

Wileda, without whose dedication and hard work TAHUTI Lodge would never have succeeded.

Jim Garvey in Central Park in 1980. He was one of the most important contributors to TAHUTI. Jim was a true Man of Honor.

Ordo Templi Orientis

OATH OA ENCAMPMENT

Gathered outside Time and Space
We offer up our hopes of Grace,
Our Oath of union into One,
Binding all beneath this Sun.
Thelema links us, Star to Star,
Tahuti calls to what we are,
For this we join, this is our Will.
Love is our Law. In Love fulfill
All striving to its just reward.
Be AL our strength and ON our Lord.
TAHUTI!

OM AH HUM!

[signatures:]
Ad Vaerum · מה איסט · רוח אור · Sub Rosa · Abrahadabra · Taceo · Sursamal Sommam · NOT · Γνοθι Σαωτου · Layla · Filius de Babalon · Serviam

TAHUTI Oath of Encampment. The calligraphy is by Jim Garvey. Allyn Brodsky wrote the text. Of the original Charter signers, Wileda, Mike Kramer and I remain the best of friends. Some signers have died. We all miss Garvey. Others have gone their own ways. All left as friends with one exception. In order: Ad Vaerum (James Wasserman) • רוח אור (Wileda) • Sub Rosa (Alan Cabal) • Taceo (Michael Kramer) • Γνοθι Σαωτου (Allyn Brodsky) • Filius de Babalon (Joe O.) • THMAIST (Jim Garvey) • Abrahadabra (William Barnes) • Sursamal Sommam (Sherri Lane) • NOT (Alan Davis) • Layla (Margot S.) • Serviam (Cathie M.)

Gurney, above, visiting Enchantments in the early 1980s, and as Osiris in Nashville, ca. 1978.

Bokar clowning above with the lovely Helen. He is one of my best friends as well as one of the most talented magicians I have known.

Michael Kramer is a Charter signer and one of the most influential members of TAHUTI Lodge. He was also master of Hellfire Camp and Khephra Oasis.

Grady and crew in Montreal. I'm standing behind Bill. Mike and Mechelle Ripple are behind Grady. Marc Desjardins is seated on floor.

Alan and Bonnie Cabal. She passed away in 2003. This photo was taken after they moved to California.

Robbie Brazil was another great friend and hard working member of TAHUTI. He established a Camp in Tarrytown called Kykuit, which closed after a time. Robbie was a Shakespearean scholar and contributed much original research to the Earl of Oxford identity puzzle. He passed away in 2010 and is missed.

David Brazil and Satra about a year before Robbie and I took them on our first trip to Oesopus Island in 1983.

The women of the Halveti Jerrahi of Spring Valley. Jane is shown top right. My hope is that Allah will forgive her for her quip about the men dancing the Zikr being the Sufis, and the women chanting at the outer rim of the circle being the Sufiettes.

Me as the Lord of Death in TAHUTI Samhain ritual, 1980.

Finita in an elegant pose—a Mistress of Tarot and devotee of Franz Bardon.

The Magical Link in the winter of 1990 outlining the history of the Church. Bishop Tau Apiryon released an additional study in 1995, which is currently available at *www.hermetic.com/sabazius/ history_egc.htm*.)

During the period I am describing, I would have been the normal choice for Bishop, as Lodgemaster and senior initiate. But I asked Grady to appoint Gurney instead so that we could share the spiritual leadership of TAHUTI Lodge rather than keep it concentrated in my hands alone. Gurney and I went up to visit Grady in Montreal in early June, where he was doing initiations for Bill Breeze's Phoenix Lodge.

Alan Cabal and Simon also came to Montreal to complain to Grady that they feared I was building a paramilitary group within TAHUTI. This was, of course, insane. However, I had become extremely concerned about the threat I perceived to American liberty. I was exposed to the survivalist movement and firmly believed that people needed to be familiar with methods of storing food, and—as a military order derived from the Knights Templar—not be afraid to encourage familiarity and skill with weapons, particularly firearms. I understood the Second Amendment to be, in Jeff Cooper's words, "Liberty's Teeth." It is the recognition of the right to be armed that allows for the retention of all the other rights acknowledged in the Bill of Rights. Cabal and Simon, however, took my ideas well into the predicate of Janet Reno's future characterization of David Koresh, leader of the Branch Davidians in Waco, Texas. Fortunately, Grady was a lot smarter than Bill Clinton. After privately discussing their charges with me at length, he was assured I could be trusted.

Grady gave me a Charter, dated June 14, appointing me his "direct representative" as the New York City Area Operations Coordinator. He wanted me to experiment with opening additional bodies and decentralizing local leadership. He asked me to offer the opportunity to start Camps to those of my most trusted members who were interested. I was happy to work within that model, because I was open to such structures by nature. My responsibilties were to oversee the satellite Camps, maintain a proper New York

City Temple (including being authorized to collect local dues from members of all area bodies), and to guarantee the highest standards with regard to initiations in all groups.

Three of the strongest members of the Lodge, all Charter signers of the Oath of Encampment, formed Camps. Michael Kramer started Hellfire; Alan Cabal started Fenris; and Sherri Lane started INRI. (Cabal could be a little nutty, as the Montreal experience indicated, but you always knew where you stood with him.) I stopped initiating at TAHUTI to give the new Camp masters time to bring in new people and build their groups.

SUMMER 1981

All of us continued to attend the main TAHUTI Lodge meeting. In July, we started the meeting with the Thelemic Middle Pillar. Gurney had expressed discomfort with the Hebrew names of the Sephiroth from Israel Regardie's version of the ritual. He and I worked out a replacement set of Thelemic names with careful reference to *Liber V vel Reguli*. The ritual is quite elegant and is included as an appendix. Later that month, Gurney conducted E.G.C. baptisms in the Atlantic Ocean near Paul G.'s apartment.

CHAPTER 15

THE CONSTITUTIONAL CONFLICTS
AND THE FIRST MOTTA TRIAL

At the very end of 1979, TAHUTI had hosted a lecture by Simon. It turned out that he was a very well-known and respected teacher to several of the principles of the Lodge, including Brodsky, Kramer, Cabal, and Bokar (a close friend to us all, but not yet an Order member). Certainly Simon and my success with the *Necronomicon* had been a delightful experience. We were discussing doing a book on Enochian magic. I had been drawing and coloring the Tablets during the summer of 1981 as a preliminary to the anticipated production. I spent untold hours working on them while listening to the Bobby Beausoleil soundtrack of *Lucifer Rising*.

TAHUTI sponsored a new series of Simon lectures on Goetic magic and the Enochian system in 1981. (Brodsky had resigned from the O.T.O. by this time.) We held events with Simon in February, July, August, and September. They were quite lovely affairs. We charged people to come and provided a nice spread of food and drink at my apartment in Inwood. We had upward of twenty people who somehow all managed to fit in comfortably. Simon's skill as a speaker was amazing and everyone had a great time and learned a lot. We split the money above expenses with him, so it was a nice, if modest, arrangement for all.

My mistake was in elevating a non-member of the Order to such a high position as an authority. The lecture scheduled for October 24 was canceled because of events that will soon be discussed. Again, it may seem curious that I would work with Simon and Cabal after the Montreal experience. My reasoning was that opinions are (since this is a family-rated book) like belly buttons:

everyone has one. Simon, Cabal, and I did not have to agree on everything to be friends and to benefit from each other's skill sets. Besides, they had made their outreach to Grady openly, rather than behind my back. Their concerns were genuine, if misplaced.

The early 1980s was the period when the O.T.O. Constitution was being discussed at length, both between New York and California and within the Lodge itself. Simon was a committed political investigator, having hunted Nazis in South America, exposing himself to a great deal of personal danger in his quest for a freer world. He embodied the "progressive" agenda and felt that the O.T.O. hierarchy was an outdated concept. In this opinion, he was buttressed by the work of Kenneth Grant. Grant had been expelled from O.T.O. in 1955 because he refused to accept the authority of Karl Germer, then functioning as OHO. Simon's idea was that Grant had actually moved in a more Thelemic direction by asserting his own authority as an initiate against the rigidity and control of Crowley's outdated structure.

This is certainly a valid point that was quite popular among many in the magical community of that era. My take on it was, and remains, that people who want to embrace the more anarchistic model of Thelema are welcome to do so, but the O.T.O. is designed as a conservative organization on purpose. In other words, our mission is to own property, publish books, enter legal contracts, and submit ourselves to the hierarchical structure Crowley proposed. We certainly all have our personal disagreements with Order policy, and are free within the organization to attempt to have it changed. At a certain point, however, one must surrender to policies with which one disagrees—or quit.

I have had my "three great hierarchical crises" during my own membership and survived each one with my integrity intact. In the first, which will be discussed later regarding my participation in a Kenneth Grant book, I "won" the argument. In the second, I submitted to the Will of the Order and learned a very great lesson about the mysteries of an important Degree. The third is ongoing. I continue to fight like hell with good humor, loyalty, and love— probably for the rest of my life.

In Simon's case, he rejected our hierarchy because it reminded him of fascism. It is ironic that the progressive agenda, while pretending to be free, actually imposes an inordinate amount of control over an individual's financial and social life. But I digress. Simon had surrounded himself with a group of nay-sayers—members who were angry about the Order for one reason or another. They had banded together and chosen the Constitutional/military structure of the O.T.O. as the focus of their rebellion. Both his own brilliance, and my having put him on a platform as a magical teacher to TAHUTI Lodge, strengthened his influence.

FALL 1981

Bloody Sunday

On October 4, some six months after the incident of the bleeding, severed rooster heads, we experienced an even more violent attack. Simon lent a sympathetic ear to three people with an axe to grind, precipitating an ugly event that came to be called "Bloody Sunday."

Mary F. was the woman to whom I had made my unsolicited advances during our Gnostic Mass practice. She had a close friend, Joe O., a sociopathic bully and a mama's boy who (perhaps tellingly) called himself *Filius de Babalon*. Mary had confided my misbehavior to Joe and he expressed his anger, first to Cabal and then in a two-and-a-half-hour telephone harangue to Wileda. I wrote him a letter expressing my sympathy for his chivalrous feelings, but criticizing him for not speaking to me directly. I also noted what I called his "willingness to cast the first stone." My diary notes that, in June 1980, I had suspected Joe of stealing pot from my home. A week after that, while drinking, he "accidently" kicked me in the head during a demonstration of a Karate move. The blow was serious enough that I went to a hospital to be checked out by a doctor and missed two days of work.

The third person was Paul G., one of the more interesting individuals to come through the doors of the New York O.T.O. A man of great self-discipline, Paul thrived in the Brooklyn underworld despite what I perceived to be a high level of personal integrity. He was forced in his own mind to compare the O.T.O. Constitution to the Uniform Code of Military Justice and felt that he did not have the freedom he required. He was the one person I regretted losing in this debacle.

We were in a Gnostic Mass. As was his habit, Gurney was not in attendance. As the Bishop of New York, he felt he didn't have to or shouldn't attend—for whatever reason. He hung out by himself in the apartment while the Mass went on in the Temple. For some period after the rooster-head incident, we kept a guard posted, so Richard was doing that duty as well. I was a member of the congregation at this Mass.

I heard a loud noise outside the Temple door, but waited until the ceremony was over before I rushed out of the room—just in time to see Gurney flying through the air like a rag doll and land crumpled on the floor. Joe O., who was about twice Richard's size, was yelling at him. Paul, who carried a gun, was looking on quietly. Mary F. watched with a crazed expression on her face. An hour later, Simon showed up. We then had a "meeting," which consisted of several hours of arguing, yelling, attempting to reason, and raging around—with periods of more physical violence. (It is important to note that the Constitutional structure and the O.T.O. hierarchy were the only subjects of the argument. My interaction with Mary F. never came up.)

As the hours wore on, Joe began screaming at me and frothing at the mouth. I was holding Satra in my arms. I looked at Joe and held up the baby to make the point that he was acting like an idiot and to just calm down. The gesture enraged him and he somehow leapt across the table like a madman, attempting to strike me. I twisted to avoid him and protect Satra, while Wileda slapped Mary, who had reached out to grab the baby. Paul restrained Joe. It was completely insane.

There was one moment when events seemed to occur in slow motion and I was able to take a careful look at the expression in Simon's eyes. I realized that he was as stunned by what was going on as I was. It was clear to me that, far from planning a physical attack on the Order with his henchmen, he was appalled. (Although we would put our relationship on hold for nearly a quarter of a century following this episode, we have since renewed our friendship.)

At one point, Joe was yelling in front of a dozen people, swearing that he was going to break into my apartment and attack and kill me. He had bragged to us that he had assaulted a person or two and gotten away with it because he had friends on the police force who believed his story rather than that of his victims. When our family returned home that day, we arranged for Wileda and Satra to visit Mike and Mechelle Ripple in upstate New York.

I went to Weiser's Bookstore, where my friend and former boss, Chip Suzuki, allowed me to pawn my copy of *The Egyptian Book of the Dead*. I took $500, and Gurney and I went to a gun store in Long Island, where I bought an Ithaca Model 37, 12-gauge shotgun. The Remington 870 was the brand of choice, but I loved the feel and balance of the Ithaca. Its particular configuration did not allow for an extended magazine. I discussed this with the clerk and he pointed out that if five rounds of 12-gauge shells were not enough to stop an attack, I was probably in more trouble than I could handle. I smiled and took the gun.

When I came home later that afternoon, I consecrated my firearm to Horus. I sat in the middle of the living room, holding the loaded weapon. I looked to the windows. I looked to the door. I looked at the hallway that led to the bedrooms. I realized that, no matter how fast Joe was, I would be able to shoot him before he reached me. I realized that all the martial arts skills and training he possessed—all the brute force he had in his favor and the fact that he outweighed me by fifty to seventy-five pounds—all these advantages were negated by the "Great Equalizer" in my hands. I knew beyond a shadow of a doubt that, if he came at me, I would kill him and never regret it, nor feel a lack of moral justification for killing in self-defense. I swore at the moment never to be disarmed as long as I lived.

The drama with Simon did cause me to become anxious about some of my higher-ranking people. Kramer, Cabal, and Sherri had all been Simon's students in one way or another and viewed him as a magical adept. I feared they might have divided spiritual loyalties. Gurney, Wileda, Laura (Gurney's wife), and I sat in Gurney and

Laura's apartment in Inwood and contemplated what we believed was the very real possibility that we would be the only four members left of the New York O.T.O.

How wrong we were! We had a meeting mid-week with the other leaders of New York and discussed the entire situation. Our fellows were repulsed by what had happened. We all renewed our commitments to build a united front as O.T.O. We agreed on a nine-month moratorium on initiation so that we could integrate and train our existing membership and clarify our mission. We felt that Bloody Sunday was a symptom of the rather extraordinary growth we had experienced in the previous several years, and a sign that we needed to regroup before bringing in new members. We agreed to consider moving to the Magickal Childe for security reasons.

The following week, we did our next Gnostic Mass at Marlborough Road, refusing to give in to intimidation. I paced outside the Temple with a machete throughout the Mass, fully prepared to kill anyone who dared attack the Lodge. (My shotgun license prohibited me from carrying the weapon around town.)

We Move to the Magickal Childe

The problem with the Marlborough Road Temple was its isolation. It was way out in Brooklyn and Michael didn't even have a telephone. I went to speak to Herman at the Magickal Childe. I told him what had happened and that we felt vulnerable and in an indefensible location. He invited us to move the Gnostic Mass back to the shop, where it had been periodically performed years before by LAShTAL. Herman would later take his Minerval initiation with us. I explained at length Simon's involvement and noted that I didn't want to put Herman in a difficult situation of "choosing" between the two of us. He was adamant that his invitation was unconditional and that, if Simon had any objections, the two of them would resolve it between themselves.

Herman later told me that Simon did come to him with a series of libels. Herman stated that Simon told him I drew blood samples from members; that the O.T.O. was a neo-Nazi organization; that we were advocating the overthrow of the U.S. government; and that Gurney and I were Motta agents. Herman, whom I adored, was known to "embellish a tale," so I am not sure how much of this Simon actually said. But I do know that he made an ugly statement to Larry Barnes' girlfriend about my holding Satra like a crucifix.

I was grateful for Herman's offer and still admire and appreciate his courage in standing with us. He was a good friend to everyone, including Simon. We packed up our Mass equipment and moved to the Magickal Childe for the next couple of years.

Our Samhain ritual went off well. My diary mentions a number of visits with Kenneth Anger at this time.

WINTER 1981–1982

In January, we formally began the New York Constitutional Study Group. We were determined to learn and understand as much as we could about the workings of the O.T.O. design. The Bloody Sunday attack had lit a fire in the Lodge to tackle analyzing the Constitution in depth.

Lon DuQuette was another passionate advocate of the Constitution. He was a Lodgemaster in Southern California and the First Emir on the Board of Directors or Supreme Council, the primary governing body of the Order at the time. The Council was composed of the Caliph, Grand Secretary General, Grand Treasurer General, and four IX°s called "Emirs." Kris Dowling had been the Second Emir. When he resigned, I was elected to replace him. Lon was a friend of Bill Breeze and Kris, and I had long heard good things about him from Grady. Mike Ripple, another Emir, called in April to convey Lon's invitation to join his Committee for the Institution of Constitutional Measures. I accepted with pleasure. All four Emirs, including Shirene Morton, were now members. I was particularly anxious to build the Electoral College and had co-signed several local Charters (with Grady) as a member of the (then non-existent) Electoral College.

Simon and I exchanged two dreadful letters. We later met in person and discussed how we could interact in future social and business settings without a public display of discord. Dylan's line still comes to mind: "And when we meet again, introduced as friends..." It was an ironic exchange, but bad manners are hardly conducive to either spiritual inspiration or publishing activities. It was not long before Simon left New York for many years on an extended series of business-related travels to the Far East.

Marcelo Motta and the Weiser Lawsuit

I also found myself pressed with more far-reaching concerns. While attending the annual Weiser Christmas Party at the end of 1981, Donald had informed me that Marcelo Motta was suing the company for copyright infringement. I felt a sense of embarrassment, as if Motta were "my fault." I also knew that I held the key to Donald's legal victory. Motta had by this time incorporated his Society Ordo Templi Orientis (SOTO) because he knew only O.T.O. could own copyrights. I explained to Donald that the O.T.O. could help him win against Motta, but the consequence would be that he would need to recognize O.T.O. as the copyright holder of the Crowley estate.

I knew from my past legal research that the law at this time required all parties who owned a joint copyright to be in agreement to file a lawsuit for infringement. Even if we did not challenge Motta's claim to a portion of the copyright through his SOTO, the fact that Grady had an even stronger claim, but refused to assert an infringement complaint, meant that Motta's efforts would fail. But that strategy involved the recognition that O.T.O. did, in fact, own the copyright. Donald agreed that it would be a wise business decision to acknowledge O.T.O. copyright. In that way, he could protect his Crowley properties from other publishers releasing competing editions, as had been the case throughout the 1970s. By way of example, there were at least three separate editions of *The Book of Thoth*.

I spent a fair part of February preparing Weiser's legal defense and submitted a brief in March with Grady's help.

On April 10, the third day of the writing of *The Book of the Law,* the day of Ra-Hoor-Khuit, I purchased my first .45-caliber, Colt 1911 pistol. I figured that, after getting the shotgun license, there were no dark secrets lurking in my past of which I was unaware. Why not apply for a pistol license? Sure enough, I received it; then I applied for the required purchase order for my weapon of choice. I carried Satra on my shoulders as we walked into a gun store in Brooklyn, a father/son moment in an unlikely urban setting. I joined the Westside Range on West 20th Street soon after. As Satra grew older, he was welcomed by the staff. I did advertising work for them for many years.

The Holy Books of Thelema

Another significant theme of this spring was that Bill, Gurney, and I offered to produce *The Holy Books of Thelema* for Weiser. We created the entire book for free in return for Donald agreeing to print it in a quality, sewn, hardcover edition, and give us artistic and editorial control of all subsequent editions. Grady had thought to create an edition of the *Holy Books* that mirrored the content of *Thelema,* the beautifully produced three small books that Crowley had put out privately for A∴A∴ members in 1909. Regardie had put out a similar one-volume group of texts published in 1972 with Sangrael Press, but it was out-of-print. Instead, Bill persuaded Grady to release the full collection of the *Holy Books* (minus those books that contained mixed Class A texts such as *The Vision and the Voice, The Paris Working,* and *The Treasure House of Images).* Bill did the design and editorial work, Gurney handled keyboarding and typesetting, and I handled art, layout, and production. All three of us did proofreading, an arduous task. Bill wrote the introduction under Grady's name, and Grady approved it and signed off with his O.T.O. imprimatur.

Wileda, Kramer, and I began a series of planetary workings. Michael was a skilled magician and we all enjoyed working together.

On April 26, I called home and Satra picked up the phone and said "Hello"! That was an event significant enough to have been recorded in my magical diary.

SUMMER 1982

Wileda and I took responsibility for the Summer Solstice ritual. It seems we had been trying to find the inspiration for the ritual for some two months without success. I knew I was after something that involved fewer words and more energy work. Grady was visiting about a week before the ritual and we were in a cab on our way to the Gnostic Mass at the Magickal Childe when the inspiration finally came.

The rite involved Wileda and me facing each other and beginning to circulate energy between ourselves. Then the group would work to amplify the energy exchange and we would all broadcast it out to the Universe. Although this particular ritual was attended by only seven people, I noted in my magical record that the energy reached such a crescendo that "it felt our heads would come off."

Wileda went back to work after two and a half years at home with Satra. In July, Mark Tranum visited and we discussed opening a bookstore specializing in metaphysical books, but also some Whole Earth Catalog-type stuff on food, energy, weapons, and survival. John Reynolds took his Minerval Degree. Satra and I took a four-day camping trip together. Another camping trip later that summer at Harriman State Park renewed my contact with Bill Siebert. He had been a disciple of Kenneth Grant. I had met him with Janice Ayers and David Smith back in the day. Siebert had become friends with Alan Davis of the Philadelphia O.T.O. By this time, I believe he had left Grant and was on his own. An amazingly talented alchemist, he had brewed up a powerful psychedelic concoction of which I took *way* too much.

FALL 1982

Wileda wrote the Fall Equinox ritual. TAHUTI Lodge was in a flurry of activity with Degree initiations, Gnostic Masses, and seasonal rituals. Satra began pre-school, which was a big step for all of us. Dennis Deem came by for a visit after some ten years of absence. He and his new wife, Lucy, were contemplating moving from the West Coast to Martha's Vineyard. Grady came back to town for his birthday bash, celebrated on October 18.

Our Samhain ritual that year was a hoot. Gurney and I had rigged up the presiding deity, the Lord of Death. Zaur, our shared magical skull, crowned a full-size, headless, research-lab skeleton that Sherri had somehow acquired and offered to me rather than discard during a move. We slit an old robe of mine and clothed the deity in it, wiring up his right arm for rigidity. He was seated upon a throne. I was standing next to him reciting Class A texts, while Gurney was hidden behind the altar manipulating the skeletal arm to pass out Cakes of Light for the communion. It was quite a production. I think Satra still remembers it.

Soon after, we had a Gnostic Mass at the Magickal Childe that was filmed by a local television crew. When it was broadcast in its edited version, it only served to increase my distrust of the media, especially where spiritual matters are involved. One hopes the day will come when a ritual can be properly presented to the public with integrity, as Crowley tried to do with the Rites of Eleusis.

The Weiser/Motta lawsuit was proceeding along its ugly path. Motta's deposition occurred on December 21 in Maine. (Donald had given his in late October.) At the request of Donald's lawyer, I had prepared a series of factual questions designed to get Motta angry. When he heard them, he knew I was involved in helping Weiser. I was told that he muttered some threats against me. The day of Motta's deposition, Donald's mother was struck by a car and killed while crossing the street in Miami.

WINTER 1982–1983

Gurney led the Winter Solstice ritual. My diary is rather scant for the first couple of months of 1983, other than to mention working on *The Holy Books*. I also learned of two other car accidents in Donald's immediate family that had taken place around the time of Motta's deposition.

SPRING 1983

Constitutional Proposals to Grady

Prior to the 1985 California court battle with Motta, which will be discussed shortly, a revisionist tendency was raging through the O.T.O. that challenged Crowley's very design of the system. I remember the Supreme Council (or Board of Directors) meeting at which it was announced that we had reached more numbered resolutions than we had members. The common refrain of the day from Northern California was that the provisions of *Liber CI: An Open Letter to Those who May Wish to Join the Order* and *Liber CXCIV: An Intimation with Reference to the Constitution of the Order* were antiquated and, in some cases, illegal—e.g., the owner of a railroad could no longer allow O.T.O. members to travel free of charge.

By contrast, I remembered the night before my Minerval initiation when Grady had handed me xerox copies of the Open Letter and Constitution from *The Blue Equinox*. He told me that O.T.O. was a dues-paying organization and that, to join, I must accept, within the limits of my understanding, *The Book of the Law* as written. I had joined *The Blue Equinox* O.T.O. in 1976. Crowley had published *The Blue Equinox*—properly, *The Equinox* III:1— in Detroit in 1919. Roughly 20 percent of the book is devoted to a series of writings describing the O.T.O., including the Constitution and the Open Letter, *Liber LII: The Manifesto of the O.T.O., Liber XV: the Gnostic Mass*, and *Liber CLXI: Concerning the Law of Thelema*. These texts were the basis for my joining the Order under Grady in 1976 and remain the reason for my continued membership.

The documents of incorporation that had been filed by James Graeb were morphing into the "new" identity of the O.T.O. Graeb, with perhaps unwitting support from my friend Bill Heidrick, was working to supplant *The Blue Equinox* design. (Heidrick is a tinkerer by nature. I would not call him a revisionist.) This had all been proceeding apace since 1979, creating a great deal of friction between the Northern California and New York centers of the Order.

In early March 1983, prior to the annual spring meeting of the Supreme Council, Breeze, Gurney, Kramer, Cabal, Bil Padgett, and I flew Grady to New York for a conference on the problem. We had developed a paper calling for implementing the Constitution over the wishes of the Northern California contingent. We showed Grady two alternate title pages. One was called "Recommendation *to* the Caliph for the Implementation of the Constitution." The other was titled "Recommendation *from* the Caliph for the Implementation of the Constitution." Ever the diplomatic Libra, Grady chose the former.

Grady was concerned that Heidrick's printing press and ability to work full-time for the Order, and Graeb's legal training made them key components of what he called the Order's "industrial base." Although he recognized that we New Yorkers were talented people with good connections in the publishing world, Grady was a very practical person. He had been a commissioned Lieutenant in charge of logistics during World War II, so he was well aware of what he perceived to be the Order's physical needs. He wanted results. Like Crowley, he also loved the rough and tumble of competition.

I flew out to the meeting in Berkeley. I spent the first few days of the trip at Heidrick's house in San Anselmo. Our friendship deepened, as it always does when we spend time together. I saw Andrea, who had moved out from New York, and I participated in her IV° initiation. I met Lola D. Wolfe and formed an instant friendship with her, as well as Jim Eshelman, with whom I had a cautious, if initially somewhat positive, interaction.

The Constitutional proposal would be part of the agenda. Lon DuQuette and we in New York had discussed this all by phone—he and his wife, Connie, being the most enthusiastic members of the Order in California regarding the Constitution. Although we had not yet met in person, the tactical plan for the meeting, as I understood it, was that Lon and I would introduce the proposal together in a mutual effort that would demonstrate the unity of both coasts.

Both of our memories are foggy about what actually happened at that meeting. Nor does my diary shed much light on the parliamentary particulars. I apparently did not realize that I needed to make a formal motion according to *Robert's Rules of Order*. Lon, it seems, either seconded a different motion—the "Los Angeles Proposal"—or did not help me to introduce what I thought was "our" motion. Quite clearly, we should have gotten together before the meeting and worked out a plan of attack. But despite our long-distance cooperation over the years, we did not yet have an established line of communication. In the long run, it all worked out, as we will soon see.

This particular meeting was memorable in another way. Phyllis was taking her formal initiation into the IV°. Because of her hostility to Grady and me, neither of us was invited. This was a highly unusual violation of Order protocol and one that would redound negatively on those who participated in her initiation. Grady was angry, especially on my behalf. I had traveled 3,000 miles to attend the meeting and he felt the honor of the Order had been slighted. He and I walked around Oakland together for hours and talked. He shared his thoughts on succession with me for the first time. He indicated that Bill Heidrick was his *de facto* choice as successor.

I spent a pleasant evening with Sally and Isaac Bonewitz on this trip. She had moved out to Berkeley, where they met and were married. She read portions of the manuscript for a novel she had written of the New York occult scene. She is a talented writer and painted a moving portrait of all involved. Unfortunately, I do not believe it was ever published.

When I got back to New York, Breeze and Gurney were annoyed that I had not properly introduced the resolution. But the chaos of that meeting was only part of the larger picture. My diary, written on the plane ride home, mentions the meeting as very positive. The concept of a constitutionally based O.T.O. was placed before the upper membership in an elegant and persuasive manner. "I believe the visit to have been a success in this respect, demonstrating the membership's [of the Council] commitment." It was too much to expect the parliamentary maneuver we designed to remake the Order so quickly. Like "entitlement reform," it may have been a hard pill for some to swallow, but it was an idea whose time was coming.

In April, *The Holy Books of Thelema* went to press after eleven months of production. The extraordinary computer program Gurney wrote to create the snakeskin pattern, formed by the word "Thelema" incrementally offset, continues to resonate.

The Beltane ritual of that year presented an interesting challenge that is worth mentioning. Scheduled as an outdoor event in Inwood Park, it involved elaborate preparations by the presiding couple, including exquisite costuming and props. However, just before the ritual, they had an argument and each demanded that the other be excluded from the ceremony! We asked them both to calm down or leave. After they left, we had a brief powwow among ourselves. Then Joe Farkas got up and did a ceremonial banishing. Mike Kramer did a powerful performance of *Liber Samekh*. We enjoyed the feast afterward and the crisis was deftly averted.

SUMMER 1983

Oesopus Island

Breeze had located Oesopus Island, the small island in the Hudson River where Crowley had spent the summer camping in 1918. Robbie Brazil and I decided to go there with our two young sons, David and Satra. The trip was timed to start in mid-August—a couple of days after August 12, the "feast for the first night of the Prophet and his Bride" (AL II:37). We had each bought an inflatable boat and both boys were outfitted with life jackets. But it was a tough haul because the boats were not quite adequate and the current was really strong in that part of the Hudson. We had invited an Order couple to join us. As they waited on shore for us to return and pick them up, they panicked and called the authorities, fearing we were in danger. This was inaccurate and annoying, as we had made no signal of distress.

We all eventually reached the island and camped the first night at the north end. The next morning, we rowed down to the south where Crowley had landed and camped. (He had paddled his canoe up from Manhattan.) We pulled into the inlet and got the kids safely occupied with our friends, climbing the rocky cliffs where Crowley had painted "Do what thou wilt" in large red letters.

Standing in the middle of Crowley's campsite, I was overwhelmed by a powerful force, as if the psychic space were peopled with the vast intelligence of Beings whose power was virtually incomprehensible to the human mind. I remember being stunned that whatever forces Crowley had contacted were still there and exposing themselves to me some sixty-five years later. Then I heard the boys in a distant corner of my consciousness and realized they needed more supervision than they were getting. I vowed to return quickly to the island alone. I came back two weeks later for a week-long spiritual retreat. I returned periodically, with Satra or alone, for several years hence.

After coming back to the City, I joined Lodge members Kent, Garvey, Cathie, Enrico, and Joe Farkas as we laid a new, black-and-white tiled floor in the Magickal Childe Temple. Herman took his Minerval on September 18. Grady was due for a visit mid-month.

The Motta Deposition

On 9/11, I flew up to Portland, Maine to give my deposition in the Motta/Weiser lawsuit. Motta's lawyer did not properly arrange for a stenographer, so the deposition was canceled. It was most frustrating because of the anticipation. The lawyer leered as he said something like: "O well, we'll reschedule for New York." I realized he was shamelessly plundering his client and felt some sympathy for Motta.

On my way home, I was aware that I had an obligation to Donald to clean up any remaining karma with him. But I was painfully aware this meant the O.T.O. would have to take responsibility for the copyrights. I was frightened by the idea, especially thinking about 100 years in the future, when I and all the people I knew would be gone. I feared the Order could become corrupt and I would have no control. But I also knew we had no choice.

Crowley's *oeuvre* deserved proper, knowledgeable, and respectful editors. I consoled myself with the thought that the most important material—works like *The Book of the Law*—would ever remain in the public domain and be available to humanity no matter what happened with O.T.O. I wrote of Motta on the plane home: "He, the Priest of Set, is the propelling influence for this foundational structure of our own success—our worst enemy, our greatest ally."

FALL 1983

I finally gave my deposition in New York on September 29. I testified for six hours, including an hour lunch break. The transcript runs some 150 pages. Sitting in a lawyer's office being asked to identify a copy of my signed Oath and Task of the Probationer was an odd experience, to be sure. The record of that testimony has proven helpful in making this book more accurate.

In December, I met the poet and artist Ira Cohen, Angus' friend from Kathmandu. Angus told me that Ira used to walk around the hills dressed in black and that the Nepalese and Tibetans whispered when they called him "the Magician." Another of Angus' friends, filmmaker Sheldon Rochlin, introduced Ira. Sheldon and Breeze would later co-found Mystic Fire Video.

Angus had started writing a treatment for a film of *Diary of a Drug Fiend* before his death. Sheldon and Ira were following up on it. We were discussing rights. I met Judith Malina and Julian Beck of the Living Theatre as part of the discussions. Our creative circle would have been the perfect place to produce that film, as we all had the requisite knowledge and experience with both Crowley and drugs. However, the financing never came through.

On Satra's fourth birthday, we went to the Egyptian exhibit at the Metropolitan Museum of Art. They had recently opened parts of their collection to the public that I remembered from visiting the museum as a kid some twenty-five years before.

WINTER 1983–1984

Hecate's Fountain, *Studio 31, and* O.T.O.

I had been approached by Weiser's to edit, design, typeset, and produce the newest Kenneth Grant book, *Hecate's Fountain,* from manuscript. I eagerly leapt at the opportunity. In the course of discussing the project, Donald agreed to help Wileda and me finance a typesetting operation by lending us the money to buy a Kaypro II computer and peripherals that we would set up to communicate via modem with a typesetting shop in Virginia. They would output our coded files on photo-reproduction paper returned overnight in rolls. I would then cut and lay out the "repro" paper on mechanical boards that would be photographed and offset printed. It was the beginning of "desktop publishing" and very exciting. Bill Breeze had pointed the way at Gandhara. (Bill was an early and important contributor to the desktop publishing revolution. He founded Cromwell Graphics Systems, which sold a disk and data-conversion computer that allowed for cross-platform access to files created by numerous proprietary software programs. He later brought Gurney into the company.)

I happened to mention the Grant project to Bill and he went ballistic. He couldn't believe I was willing to work on a Kenneth Grant book. Didn't I realize that Grant was an "enemy" and making false claims? I was dumbfounded. How could I possibly care about Grant's claims in a commercial venture? Breeze called Bill Heidrick, who made a rare phone call to me. (Heidrick is notoriously the recipient of phone calls.) He was upset as well. I was stunned, to say the least. Then Grady called. He said he had heard I was doing the book and wanted to discuss my ethical reasoning. I explained that, as the proprietor of Studio 31, I was a servant of Tahuti, the Lord of all communications, both truth and lies. If I were to limit myself only to working on books that told the truth, I would be reduced to creating endless editions of *The Book of the Law.* That would be fine, even desirable, but hardly how a book designer could earn a living.

I think Grady generally understood the seriousness I attached to my profession, that I considered it part of doing my True Will. This incident still feels like a tempest in a teapot, but it would have ended my O.T.O. career had Grady insisted I not work on the book. In fact, I cooperated in the effort to get Grant to call himself the head of the "Typhonian O.T.O." so as not to infringe on our name. Further, as an O.T.O. member, I was delighted when Heidrick was able to pressure Weiser to drop the book. But as Studio 31, I absolutely refused to reject the book. (Grant, later still, changed the name of his group to the Ordo Typhonis or "Typhonian Order" so as not to infringe on our trademark rights in O.T.O.)

I will add that, in the initial editorial correspondence with Grant, I found him polite and professional. Years later, I licensed several images from him and Steffi for my book *Art and Symbols of the Occult* (revised as *The Mystery Traditions*) and again enjoyed a cordial working relationship with him. As the O.T.O. progressively secured all legal rights, I remember Grant making the transition to the Typhonian O.T.O. in a seamless and polite manner (a compromise suggested to him in a letter from Bill Heidrick). He always struck me as above the fray, unlike the coarse and arrogant John Symonds with whom he occasionally collaborated. When Kenneth Grant died in 2011, I was genuinely sorry and we dedicated a Gnostic Mass in his honor. Donald and I squared away the computer loan with other projects.

Maine Lawsuit

The trial began on March 1, 1984 before the United States District Court, District of Maine, Southern Division. It was my mother's birthday and I had planned to visit her, but the trial date was moved up and I had to reschedule seeing my parents.

Motta had accumulated another wealthy disciple or two and mounted a full-fledged legal challenge to Weiser. Bill Breeze and I went up to Maine for the trial and stayed at Donald's house. Donald arranged to fly Grady out to testify on his behalf. A big snowstorm had blanketed the East Coast. Grady had to spend the night in the Boston airport, an event that would lead to serious health consequences down the road for him. Motta made his case for infringement. Then Grady demonstrated his *bona fides* and testified that he did not wish to participate in a legal challenge against Weiser. Motta's lawsuit thereby failed on precisely the grounds I had earlier outlined to Donald.

Motta refused to make eye contact with or speak to me throughout the proceedings. Motta subpoenaed my diary for the period 1975–76, as mentioned in my book *Aleister Crowley and the Practice of the Magical Diary.* I explained there that, although I thought I could contest the issue on First Amendment grounds based on the diary having been a protected exercise of religion, Weiser's lawyer begged me not to. We arranged a compromise in which he, as an officer of the court, read the diaries in search of evidence that I was involved in conspiratorial behavior with either Weiser or Grady against Marcelo. Obviously, that was not the case. I was permitted to sit with the lawyer as he read. His eyes bulged at the post-marital sex and drug chaos of those months. If it hadn't been such a violation of my privacy, it might almost have been funny. No copies were made of the diary.

The Maine decision incorporated a devious twist in the road originating from Weiser. It is customary for lawyers to write proposed opinions for a judge to review. After weighing both sides, the judge chooses the one he will support, and uses that lawyer's opinion as the basis for the written opinion that he edits and shapes as his own. Weiser's lawyer, James Erwin, attempted an unanticipated end run around Grady. Judge Gene Carter's opinion stated that—on the basis of the evidence submitted in the case (primarily by Motta's team)—the O.T.O. was essentially an idea in Crowley's mind. Since neither Crowley nor Germer had ever legally incorporated the Order, the O.T.O. was an "unincorporated association." In Maine, an unincorporated association is unable to "take by bequest," i.e., through a will. (In California, where O.T.O. had its most real connection, it could.)

Further, Motta had so clouded the issue of membership that the Court was unable to determine by what criteria membership was defined. Since our participation in the case was limited to merely helping Donald by denying Motta the ability to present himself as the sole owner of copyright, the Court was unable to "identify a chain of successorship which has the exclusive right to use of the O.T.O. associational name." It remained for us to prove our right to that in the battle to come in California.

Grady, Bill, and I were mortified. For what it is worth, Donald Weiser and I remain the closest friends. I have "forgiven" him for what he and his attorney tried to do. It was obviously the self-interested act of a businessman who had invested and made a lot of money in the free-for-all of the status quo of the Crowley literary corpus (and had thus kept alive the torch of Crowley's teaching for a generation). The problem rested with the copyright chaos Crowley had left at his death in 1947, which neither Germer nor Grady (by this time) had managed to repair. After Grady won the copyrights in the U.S., as discussed in the next chapter, it would remain for his successor, Caliph Hymenaeus Beta, to secure the copyrights worldwide. The Order spent some two decades in courts throughout the world, at a cost of many hundreds of thousands of dollars. But we have accomplished the task with which we were charged, thanks to the leadership of the Caliph and the Order's determined support of his effort.

During the Maine trial, Motta was accompanied by Martin Starr. Martin was his chief disciple at this time, a very young scholar and magician with passionately held beliefs. We ran into each other in the hallway at one point. I offered my hand, which he refused to shake. I was the enemy.

SPRING 1984

Grady came back down with us to New York. He led the Spring Equinox ritual, in which he divined for the Word of the Equinox. Four people stood at the quarter points invoking the Archangels. Grady stood in the center of the Circle doing *Liber Samekh*. Joe Farkas circled around in one direction chanting "AL." Morgana walked in the opposite direction chanting "LA." Joe came to the center on Grady's signal and opened *The Book of the Law*. Grady dropped his Ankh-f-n-khonsu seal ring from Crowley on the book. The Word for that period was "the sign." Soon after, Grady returned to California and we learned he had been hospitalized with pneumonia and heart trouble stemming from his ordeal in the Boston airport.

It is so interesting to reflect on just how early this period was in the development of the modern Thelemic movement. While researching this book, I came across a report I had submitted as Second Emir to the Supreme Council on March 22, 1984. We found a Spring Equinox greeting from Crowley to Grady dated "Anno 40." Grady had saved the envelope, postmarked 1944. (He brought it to Maine as part of his documentary evidence and I saw it for the first time while he was visiting.) This letter and its postmark resolved our long-standing question about the technical beginning of the Thelemic year. Had Crowley intended our New Year to begin on April 8, the first day of the writing of *The Book of the Law*, his Spring Equinox greeting in 1944 would have been dated "Anno 39." The Supreme Council resolved to acknowledge the beginning of the Thelemic year as the Spring Equinox—marking Crowley's successful performance of the Supreme Ritual and the Equinox of the Gods.

I led the Hadit ritual for the second day of the writing on April 9. An incredible burst of energy came through that startled me and opened a verse of *The Book of the Law* that had long puzzled and troubled me. Chapter II, verse 63 begins: "Oh! thou art overcome: we are upon thee; our delight is all over thee…" My reading was preceded by the Banishing Ritual of the Pentagram, the Star Ruby, A Ka Dua chanting, the Thelemic Middle Pillar, and "wine and strange drugs" (AL II:22). I went into a state of ecstasy when I vibrated the word "Oh!" It was the opening of a previously mysterious arcanum.

At the end of May, the original manuscript of *The Book of the Law* was returned to the O.T.O. It had been in the Germer Library and survived the 1967 Brayton robbery. Sascha Germer may have given it to a neighbor, or Mr. Gualdoni may have somehow misplaced the carton in which it was stored while Grady was picking up the material in 1976. Thus it had also escaped Phyllis' clutches. The whole thing remains a mystery. In any case, it was discovered in the basement of a house in Oakland. When that house was sold, the new owner, Tom Whitmore, who was going through some cartons the previous owners had left behind, found the manuscript. He met Heidrick through a mutual friend in the O.T.O. and decided to return it to the Order. He first contacted Regardie, who confirmed that Grady was the legitimate representative of the O.T.O. It came back to us after nearly twenty years absence. The Tibetan Buddhists refer to such hidden scriptures that magically resurface when needed as *Termas*.

SUMMER 1984

Gurney and I founded The Holy and Apostolic Church of the Blessed Antichrist in response to Wileda's thought of sending Satra to a nearby church school. They asked her what church we belonged to. I was annoyed with the whole thing, but thought: "Well, what church *do* we belong to?" The Holy and Apostolic Church of the Blessed Antichrist was the answer. Gurney and I designed a business card for "Reverend Death," the identity of each member.

It was a church of the business card—the sole qualification for membership was laughing when you saw the card. Inclusion within the church was restricted to those who had one of the 500 cards we printed. We used some very odd typography, spending hours and hours in Gurney's type shop to perfect the card. Our goal was

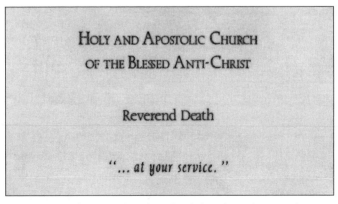

The Holy and Apostolic Church of the Blessed Anti-Christ.

to design a card that would appeal to a hip young undertaker. For example, we set "at your service" in both quotes and italic type, a real stylistic no-no. We then compounded the typographic travesty with the use of ellipses. The entire card had ninety-three characters. There were forty-five letters in the name of the church, and thirteen in the name Reverend Death—seventy-seven letters altogether. It was printed on a kind of translucent parchment that reminded us of Zaur in candlelight.

One day, I came upon Bokar sitting in meditation at the Manhattan terminal of the Staten Island Ferry. (He was working on a practice in which he would spend a period of several days in meditation—from the time he awoke till he went to sleep.) Soon after, as he was walking near Astor Place, he had a vision about finally joining the O.T.O. He came home and called me. Curiously, an initiation was scheduled for that evening. My rule was that, as soon as I turned on the faucets to draw my bath, I ceased answering the phone, determining that moment as the start of the ritual. As I turned on the faucets that day, the phone rang. Happily, I made an exception. I informed Bokar of the time and location and he joined the Order that night. Rules, after all, are made to be broken.

I met Harvey Bialy, a Thelemite and molecular biologist, through Bill Breeze. Harvey was a poet and friend of Kenneth Anger who had appeared in Anger's 1966 film *Invocation of My Demon Brother*. Harvey was also in an interracial marriage and our families became friends.

On my thirty-sixth birthday, Wileda, Satra, and I went to a beautiful park on Staten Island where I took some magic mushrooms. We were having a lovely time. A woman rode up on a horse and generously offered Satra the chance to ride it. What a great day.

Soon after, Grady went back into the hospital with heart trouble for a second time.

During an evening's study with Wileda, Finita, and Jorge, we discovered the dynamics of the Mobius strip as illustrated in *The Book of Thoth*. We felt the diagram revealed itself to us. The Hé and Tzaddi switch is an inescapable component of that rather cosmic geometry. The folds of the Mobius strip are also suggestive, of course, of the shape of the DNA molecule discovered later in the 20th century, as well as of the lemniscates above the Magician's head. (Bill Heidrick notes that this paragraph was definitely not written by either a physicist or a mathematician. But I hope the reader gets the general idea.)

In August, I returned to Oesopus Island with Satra, Robbie, and David. Satra did a full session of yoga and meditation with me for the first time and there was much improvement in his swimming skills. He spent several days chopping at a fallen log. He was very determined to cut through and kept at it with great persistence, especially for a four-and-a-half-year-old. It was taking a lot longer than either of us anticipated, but he continued on. Finally, nearly crying with frustration, he broke through at last. I gave him an "Oesopus Island Chopping Award," written with a felt-tip pen on a paper plate we found. It was a great honor. Later, Wileda met up with us and we drove to visit Dennis and Lucy in Martha's Vineyard.

FALL 1984

We celebrated the fifth anniversary of the founding of TAHUTI Lodge on the Fall Equinox.

I began working on a new book, to be called *The O.T.O. Handbook.* It was a collection of O.T.O. papers, mostly from *The Blue Equinox,* which had been out of print for some time. I began to write a history of the Order. I started the project in September, conceiving of it as a 160-page book. In time, I called upon the assistance of Bill Breeze. After he became Caliph in 1985, he asked to take over the editorial work. Steve Santiago, a member of the Lodge, offered to invest in the printing and *The Equinox* III:10 was born.

There was a shakeup in the organization of the New York E.G.C. at this time. Gurney had gotten sloppy in his Mass scheduling and I appointed Joe Farkas to take over. Joe did a good job for a time, until he started squabbling with Herman. This was not difficult, as Herman could be "challenging." Farkas wanted to move things out of the Magickal Childe and begin conducting closed, members-only Gnostic Masses in Jersey City, New Jersey. That was unacceptable, so I took over the leadership of the New York City E.G.C.

Soon after, I learned that Motta was planning to sue me personally for colluding with Grady in 1976. This was at the same time that we were preparing a major lawsuit against Motta in San Francisco, whose outcome would be historic. It is discussed in some detail in the next chapter.

Ehud Sperling of Inner Traditions offered me a job as Operations Manager, my first real job in seven years. This was at a time when Soho Studio was getting busier. I was trying to cut my hours back even further and had managed to reduce them to under twenty-five. Although I wanted to cut back to twenty, the needs of the Studio forced me to increase my hours to something more like thirty. Meanwhile, Studio 31 was doing quite well and the situation was becoming unbalanced. Ehud had been a big client for several years. I obviously loved the publishing business and had (and have) great admiration for Ehud's skills. I decided to take the job. It would provide a unique opportunity to learn about computers, as Ehud was working with a small software development company to build a custom publishing program. I would interface directly with the programmers, in addition to managing the business. It was fascinating. We agreed I could keep a freelance effort going as well, with limited book design and production.

*** *** ***

CHAPTER 16

THE SAN FRANCISCO LAWSUIT

WINTER 1984–1985

THE NEW YEAR BEGAN WITH a painful personal crisis that overshadowed much else during this period. There is little diary activity.

After some four years as Second Emir on the O.T.O.'s Board of Directors or Supreme Council, I resigned in favor of Bill Breeze. (The position of Emir no longer required the holding of the IX°.)

Gurney and I put the finishing touches on the type and design for our diagram of the structure of the Order according to the Triads of the Constitution, as outlined in *Liber CXCIV: An Intimation with Reference to the Constitution of the Order*. The New York Constitutional Study Group did the research and Gurney's masterful typography brought it to life. The diagram is included in the appendices.

SPRING 1985

Things had become much calmer in the New York Occult scene and our security situation had improved. Herman needed to convert the Temple space into a storeroom for inventory, as he had begun to do more publishing. TAHUTI Lodge moved the Temple back to Brooklyn. We reactivated Marlborough Road with a celebration of the Holy Days (April 8, 9, and 10—the "three days of the writing of the Book of the Law" [AL II:38]), along with a large group of I° initiations.

We located a copy of the 1917 O.T.O. Constitution, probably through the research efforts of Bill Breeze. It was an exciting discovery and one that was included in *The O.T.O. Handbook*. It had been written by Theodor Reuss in 1906, revised and re-issued in

1917, and was previously unknown to us. It added a new dimension to our understanding of the Order's design.

The San Francisco Courtroom

On May 11, I found myself once more at an airport about to fly to San Francisco for the second Motta trial. During the 1984 trial in Maine, Breeze had brilliantly strategized to serve Motta with a subpoena for the comprehensive lawsuit we had originally filed in March 1983 in the Superior Court of the State of California, County of Alameda. The case had since been moved to the United States District Court for the Northern District of California in San Francisco.

Our complaints were that Motta was violating the names and trademarks of Ordo Templi Orientis with his use of the name and logo of Society Ordo Templi Orientis (SOTO), and that he was misleading and confusing the public thereby. Moreover, we maintained he had committed libel against the named individuals with pernicious and false statements in his published works. Finally, that he was violating the name of Thelema Publications as used by Helen Parsons Smith for many years by his use of the name Thelema Publishing for his Nashville company. The suit had been started as a libel action by Breeze and Kenneth Anger, but grew in scope after Grady was added, along with Heidrick, Phyllis, Helen, Regardie, and myself. Breeze, Kenneth, and Regardie were ultimately dropped to reduce costs. The suit was heard by Judge Charles A. Legge.

I called Dan Gunther just before traveling. There had been some years of silence between us. His first child, Dylan, had just been born that week. I remained in San Francisco for seven days. I was in quite a state. Staying at Heidrick's house was chaotic and wearing on my nerves. Although I was a regular drinker, I did not dare take alcohol during the court's lunch break, because I was terrified of its effect on my stomach. Acid indigestion is not conducive to sitting all day in a courtroom, so my daily lunch consisted of cheese sandwiches and glasses of milk at a nearby bar.

I had met Dr. Michael Aquino through correspondence in 1975. He had reached out to Weiser for help in conducting a raffle to raise funds for a legal case involving one of the members of the Temple of Set who had lost her job because of her religion. The elegance of his presentation encouraged me to press his case with Donald. We did help him with a limited-edition copy of the recently published John Dee book, *A True and Faithful Relation*.

Michael was later to become a friend of Heidrick's and Grady's. They decided to play on Motta's extreme paranoia. Michael appeared in the courtroom as a spectator in his full-dress uniform as a Lieutenant Colonel in the U.S. Army Special Forces. It was a pleasure to meet him finally, and I appreciated his sense of humor in teasing Marcelo. He and his wife, Lilith, invited me to dinner at the Officers' Club at the Presidio military base and we later enjoyed a lovely evening in their San Francisco home. Their hospitality and kindness that evening were a lifeline to a very uncomfortable soul. I remain forever grateful to both of them.

Martin Starr had left Motta at this point and decided to assist us in the lawsuit. I knew that he was deeply troubled by all that was happening and reached out to him. He had become a different person after the Maine lawsuit the year before, arriving at a personal realization that Motta's abusive behavior was a symptom of his deepening psychological instability and alcoholism rather than a needed corrective to Martin's behavior. Gurney, Daniel, and I had all previously reached the same conclusion about his treatment of each of us. In fact, we were all correct in both instances.

Motta was a very difficult and harsh teacher, and we were a bunch of young and stupid, undisciplined kids who needed adult supervision. On the other hand, as time went on, Motta became more unbalanced. I had parted company with him in 1976. Dan did the same in 1978. Gurney left in 1980. Martin did so in 1985. Martin provided damning evidence that hurt Motta's case, including testimony of his disregard for proper research conventions, his abusive temperament, and his active alcoholism. Martin also provided a copy of a violent letter Motta had written to Jeremy Charles Ellis that will be discussed shortly.

Grady's testimony was excellent on direct examination. The next day, under cross from Motta's lawyer, he became disoriented and was rushed to the hospital for hydration and care. He returned two days later and the cross-examination resumed. He did an excellent job. However, the following day, Saturday, he had to be readmitted to the hospital.

I wish to put myself on record as one of the few human beings ever to have seen Bill Heidrick in a suit and tie! His testimony was thorough and methodical. The documentary record he submitted in evidence was meticulous and heroic in scope, providing a history of the O.T.O. in America since the 1930s.

I was deeply troubled by Motta's isolation. There was Grady, surrounded by a group of adoring friends—people who looked up to and after him and enjoyed his company. Marcelo, who had such a wealth of information to contribute, was all alone. It was thoroughly depressing. Someone had circulated a letter from the archives that Motta had written to Germer many years before. Motta was pouring his heart out as a young man to his Instructor. His letter was embarrassing and I was offended that it had "made the rounds." I went up to him at one point, a technically ill-advised act under the circumstances. I spoke to him on his side of the courtroom and assured him I had had nothing to do with circulating the letter. He looked at me for the first time since Brazil and told me he knew I would not have been involved. He added that I had misconstrued his statement about his having magically murdered Fred Mendel. He explained that what he meant to say was that the Thelemic hierarchy had punished the lack of integrity in the company's publishing program. I thanked him and left. I was criticized for having endangered our position that the letter may or may not have been leaked. I didn't care.

The one good thing I can say about Phyllis Seckler—other than to remember her charming smile when she wanted to be friendly—was that she held herself in check during her testimony. She had built up so much resentment against Grady that we all feared she might turn on him from the stand, and she did not. She was forced to make an eight-hour round trip to her home to retrieve her diaries, which discussed the Library theft. Her son, who was never an Order member, was forced to testify regarding the boxes of material, technically known as the "Whitmore Recovery," in which the manuscript to *Liber AL* was found. I sympathized with Phyllis for the invasion of her family privacy and the difficulty of her time in court. My otherwise negative assessment of her will always be weighed against her good behavior in the courtroom during that trial.

Helen Parsons Smith also handled herself well on the stand. To me, she will always be the Grand Dame of Thelema.

As I testified, I added an impassioned short statement into the court record about how sad it was that such a small group of people could be spending all our energies and money fighting each other from Maine to California—that I wished we could cooperate and use our resources to advance Thelema. I was still too inexperienced to understand that this was exactly what we were doing—painful as it was.

The general sense of the behavior of the O.T.O. members during the San Francisco trial was fraternal. We backed each other up and presented ourselves as a unified group of co-religionists, able to put aside our personal differences for a common purpose.

Marcelo Motta's Role in the Development of O.T.O.

People have often asked about Motta and my opinion of his fall. Was he a Black Brother? How could a high initiate, a man I still consider to have been a Master of the Temple, act the way he did? Can a Master of the Temple be an active alcoholic? These are all complex questions that turn on the very nature of Initiation and the Mysteries.

I believe we were all used in service to a greater power and a greater destiny. Motta, in particular, was the Worthy Opponent. His legal action against Weiser in 1984 had failed. But the company's legal betrayal of O.T.O. had resulted in a judge accepting that the Order was "an amorphous set of ideas and rituals," "nothing more than an idea in the mind of Aleister Crowley." The flawed Maine decision had demonstrated to the entire O.T.O. leadership that we were vulnerable unless we cleaned up our act.

The lawsuit in California gave us our own day in court to prove that we were the real O.T.O.—Crowley's O.T.O. Heidrick did yeoman's work in integrating the Constitutional approach. Before we knew it, all the founding documents had been placed in evidence to show our *bona fides*. Motta's development, the SOTO, was totally revisionist. We looked very much again like the Order Crowley had designed and I had joined. All the fuzziness and fluidity of identity between Constitutional and non-Constitutional thinking began to disappear as the discovery process in the California lawsuit proceeded. Revisionism was no longer "cool."

We needed to overturn the Maine court's embrace of the Weiser legal position by showing two things: first, that we were a dues-collecting, property-owning, incorporated legal entity with a contact address and phone number, an answering-machine message, membership rolls, and a series of publications; and second, that the basis of this effort was Crowley's *Blue Equinox*. I rejoiced inwardly to see the "Recommendations to the Caliph" instituted in an even stronger form than my mishandling of the resolution could possibly have accomplished. Judge Legge found that we were indeed the O.T.O. as described in *The Blue Equinox*.

I do not believe that, without the challenge represented by Motta's threat to our very existence, this would have happened so quickly and definitively. I felt then, and continue to feel, that James Graeb was disloyal and in pursuit of a flawed agenda. As my former friend Jerry Cornelius once made very clear, Graeb perceived himself as bringing down the Order in the way Crowley described his bringing down the Golden Dawn in *Liber LXI: The Knowledge Lecture*. I think Grady and Heidrick were both manipulated into excusing Graeb's machinations under the rubric of practicality. Motta blew all such revisionism out of the water. No one but an extremely powerful magician could have so efficiently effected the redesign of Ordo Templi Orientis as he did. We owe him a great debt for purging and cleansing the Order. By challenging us so vigorously, he forced the O.T.O. to correct itself.

Let me state clearly that I have always accepted Motta's claim to have been the Praemonstrator of A∴A∴. I will add that had he and Grady been able to work out the agreement I tried so hard to help them craft, the entire modern fallacy of A∴A∴ "lineages" would never have developed. That unfortunate conceptual model was born in 1976.

On the other hand—so that there is no misunderstanding whatsoever—Motta was a dangerous man. By way of example, he appointed Jeremy Charles Ellis as his London representative in 1978. In 1982, Ellis was arrested and convicted of trying to fire-bomb the Routledge & Kegan Paul warehouse in an effort to destroy copies of the Grant and Symonds edition of Crowley's *Confessions*. Motta's inflammatory letters are believed to have encouraged him. Ellis pleaded guilty and was sentenced to a year in prison. After his release in 1983, he died of a drug overdose at age twenty-six.

Ellis was also rumored to have been responsible for attacking John Symonds—a dastardly slanderer, but a frail old man. Ellis may have acted on his own. I have a copy of a letter that Martin Starr introduced into evidence that Motta sent to Ellis on June 12, 1981. Motta wrote: "If English judges are honest, Symonds will lose his suit. If he does not, English law is the puppet of sinister interests, and in that case I want Symonds executed as an example to other thieves." In the same letter, Motta chastised Ellis: "If you had sued Symonds ten months ago, when you were ordered to, or if you had broken his neck, which he thoroughly deserves, the other thieves would have stopped at once." Motta had become increasingly unbalanced and violent as he grew older. Against all the nasty things he wrote to me, this letter to Ellis—five years after Motta and I broke contact—is an order of magnitude more perverse. Whatever good Marcelo Motta may have done was balanced by his flaws. I believe he died a fallen adept in August of 1987.

Chapter 17

Grady's Death and Bill Becomes Caliph

Summer 1985

July 12, 1985 e.v.

Grady died on July 12, 1985 as the result of lasting complications from the harrowing flight and overnight confinement at the Boston airport in 1984. On the day of his death, we received word that we had won the Motta lawsuit. The Federal Court recognized us as the real O.T.O., with ownership of the copyrights, names, and trademarks of the Order. Grady, Helen, Phyllis, and I were each awarded monetary damages for the libels and slanders against us. (As I later wrote in my diary, I was rich in never-ending, if uncollected, accounts receivable.)

Satra and I returned to Oesopus Island on July 28 for a quick two-day stay. There is a mental hospital along the route and, as we passed by it, I was aware that I was at the end of my tether. I desperately needed that which I knew I would find on the island.

In August, Ehud began discussing his plan to move the company up to Vermont. He had vacationed there for some years and had a dream of living there one day. The idea opened a whole new vista of potential for my future.

Fall 1985

Election of Bill as Caliph

I had long supported Bill Heidrick as Grady's successor after Grady's nod to me on the subject. Lon DuQuette's name had been proposed, as had mine, but we both had some baggage. Phyllis proposed Jim Eshelman. Helen called me to see how I felt about Eshelman. I told her that I would gladly support Heidrick, but would resign if Eshelman were elected. Helen then proposed Bill Breeze. She stopped me in my tracks. We discussed that option for an hour. What a perfect breath of fresh air that would be. I enthusiastically and unreservedly joined her in supporting him. Heidrick was and is a good friend and would have been perfectly acceptable to me. Under his leadership, we would have had a small Order that sustained itself well, but little else. Breeze was expansive and innovative, a brilliant visionary and experimental. He has proven to be an excellent choice. Thank you, Lady Helen.

James Graeb conducted the meeting of IX°s (later called "Elector IX°s") who would elect Grady's successor according to the instructions in his will. Jim's masterful handling of that election was extraordinary. There were very passionate feelings among the eleven people present. Somehow, Jim patiently and methodically led the meeting to a choice that was definitely not his own, but that was unanimous after eight long hours. That unanimity has served us well since, and we owe Jim a great debt. (In fact, we repaid it many times over by not expelling him, despite some of the most outrageous behavior of any member of the O.T.O.—at least until 2003, when his actions simply became too extreme to tolerate.)

When Bill became Caliph, he asked me to become the Grand Secretary General of the Order. The immediate period after the election was difficult. It included a combination of political intrigue, hurt feelings, and grief over the loss of Grady. There was suspicion of Bill as a young and unknown member thrust into a position of leadership after the death of the person who was a father figure to us all—complete with a long white beard. It was a time of terrible uncertainty and danger for Bill. He needed a trusted ally by his side. His elevation also caused a terrible disruption in his personal life. Within six months of the election, his greenhouse apartment in Greenwich Village was torn down and Cromwell Graphics Systems closed. Bill quipped that he felt like a reformatted hard drive.

Bill insisted that I step down as TAHUTI Lodgemaster in order to fulfill my Grand Lodge duties as GSG. This was a painful transition. I had thoroughly identified myself with the Lodge. Now, I was moved into a position of national and international leadership. Despite my intense and heartfelt friendship with the many brothers and sisters whom I have loved since, I was never to regain the feeling of belonging to a small localized community of peers that I had enjoyed for my six years as Master of TAHUTI Lodge.

The loss of Grady was a significant point of personal spiritual growth for me in another way. Grady was an Elder. A young person on the mystic path seeks teachers—generally an older person of the same sex with whom he or she identifies and looks to unconsciously as a model—much like a parent. Grady would be the last of these figures for me, except for Harry Smith, who died in 1991. But Grady was my leader. I used to call him "Chief." It was funny, because he was one-quarter Cherokee. But the name also suggested Secret Chief. It was a term of affection, respect, and some humor. Since his passing, I've never been able to "look up" to anyone in the Order. This is not to imply any lack of respect to anyone in current leadership. Far from it. I have enormous respect for the Thelemic leadership worldwide. However, with Grady, Motta, and Harry gone, so is my youthful period of the Quest. (I find that many "look up" to me, which is a strange phenomenon for someone who feels a preternatural sense of youth.)

I was a short-lived GSG to be sure! I was certainly a loyal right-hand man, but the world's worst correspondent. It is just not my "thing." It was almost comical. I lasted about a year.

Gurney was made a IX° and became TAHUTI Lodgemaster. I insisted on giving him as much room as possible. He certainly did not need me around on a regular basis, as he knew what he was doing. He lived in an apartment one floor below the Marlborough Road Lodge. He oversaw a large renovation project of the Lodge space that went on for months. Kent Finne was in charge of the construction, and Lodge members like Nancy Riggins, Morgana, and Jim Garvey contributed the most work.

In November, my family traveled up to Rochester, Vermont to see where Ehud planned to move the business. It was a natural paradise and we all loved it. However, the next month, with great sorrow, I decided not to relocate. I felt I would be trapped in Vermont if there were ever a problem with my employment. In the City, the publishing company was located on the 6th floor. There was a graphics company on the 3rd floor. I used to joke to myself that if anything ever went bad with Inner Traditions, I could find another job before the elevator reached the lobby. Moving to Vermont represented too much loss of flexibility. Ehud was supportive. He offered future work and recommendations to other publishers for Studio 31. I stayed with the company through the spring, helping them prepare for the move, and remained close at hand until they finally did move at the end of July 1986.

Nancy Riggins

Nancy had moved up from Florida that fall and was living at Craig and Morgana's house in New Jersey after Morgana and Farkas split up. It was a scene of much madness and chaos. Morgana was a talented magician, but a severe alcoholic and very unbalanced. We were close friends and she worked at Studio 31 for a short, but productive period. I liked Nancy and was afraid that she would wilt under Morgana's insanity. Nancy was a breath of fresh air for the Lodge. I introduced her to Robbie Brazil in an effort to keep her around. It worked. Nancy, Wileda, Satra, and I were good friends as well. Nancy became an essential and hard-working member of the Lodge.

Nancy and I had a fun experience on Saint Patrick's Day, 1986. We somehow wound up going to an Irish bar together. I was familiar with the theories of Godfrey Higgins and other 19th-century esoteric historians who considered the Irish to be one of the lost tribes of Israel. I had never felt such a connection until that night in the tavern. The family-centered communal celebration seemed so very familiar. I wondered if these speculations were correct. A man with a mustache dyed green for the holiday was drunkenly hitting on Nancy. She asked if I would pretend to be her boyfriend to keep the wolves at bay. I did, and indeed it was a very natural way to relate to her.

SPRING 1986

On the Spring Equinox, I left Inner Traditions and rented a commercial space on 23rd Street from Superior Computer Services. Marc Barash and Michael Dillinger were the software developers with whom I had worked during my year and a half with Inner Traditions. We were close and tested allies. They were into a kind of positive thinking and demonstrated to me that I already had enough work in Studio 31 to take the leap to full independence. They suggested an affirmation that went something like this: "I am playing a game. I am playing to win. Failure is not an option in my game. I am playing 100 percent of the time with 100 percent of myself." How much it reminded me of the command from *The Book of the Law*: "thou hast no right but to do thy will. Do that, and no other shall say nay" (AL I:42–43). This was the first time I actually rented professional space to fulfill my business needs. Wileda moved her computer in and ran Royal Type. We would do many fine projects together. Morgana also joined us, helping me with graphic production.

On April 13, TAHUTI sponsored a lecture in Manhattan by Robert Anton Wilson. His topic was Giordano Bruno. He later came for a visit to the Lodge. We showed him the Temple with Michael's beautiful murals. He was most impressed. We then gathered downstairs in the living room of Gurney's apartment. As GSG, I felt responsible for providing him with a cordial environment, as we seemed to have a natural philosophical alliance and he was a powerful figure. We sat him down in an easy chair and all of us gathered around as he regaled us with stories. We all asked questions about his books, with which everyone was familiar. At a certain point, Nancy tired of the conversation and turned on the stereo! I was mortified and got up to speak with her. She said she thought Wilson was pompous and tedious, and we could go into the other room if we wanted to listen to him pontificate. Dumbfounded, I moved our group of acolytes into Gurney's bedroom, while a considerable portion of the membership hung out in the living room listening to music and talking. (She hasn't changed a bit after our now two decades of marriage.)

On June 1, 1986, Wileda and I performed a Gnostic Mass wedding for Craig and Morgana. Satra was the ring bearer, dressed in a suit and tie. This was the first Mass we had done for many months and a lot of practice had gone into it. Wileda and I had had a difficult year, but this turned out to be a particularly powerful Mass. Nancy had earlier asked if she and I could do the ritual together. I somewhat reluctantly told her that Wileda and I were an exclusive team. I have a clear visual memory of looking at Nancy during the communion and thinking she was far too young to be able to sustain that kind of energy with me. How little did I know! (During wedding Masses, it is customary to have only the Bride and Groom communicate, but Craig and Morgana asked to have a full communion of all present.)

SUMMER 1986

Equinox III:10 came in from the printers. Helen Parsons Smith had turned over the name Thelema Publications to the Order, so the first edition was published under that imprint. The book was a far more ambitious project than I had originally conceived. It included the core O.T.O. documents as planned, but Bill added a number of A∴A∴ papers as well, along with letters from *Magick without Tears,* the text of *The Book of the Law*, and various other writings by Crowley, Wilfred T. Smith, and Frater Achad. My essay on the History of the O.T.O. appeared, as did the diagram from the New York Constitutional Study Group. The court decision from California was included, as was a tribute to Grady. Bill wrote an extensive introduction and showcased a group of contemporary Thelemic poets and artists, along with a section on Kenneth Anger's films. It was truly an Equinox in the tradition of Crowley.

Later that summer, Wileda, Satra, and I moved up to Tarrytown, where Robbie lived. He helped us find a place—a single-family house that was broken-down and neglected. With a lot of hard work and Robbie's expert assistance with renovation, however, it was quite lovely by the time we moved in. We saw a lot of Nancy through this period. I got my monthly commuter pass and took the train to and from Grand Central Station each day. It was a nice change to be living outside of the City for the first time in fourteen years.

A legal publisher in Larchmont who was a client informed me that he was making a big expansion and could provide a great deal of steady work. This was most welcome news. He had purchased a very sophisticated software program, a precursor of desktop publishing. He set up a Linotron 202 typesetter and a VGC stat machine to process the photo-reproduction paper used for paste-up into camera-ready mechanicals for the printer. He was doing a professional magazine called *Tax Times* that explored IRS law and policy. I was named art director and spent some eighty hours a month on production with a crew of two others. I learned the software and the operation of the 202. I was familiar with the VGC stat machine, as we had one at Soho Studio and they were quite common in those days.

That was the summer I stepped down as Grand Secretary General. Bill was secure enough by this time not to need me in a position for which I was temperamentally unsuited. Tony Iannotti had served as GSG before me and done an excellent job. He returned to the position with my gratitude. He and I had met a year or so earlier when he visited me in Staten Island. We had taken a long walk together and come upon a mass of scrap metal that had somehow fallen into the street. The pieces were heavy, so we had to lift them in unison to move them to a safe location out of the path of traffic. I remember thinking that, while we hardly knew each other yet, we were Initiate Brothers engaged in a random act of good citizenship. I believed this would bode well for the Order.

For the first time in many years, I was without an official O.T.O. title. I was reminded of Grady referring to himself during the 1950s and 1960s as "just another IX° Indian running around the old O.T.O. reservation." Bill and I did discuss activating other Constitutional bodies within the Order, such as the Grand Tribunal. He suggested I might lead that.

I produced at least two issues of *The Magical Link* as GSG, including one in which I shared the method for making the Cakes of Light that alchemist and *Necronomicon* freelancer Khem Set Rising had suggested. It involves the "thick leavings of red wine"

(AL III:23). Khem's method was to heat port wine over a very low flame for up to seven hours, leaving a sweet gooey residue that makes an excellent bonding agent for the Cakes and tastes great. In previous years, LAShTAL members prided themselves on how bitter and awful they could make their Cakes taste. Andrea had gone to the hospital once after eating one, because she had an acidic stomach and the LAShTAL Cake had burned her. By contrast, Wileda and I couldn't keep Satra from raiding our Cakes when he was little because they tasted so good.

I turned thirty-eight that summer. In July, Satra and I went back for another very short retreat at Oesopus Island. I had a moment to contemplate another year of intense change. Leaving the security of Inner Traditions for the independence and risk of Studio 31 was both an exciting opportunity and a daunting challenge. I wrote in my diary that I had moved from being a dependent employee to a dancer. Yoga, meditation, and contact with Nature in our island sanctuary was just what I needed. On the trip home, Satra and I saw a license plate reading "DANCER 31"—a positive cledon indeed. "The hunter returneth not but with quarry after the measure of his intention."

FALL 1986

In September, I traveled up to Vermont to do a training session for Ehud's new crew on the operation of the publishing software. It was a productive trip that helped get them off to a good start. I enjoyed gaining a sense of intimacy with the new incarnation of the company.

On my return, I picked up another large client in my building, a scientific publisher who would help in many ways. I was also hired to draw a seven-sided figure as a corporate logo for a rather visionary woman. She thought it might best be done by computer. At the time, I was confident in my ability to make a more accurate, better-executed drawing using Rapidograph pens. We were both thrilled with it.

I am less enthusiastic to report that a theme runs through these years of diaries of my ongoing battle with alcohol. I fought

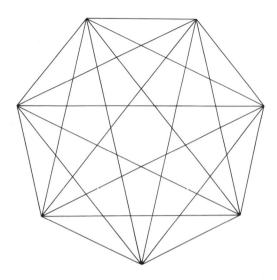

The Septagram is a symbol of the planet Venus.

it constantly—stopping, starting, having bad experiences, stopping again. It was an endless and continuous depressing struggle for me. One instance happened in October. I had stopped drinking for a time, but now Michael Kramer and I were in a bar having a couple of drinks together. Out of nowhere, an old drunk walked up to me and started screaming curses in really vile language. The bartender was about to go ballistic when I managed to calm them both down. I turned to Michael and told him it was my HGA trying to correct my behavior.

In November, a major structural problem developed in the house in Tarrytown that forced us to move out very quickly. Lee Downing, an O.T.O. sister living in Park Slope who rented out the top two floors of her building, welcomed us in. Bill had rented both floors before we took the third. He had helped Harry Smith during a terrible crisis, inviting him to live on the second floor and thus probably saving his life. Then Tony Iannotti and Nancy B. moved from California with the O.T.O. archives and took over the second floor. Bill left town for a spell and Harry moved in with Allen Ginsberg.

I purchased my own VGC stat camera at Studio 31.

WINTER 1986–1987

January began auspiciously enough, with a series of VI° initiations in Los Angeles. We were committed to filling in all the O.T.O. Degrees properly. This was an especially revealing moment for me, because I was aware there was an oath of obedience involved. I had been concerned about it earlier. Although I would have laid down my life for Grady, I was uneasy about some of his choices of personnel. There was never a question of my personal loyalty to him. But the idea of pledging myself to an uncertain hierarchy was of concern. That issue was resolved by Bill's leadership. We often disagree about things to this day, but I have never ceased trusting his judgment.

Lola, Graeb, Bill, and I were the candidates. Eshelman played the role of Initiator. Lon, Helen, and Phyllis all participated. The next day, Eshelman and Anna Kria did a Mass. I liked her. Kenneth Anger attended and mentioned that he wanted to join the Order and film the Mass. Several of us were invited to visit him in his Hollywood home close by.

Bill and I flew back East together. We discussed establishing TAHUTI Chapter of the V°, with either Gurney or myself as the Most Wise Sovereign. I was excited about seeing the Order grow along Constitutional lines.

SPRING 1987

Finita invited Satra to spend the summer in Argentina. Wileda and I were justifiably concerned, of course, but happy for him to have that opportunity. The plan was that he would fly by himself and Finita would meet him at the airport in Buenos Aires. He began playing Little League Baseball that spring.

On May 2, Tony, Gurney, and I gave a public lecture for TAHUTI Lodge. It was a successful outreach effort to explain Thelemic philosophy. It was well-advertised and well-attended.

The next day, I performed the Deacon role in the Gnostic Mass for Kent and Cathie Finne. The Saints portion of the Collects was unusually powerful. When I reached Grady's name, which we added after he died, my tears obscured the words of the script.

Gurney invited me to take a more active role in the Lodge leadership. I was grateful for that and happy that he felt secure enough in his own leadership to invite me to share it.

In May, Satra and I went back to Oesopus Island with another father and son, a colleague from the magazine production crew. This was another very short visit, but even such brief interludes in Nature were a lifeline for an urban adept.

SUMMER 1987

Wileda and I spent the summer arranging for financing to lease a Linotron 202 and purchase the software program to drive it. This was an ambitious undertaking, costing over $50,000. The output service in Virginia, even with overnight delivery, did not allow us to do fine tuning and quick corrections on deadline projects. Our current system worked fine for books or projects with decent lead time, but we had been seriously compromised several times on deadline-intensive work. Since my VGC stat camera could double as a type processor, we had a part of the problem solved already. With the help of a very good client, we were able to arrange everything over the next several months.

Bokar began to work at Studio 31 over the summer. What a lot of fun we had. He was highly skilled and very fast in his work.

Satra spent a month in Argentina with Finita, both in her apartment in Buenos Aires and on her family farm in the interior of the country.

FALL 1987 (PART ONE)

We held a magnificent series of V° initiations in New York, made possible by the generosity of our California brethren. Lon, Connie, Lola, Leroy Lauer, Doug and Karen James, and Jim Eshelman all came into town to help us set up our first proper initiation. Grady and Kris had essentially read me into the degree years before, and

Grady and I had initiated Michael Kramer in a rather improvisational ceremony. Gurney had taken his V° out West. Writing about the generosity of these folks two dozen years later still conjures a sense of gratitude and appreciation for the efforts they made on our behalf.

Lon was in charge, as the most experienced V° initiator, and Gurney and I were the two chief officers after Lon and Leroy helped get us up to speed. Connie and Lola rotated the female role, as there was no one in New York yet of sufficient degree. Our candidates included Wileda, Kent, Garvey, Bil Padgett (who traveled in from Atlanta), Finita, and Jorge. Lon and Connie stayed with Kent and Cathie, and then with Wileda and me. It was a pleasure to have the opportunity to get to know them better. I was given the KRE degree as Past Master of TAHUTI Lodge.

On the day of the Equinox itself, Gurney and I passed the leadership of TAHUTI Lodge to Kent. It was the Lodge's eighth-year anniversary.

* * *

CHAPTER 18

GURNEY'S DEATH

FALL 1987 (PART TWO)

THROUGH A COMPLEX SET OF CIRCUMSTANCES, Gurney and I became aware of a heroin buy point near East 25th Street and 1st Avenue, close by my office on 23rd Street between 2nd and 3rd Avenues. We started out using the drug recreationally, as we had both long enjoyed it. What began as a bit of a lark, however, gradually became a problem for both of us—Gurney would die from it and I would join Alcoholics Anonymous. Our "little adventure" lasted some fifteen months. I never used a needle during this period. Gurney only did a couple of months before he died of an overdose. We had constant discussions of the various oaths we were breaking in O.T.O., yet we believed in some twisted way that we were working within the parameters of Crowley's teaching in *Diary of a Drug Fiend*. It was a constant searing topic between us.

In October, a horrific alcohol-related incident occurred. One of my girlfriends lived in a high rise. We drank too much and left a window open. Her cat slipped on a poster board while walking past the window and fell eleven floors to the concrete below. Somehow, her broken little body survived the night. I received a hysterical call at my office the next morning and saw the dying cat just before the vet came to put her out of her misery.

In the same week, I spent the evening in a bar with Robbie. He was an extremely competitive guy who apparently decided he was going to "keep up" with my drinking—an idiotic stance to take with someone who had developed a tolerance to alcohol. After we left the bar, he started throwing up into garbage cans and off the curb. I was disgusted with myself. Robbie had been attracted to O.T.O. by a lecture I had given at the Magickal Childe. As the representative of a spiritual Order, I was watching my own flaws and bad example manifesting in front of my eyes through the suffering of my friend.

Meanwhile, the "wise" were still trying to understand the Hé and Tzaddi switch. In the text of *The Book of Thoth* (page 78), Crowley describes the white light descending upon the Emperor as coming from Chokmah and being exerted on Tiphareth. This completely contradicts the position of the card on the Tree of Life on page 268 and the table given on page 278. Further, the astrological attributes given for Hé and Tzaddi on page 268 are different from those on page 278. Of the three different instructions given, which was correct? If the Emperor no longer falls on Path 15 between Chokmah and Tiphareth, does that mean the magical image of the New Aeon Emperor Card is incorrect? Adding more confusion is the Class A verse in *Liber VII: Liber Liberi vel Lapidis Lazuli* attributing the image of the classical Star card to the English translation of the Hebrew letter Tzaddi, the fish-hook. "Only one fish-hook can draw me out; it is a woman kneeling by the bank of the stream" (*Liber VII*, V:5).

In December, I noted that I had been using heroin steadily for a month. What is interesting is that I had stopped drinking after the horror of the dead cat. I thus gracefully made the transition from the frying pan into the fire.

I suffered from constant back pain at this time. My lower back issues had been going on since I had experienced a mysterious debilitating spasm in December 1984. This was a further inducement to use narcotics, as they helped mitigate the pain. I was also seeing chiropractors. Tony Iannotti gave me a large bovine vertebra as a magical charm for health.

On December 13, Gurney, Tony, and I did a second symposium for the Lodge that brought in eight new Minerval candidates.

In the wonderful world of business, I was involved in setting up and learning the typesetting machine and software we had finally acquired. There was an initial interface problem in getting the software to operate the hardware. We went through weeks of the standard maze of the software people blaming the hardware people and vice versa. I'll never forget one of the techs remarking on my calmness and politeness in the face of such frustration. I remember thinking to myself something like: "Well if you were as stoned as I am, perhaps you'd be calm and polite too." We finally found a third supplier, a brilliant interface specialist named Irwin Marcus, who solved the problem perfectly.

WINTER 1987–1988

Gurney did the Invocation to Pan for the Winter Solstice using Crowley's "Hymn to Pan." Harry Smith was invited and we allowed him to tape-record the ritual—the first and only time electronic recording was allowed in a ritual. We have since transferred the tape to digital format and posted it on the website for this book. While Gurney's performance was masterful, I could detect that it was ever-so-slightly flatter than the other times he had done it, heroin having taken away some of his edge.

On December 24, I noted in my diary that I had acquired a habit. I had symptoms of illness when I stopped my drug use, especially on the second day. Such symptoms could instantly be alleviated by using again. Surprise! Here's hoping the third time was a charm.

Gurney's wife, Micheline, declared her intention to leave him. A Canadian, she was visiting her family in Montreal for Christmas and told him over the phone. He was devastated.

On New Year's Eve, I came up with a brilliant plan that is perfectly indicative of how little I understood my problem. I had stopped using for a week and thought I had a clear mind. I decided to institute a merit system for drug use tied to my gross billing. I would allow myself one bag of dope for each $1000 of work I billed. I have to laugh as I record this.

1988 was an increasingly difficult year for the Lodge, especially for Kent. We had gotten used to socializing at Gurney's place after events in the Temple upstairs. It became increasingly obvious to everyone that something was wrong with him. I was further out of the daily workings of things, so my problems were less evident to Lodge members, with certain exceptions among my closest friends.

On January 15, I was boarding a plane for Los Angeles to help with another round of VI° initiations, including Gurney's. I left the day after Wileda, Bokar, and I had successfully run our first full book through the new typesetting system, a beautifully illustrated coffee-table catalog of the work of artist Georges Braque that was published by Konecky & Konecky.

I was to be staying with Lon and Connie. Lon picked me up at the airport and announced that Dr. Alan Miller (aka Christopher S. Hyatt) of Falcon Press was coming to dinner. I was less than enthusiastic about meeting someone new after a long plane flight, but Saint Lon took me to a bar, to my great relief. (Apparently my month-plus of non-drinking had ended.) When we got to his house, I was feeling much better. Alan showed up right on time. That was the first good thing I could say about him—promptness equated to politeness, which was a rare quality among our set back then. The three of us and Connie had a perfectly wonderful evening.

Discussing my relationship with Alan Miller would take a book of its own. Suffice it to say that he was one of the pivotal people in my life. As a highly trained psychologist, he was enormously helpful in bringing me to detect my emotional patterns. As a businessman, he helped me to become more successful in my handling of money; he also provided a great deal of work. I credit him with having launched me as a writer after I left drugs and alcohol behind. It saddens me to think that my stopping drinking negatively impacted our friendship. He was, himself, a problem drinker and resented me for embracing sobriety. People on the front lines of substance abuse sometimes equate those who become free as traitors. Certainly that was his attitude toward me. Interestingly, Alan was a Cancer, Leo Rising, Scorpio Moon, exactly like Motta.

The VI° initiations were a success and we had a lovely visit with our California Brethren. Gurney and I had both been clean for a couple of weeks. He was further blessed by a mental-health interlude with a lovely California damsel from the Order.

On the plane ride home, I was acutely aware of the expanding universe of my obligations: the Order, my family, my spiritual work, and now the banks. Our monthly expenses were high, with the loans and leases added to everything else. I was conscious of, and grateful for, the healing Gurney and I had been given by our visit to California. Bill appointed me as Publications Secretary of the Order, my first official title in some time. It was essential that I maintain physical, mental, and spiritual health at all costs.

We learned that the U.S. Supreme Court had declined to hear Motta's appeal of the San Francisco Federal Court decision. We had thus legally won the Crowley copyrights in the United States, as certified by the highest court in the land.

SPRING 1988

On the Equinox, I took an oath to stop using drugs until after the Holy Days in April. I had apparently been keeping a calendar of my heroin use during the previous six to eight weeks (although I cannot locate that record today).

I experienced another particularly powerful energy as Deacon while invoking the Saints. I described their presence as "palpable," in my diary, "more so than ever before." This was confirmed by Order brother Patrick King, who said he was stunned by the energy in the room. Satra and Amélie Le Gallic asked to be able to play the Children roles for an upcoming Mass. (Amélie had named her kitten "Satra.")

In May, we began our first series of Crowley's Rites of Eleusis. We organized the Rites through the Chapter. Each member of the Chapter volunteered to be responsible for one of the seven deities. We would each assemble our own cast from the Man of Earth members and handle our own props. If we had a problem, we would discuss it in Chapter and help each other to find solutions. It was a terrific system and I remember three successful series. I began the first series as Saturn. Bill played viola and it was the most exquisite use of ritual music I have ever experienced in O.T.O. The next rite occurred a week later, with Kent as Jupiter, then Tony as Mars, Bill as Sol, Wileda as Venus, Gurney as Mercury, and Cathie as Luna— a rather ambitious schedule for our first series.

I decided on a solitary retreat to Oesopus Island to deal with my drug issue. I expressed a real hatred of heroin for the first time in my diary and decided to seek a doctor's help in getting a prescription for tranquilizers. I went to the island for three days at the end of May. It was an uncomfortable experience, more about self-mortification than the spiritual peace and unity with Nature I had previously sought. I brought no food, no drugs, no coffee, no cigarettes, no booze, no books. I was aware that this was something of a desecration of my Holy Place, but I trusted it would be okay. I noted that I had been on a steady heroin diet since October, with breaks for the VI° trip and between the Spring Equinox and the Holy Days. I wrote that heroin smoothed the rough edges of life, but "those rough edges are the hand and foot holds of the lusty climbing goat, His means of reaching the pinnacles of joy and freedom." At the end of those three days, for the first time ever, I was relieved to leave the island.

We decided the rumors of Motta dying in August 1987 in Rio were probably true. Although there was yet no "proof," Martin forwarded copies of pronouncements by Motta's few remaining followers accusing each other of thievery. We concluded he must be dead.

Satra was chosen as one of three children from his school to do an interview for the *NY Times*. Asked about what he liked best about his parents, he replied that what he liked best about his Mom was her taking care of him when he was sick; what he liked best about his Dad was the camping trips they took together.

Summer 1988

I did the Solstice Gnostic Mass with Dora as Priestess, Gurney as Deacon, and Satra and Amélie as Children. Wileda was upset with me for having violated a promise about drugs. After the Mass, Gurney and I managed to score. On the way home, I took a spill and broke my arm. My fortieth birthday two days later was a trip. Looking at myself in the mirror with the broken arm in a cast, I understood that I was seeing a perfect image of my inner state manifesting itself in three dimensions. My work involved using both hands to manipulate a T-square on a light table, so it was a challenge. One must see a certain humor in the chaos continuing to mount.

The Dawning of the End

A week after my birthday, I drove up to visit Robbie by an alternate route so I could drop Wileda at a friend's. When I passed the exit to Montvale, New Jersey, I thought of Mary and was seized with an overwhelming need to contact her. (We had not seen each other since 1971.) The next day, I decided I would try to track her down through her mother. On my way to score that morning, I passed by Weiser's Bookstore, which had moved to 24th Street and Lexington Avenue. I ran into two employees on the street who mentioned that I had received a phone message. I went into the store to learn it was from Mary. She had left a number. I saw her soon after with Wileda and Bill. She could tell I was high. I learned that she had two kids, that she was divorced from their father, and that she had moved from Colorado to New York.

Two more telling indicators of the changes looming on my personal horizons were also to occur this summer. The first was attending a Leonard Cohen concert on July 6 at Carnegie Hall with Wileda and Tony and Nancy B. I felt a compulsion to consume a great deal of alcohol during the concert and was quite aware that it was a completely abnormal hunger. I reject the idea of celebrity worship, but certain people have connections with larger numbers of people with whom they do not have a personal contact. Leonard Cohen has been an influential character in my life, despite my never having met him. This concert was an awakening to the increasing severity of my drug and alcohol problem.

The second event was a breakfast meeting with Dr. Joe Gross—an intimate friend of Harry Smith, as well as his physician and a devoted student and loyal disciple. I asked him to prescribe tranquilizers for me in an effort to get some order in my life. I asked why he thought I was so anxious and what the effect of alcohol use was on my health. He carefully explained that, at first, alcohol coats the nerves and thereby induces a feeling of well-being and relaxation. But as a person continues to drink over a period of time, alcohol damages the natural nerve coating and therefore the person needs to drink to restore a sense of normalcy. The true definition of a vicious cycle. I got the message on a very deep level.

I was reminded of a book by Jim Carroll called *The Basketball Diaries,* in which the author describes being aware of needing to take large and expensive amounts of heroin just to feel normal. (I held to one to two bags a day, $10 to $20, rarely straying to a third.)

My month of July was quite good after the Leonard Cohen concert. Gurney and I made a pact together. I stopped both alcohol and drugs and worked on healing visualizations for my arm, along with a rigorous program of spiritual exercises. I noted in my record that Bill was getting mighty sick of Gurney's and my behavior. I learned that Ken Patton, the typesetter of *The Commentaries of AL,* had died.

In August, things again went in the wrong direction regarding drugs. Then, in the middle of the month, I learned that my beloved Uncle Sonny had lung cancer. Gurney and I made another faltering pact at the end of the month. I had a most disturbing experience one morning after deciding not to use dope that day. I literally watched my feet begin walking toward the score scene despite my intention—as if I were an automaton at the mercy of an alien force. I was helpless to intervene.

In early September, Bill became increasing frustrated by my addiction and demanded that I seek professional help from certified drug counselor and O.T.O. member Steven Fox. He threatened to strip me of my duties in the Order if I was unwilling to accept treatment. Although I was loathe to see a counselor (even though Steven and I were and are friends), I was exhilarated by what success in this battle would mean for me as an initiate. I bargained with Bill for two more weeks. If I couldn't defeat this alone by the Equinox, I would start treatment with Steven. On September 7, I called heroin a "most worthy adversary that has been kicking my ass for close to a year."

FALL 1988

I did not achieve successful mastery in those two weeks, so was now committed to counseling, "which I think I can stomach less than stopping." Steven and I began a weekly dinner together, my treat. (Far be it from me to have visited him as a "patient.") It was the beginning of my sobriety. I was proud, at least, that this could all occur within the bonds of the Order, that we had developed the capacity for healing members in trouble.

I was consecrated a Bishop of E.G.C.

In October, I went to Florida to see my uncle. We discussed death. I admired his courage, both in pursuing treatment and in accepting the fact that it might not work. I went on the boat with my father and did some swimming.

In November, Steven and I had one of those funny "therapeutic" interactions in which my arrogance was fully on display. Discussing alcohol, I said something like: "I can stop anytime." He said: "Well prove it. Stop for three months." I disdainfully replied I would stop for six months, just to prove that I didn't have the problem he thought I did. (I am not making this up.) However, since I refused to think of myself as someone with an intrusive malady, and since I remembered a wedding nearly twenty years earlier at which I was unable to toast the bride and groom because of my no-drinking pact with the guru, I insisted I could drink at rituals and appropriate social occasions. Steven agreed, but suggested I limit myself to two drinks in such case. I agreed to that.

After one particularly dramatic evening a week or so later at my cousin Pete's, celebrating our reunion after ten years with two glasses of wine, I realized two drinks were not enough. Two days later, I found myself seeking dope. Toward the end of the month, I was drinking again—astounded that I had lost my ability to stop at will.

In the beginning of December, Wileda and I celebrated our tenth wedding anniversary in Montauk on Long Island. It was a beautiful respite and acknowledgment. I swam in the ocean one night in an ecstatic bio-energetic healing, probably the only person in the water at that time north of at least Virginia.

WINTER 1988–1989

Despite some real progress on the drug front, I had a really bad scene with Wileda over scoring heroin with Satra on the day of the annual Weiser Christmas party. I had been laid up with severe back pain. Like much else in the world of substance abuse, heroin seemed like a good idea at the time. It wasn't, and I would pay. Wileda had had enough. (In my defense, I will add that I considered asking Satra to conceal where we had been, as I knew Wileda would ask when we three met up at the party. But I did not want to encourage our son to be dishonest with his mother.)

I persuaded Wileda to see Steven with me rather than ending our marriage. I wrote in my diary that I cursed the day I smoked my first joint. I later told a story in an article in the summer 1989 issue of *The Magical Link* (*Diary of an Ex-Drug Fiend*) about what happened when Steven craftily seized this opportunity to force me to attend Alcoholics Anonymous meetings on a weekly basis as an "incentive" for Wileda not to leave. She agreed. I was appalled, but had little choice. He handed me the AA *Big Book*. I recoiled as if it were a reptile. Raging inside at the thought that he dared call *me* an alcoholic, I accepted it graciously in front of her, vowing to myself never to read it, knowing exactly on which shelf of my library I would place it—with the other unloved books, received as gifts, that I was obliged not to discard.

As it turned out, I had nothing to read on the return subway ride to Brooklyn and I opened the *Big Book*. I would not put it down for three days. It finally explained all the agony and conflicts around my problem. I was an alcoholic. It was just that simple. And everyone knows an alcoholic can't drink (or take heroin). True, I had not been lying in a doorway begging for change or prowling the streets for robbery victims. But with the help of that book, I understood alcoholism for the first time. It was the beginning of a very positive change in my life that brought long-lasting benefits.

I went to my first AA meeting right after Christmas weekend. While I was none too pleased at first, there was something about the gaiety, clean auras, and bright eyes of the people at the meeting that I admired and enjoyed. It brought a sense of hope.

At the same time, Gurney began lying to me. He told me that he had stopped drinking and had kicked dope—the desire having simply left him. I was amazed and felt like a complete idiot. He could do it by setting his will to the problem, while I "needed" AA. It was totally humiliating.

On Satra's ninth birthday, I felt as if I was able to give him the best present I could, the promise of a new life. I was aware that AA shared the same initials as the Order I had long held so holy.

On January 4, we were burglarized and lost thousands of dollars of possessions. I found myself in a state of overall acceptance about the loss, aware of the bad karma I had been accumulating. I was less sanguine about the loss of my Colt 1911. That has plagued me since. The thought that a criminal has my treasured, consecrated weapon still turns my stomach.

On January 8, I had a long battle with heroin desire. It came again with renewed intensity on January 9. I had a session with Steven and couldn't wait to get out and score. I bought two bags, snorted one, and flushed the other down the toilet. That was the first time in my life that I had ever done that. I also understood that, in taking the heroin after nineteen days of sobriety, I was consciously cooperating with the Dark Side.

On January 10, I asked Mary if I could spend the night at her place because of an argument with Wileda over the drugs. Mary and I had a couple of drinks together and renewed our decades-old love affair. On January 11, I did what I hope was my last run. January 12 began my first day of sobriety . . . again.

I learned that my Uncle Sonny was really sick and made plans to go see him. Mary helped me pack, as I was beside myself. On January 14, he died. I drove down to the funeral with my cousin Maury (Pete's brother) and his wife, Marcie. I found my father very bitter toward life and God.

On my return, I was grateful that Wileda had held down the fort in my absence. She had cared for Sonny too. She and Satra left to spend some time with family in New Jersey. Mary came to visit the office as I was finishing Israel Regardie's *Healing Energy, Prayer, and Relaxation* for New Falcon Publishing. Later in the week, we discussed doing a series of magical workings together. A new phase of my spiritual life was about to begin. I do not believe I would have been able to maintain my newfound sobriety without the help and healing Mary brought.

One final story about my drug use. After returning home from Florida and discussing my three-day "slip" with Steven, I told him that I had used dope as soon as I left our last session. He looked really surprised and puzzled. He said: "Why didn't you say something? You're coming here to get help with drugs. I would have helped you." I was stunned. I could not believe he would have expected me to talk to him about my drug craving! I had spent some twenty-two years lying, hiding, and "managing" my drug use in a very private manner. I realized I had entered a new stage of my life. I promised him then that, if I ever felt that way again, I would talk to him before using. My Angel's gift these last twenty-three years is not having needed to make that call.

In mid-February, I completed my essay on the Middle Pillar as a group working, which was added to Regardie's *Healing Energy, Prayer, and Relaxation.*

Gurney's Last Days

Around February 24, Gurney and I spent a magical evening together, many hours in conversation. We started at dinner, then went to my apartment. Afterward, I drove him to his place and we continued talking. It was the most intimate and relaxed evening I had spent with a friend since college. But he said something that scared me. He said he wished he could go back to the old days in Nashville with Dan, when he had the guidance and companionship to pursue his spiritual work. I was troubled, because I felt that we were too old for that kind of nostalgia, that he should have been fully committed to his current spiritual work.

On February 25, Kent and I had a long talk about Gurney's insanity with money. He was always short and always borrowing from friends, yet he earned more than most of us. Knowing he had quit heroin (because he told me), I became terrified that he was actually using cocaine, God's answer to making too much money. I was genuinely afraid he would die of a heart attack.

On February 26, I spoke to him, openly sharing my concerns, letting him know how important he was to me and all of us. He confessed that he had been lying to me for two months—that he not only had not stopped using drugs, he had started shooting them. He showed me a whole box of needles and paraphernalia.

I talked to Bill, Steven, and Kent. We set up a meeting at my office on February 27. We caravanned over to Gurney's to confront him. It seemed to have worked. Bill read him the same riot act he had read me—"fitness to serve on committees" and all that. Gurney agreed to begin therapy with Steven and submit to drug testing.

Steven wanted us to institutionalize him forcibly. He felt that Gurney's addiction prevented him from connecting with his True Will. I vigorously rejected this option as being counter to his autonomy as an initiate. This was exactly the stance I had taken with John and Merrie in 1971. Bill agreed with my position. Gurney went to live with Kent and Cathie, who nourished and nursed him back to health. But it was becoming pretty grim. He continued selling his superb collection of Crowley books and frantically trying to "borrow" money from everyone he knew. Bill and I realized with horror that, since AIDS had surfaced around 1985, we would be hard-pressed to introduce any visiting Order sisters to him because he had been sharing needles with street people. Then he stopped going to Steven for therapy and began to disappear for long stretches of time.

On March 11, Kent was forced to move the Lodge equipment out of the Lodge space above Gurney's apartment. He arranged it quietly, without Gurney's knowledge. They spoke the next day and Gurney, of course, understood that Kent had had no choice and had acted correctly.

On March 18, I was lying in bed with a bad back for the third day. Kent had asked me to perform the Spring Equinox ritual after he moved the Temple. I felt honor-bound to help the Lodge and especially wanted Mary to see a full-blown magical ceremony. I decided to perform the invocation of Horus from the Supreme Ritual for the first time. I swore I would do it in a wheel chair if I couldn't get out of bed. Horus was ever present. On March 14, I replaced my 1911 pistol. I also found a beautiful heavy brass Ankh at the Magickal Childe. But I was a having an agonizing time preparing for the rite on such short notice and in such pain. On the day of March 19, I spent a long time in prayer prior to leaving for the Temple. The ritual was superb.

Later, Wileda read her version of the riot act to Mary and me. She presented an either/or ultimatum about us. I had a very different view, because I loved them both and especially Satra. On March 20, I moved in with Bill.

On March 24, after we had searched for Gurney for a week, calling hospitals and morgues and prowling the streets, Bill finally learned that he had been found dead from an overdose. He died on the Ides of March. He was found with $250 in his pocket, so he had definitely *not* committed suicide. There had been a run of unusually strong dope on the streets of New York. I sobbed uncontrollably for the first time in my life.

A memorial Mass was planned for April 2. On March 28, I got a call for Richard Gernon at Studio 31. Because he had given my office as a credit contact phone number, I cautiously accepted the call. A florist had a bouquet of flowers from Donald Weiser to Richard Gernon for the funeral of James Wasserman and wanted to schedule delivery. I gently corrected him. That day I spoke at an AA meeting for the first time.

On March 29, Kent and I initiated Mary into the Minerval Degree. She and I had begun intensive work on the Mass against the possibility of doing Gurney's memorial service. But Bill wisely decided that, since Wileda and I had split up, the best course of action for the emotional well-being of all concerned was to ask Kent and Cathie to do it instead. Bill initially intended to perform the Deacon role himself, but I somehow wound up doing it.

* * * *

A HUGE CHANGE CAME OVER TAHUTI Lodge and, in fact, the entire Order after Gurney's death. The relaxed attitude toward drugs that had been a hallmark of O.T.O. since Crowley's day changed overnight. Steven Fox wrote an article making a therapeutic outreach to people with a drug problem that was published in the spring 1989 issue of *The Magical Link*. I wrote *Diary of an Ex-Drug Fiend*, an account of Thelemic sobriety, that appeared in the following issue. The long lines of people snorting cocaine disappeared from O.T.O. parties and the excesses of our earlier years were curtailed.

I have long thought that Gurney's death was a sacrifice for the benefit of the Order. By forcing us to clean up our act, he paved the way for an increased efficiency and coherence in the Order. It has certainly worked that way in my case. As I wrote in *Diary of an Ex-Drug Fiend*, my Brother walks within me now. The Order is growing under Bill's leadership and we are ever alert to psychological problems within our membership. By keeping a strict zero-tolerance policy on drugs at Order events, we have also avoided the tangle of legal problems that would inevitably have damaged our work.

Gurney offered us the example of one of the most powerful, learned, and talented magicians ever to have been a member of O.T.O. falling to the deadly consequences of addiction. How I managed to survive is a mystery for which I am both grateful and responsible every day of my life. I have been granted a reprieve from the death sentence that claimed the life of my best friend and must ever be aware that I have an obligation to repay that gift.

EPILOGUE

THE BEAT GOES ON

So THERE IT IS. Many joys, many sorrows, much inspiration. I think the O.T.O. represents a positive force in this world and am honored to have participated in its modern development. There was a great deal of color and passion in the more free-wheeling days of my memory. But there was more danger as well, and some of the good people we lost might still be around in the Order as it is constituted today. I think, for me, the most important feeling I have is that Grady would be proud of our accomplishments.

I hope the same might be said of Marcelo. O.T.O. and A∴A∴ have finally properly allied again as the spiritual partnership Dan, Gurney, and I so hoped for in July 1976. When we three joined O.T.O., there were at most a dozen members—if you were generous enough to count those who had stopped paying dues and were no longer in contact. As of 2011, there are over 4,000 active members in some fifty countries. A∴A∴ has initiates functioning throughout the world. The Grades of the Order are being populated by qualified and tested magicians.

Publications like *The Holy Books of Thelema, Liber ABA,* and *The Equinoxes* have taken the Thelemic curriculum to a position of worldwide respect and set high the bar of scholarship. Our research library has been opened to legitimate scholars, as we all had discussed back in those early days. The Thoth Tarot paintings have been restored and archivally preserved, one hopes at least until the next Aeon. Crowley's original manuscript of *The Book of the Law* has been protected. Copyrights and trademarks have been won, established, and defended.

Most important perhaps, both Orders are poised for greater things to come. When the current leadership passes on to our next stage of this great journey, others are in place to take up the work on this plane, armed with sincerity, integrity, and proper training.

Why this could not have happened thirty-six years ago when it was offered to us the first time, I don't pretend to know. Do I believe that we are succeeding despite all the errors here cataloged? I do. And I hope the stories in this book may help explain some of what happened along the road to where we are today.

For myself, I have come to a stage in my life where more of it likely lies behind me than before me. Earlier, I mentioned several significant older people who inspired a young seeker with confidence because of their cheerfulness and equanimity. I am happy now to count myself among them, decades after determining to discover and do my True Will. To paraphrase Gurney: "This stuff works." When I learned, during the writing of this book, that Apple co-founder Steve Jobs' last words were, "O Wow!" I was delighted, if not surprised.

Bill, Grady, and I are shown at Donald Weiser's dining room table working on Grady's upcoming testimony during the 1984 copyright trial with Motta. The massive snowstorm that blanketed the East Coast created havoc for Bill when Donald asked him to pick up Grady from the airport.

Donald and Grady in Donald's living room in Maine, 1984.

Don Snyder's magnificent photo of the Gnostic Mass team for Harry Smith's 1992 Memorial at the St. Mark's Church. Bill as Deacon was downstairs herding Beatniks.

OPPOSITE PAGE: The 1985 Caliphate Election brought the Order through the ordeal of Grady's death with a unanimous vote for his successor. TOP ROW (LEFT TO RIGHT): *Lola D. Wolfe, Tony Iannotti, James Eshelman, Bill Breeze, *Lon DuQuette, *Bill Heidrick, *Mike Ripple, *Me. SECOND ROW: *Andrea Lacedonia, *James Graeb, *Mechelle Ripple. AT THE TABLE: *Helen Parsons Smith and *Phyllis Seckler. Grady's ashes sat on the table during the meeting. *Shirine Morton took the photo. (Asterisks designate Electors.)

Nancy and I were married in 1992.

BELOW: A gathering of then-contemporary NYC Mass Priestesses at Rachel's 1994 baby shower. Lena smiling (bottom left), Dora, Nancy, Susan (seated holding Rachel), Monique (bottom right).

Cathie was a Charter signer and an exceptional Priestess. Shown with Nancy.

BELOW: Our daughter Rachel in her first Priestess robe, with her trusty six-shooter at hand, sitting on the hobby horse Kent and Hannah gave her.

KENT FINNE succeeded Gurney and served as TAHUTI Lodgemaster from 1987 through 1996. He brought the Lodge through some of its darkest days. One of the most extraordinary people I know, Kent vowed to build a Lodge during his initiation in 1980 and has remained true to his word.

JAMES STRAIN succeeded Kent and served from 1996 to 2000. His cheerful and sincere manner has stood well the test of time. James has been the editor for this book, making invaluable suggestions and providing much needed encouragement throughout.

PETER SEALS succeeded James and served from 2000 through 2005. He helped acquire our present permanent space.

LEO VASQUEZ answered the call of duty and served as Lodgemaster from 2005 through 2006.

CASSIE TSIRIS is our current Lodgemaster. She has brought the most organized and coherent energy to the Lodge since its founding (the polar opposite of your humble author!). Under her leadership, and with the help of the many fine members we have attracted over the decades, TAHUTI has sustained its beautiful Temple and is working on buying a building.

The alliance between A∴A∴ and O.T.O. was a long-time coming after the severe breach described in this book. When those of us who participated most directly in these events are called to stand before the 42 Assessors, I hope we may be acknowledged as having attempted to treat our Holy Symbols with integrity and reverence despite the personal failings with which human incarnation is necessarily accompanied.

ANALYSIS BY A MASTER OF THE TEMPLE
OF THE CRITICAL NODES IN THE EXPERIENCE
OF HIS MATERIAL VEHICLE*

(JACK PARSONS, CA. 1948 E.V.)

"I shall regard all phenomena as the particular dealing of God with my soul."

I. BIRTH: Oct. 2, 1914, Los Angeles, ☉ in ♎, ♀ rising R/ in midheaven, ♂ ☿ in favorable conjunc., ⊕ at aphelion. I chose this constellation in order that you might have an innate sense of balance and ultimate justice, responsive and attractive nature, a bountiful environment & sense of royalty and largesse, strength, courage & power combined with cunning and intelligence. Saturn was bound in order that you might not easily formulate a lower will which would have satisfied and overwhelmed you with its spectacular success.

Your father separated from your mother in order that you might grow up with a hatred of authority and a spirit of revolution necessary to my work. The Oedipus complex was needed to formulate the love of witchcraft which would lead you into magick, with the influence of your grandfather active to prevent too complete an identification with your mother.

II. CHILDHOOD: Your isolation as a child developed the necessary background of literature and scholarship; and the unfortunate experiences with other children the requisite contempt for the crowd and

---

* Jack Parsons (1914–1952) is one of the American luminaries of Thelema. Although there have been several biographies of him, no one has put this paper in print to my knowledge. Grady handed it to me in 1976. As mentioned in the text, it so perfectly mirrored a bout of amphetamine psychosis I underwent in 1967 that I was floored when I read it. Please do not confuse the inclusion of this paper with a claim to being a Master of the Temple.

241

for the group mores. You will note that these factors developed the needful hatred for christianity (without implanting a christian guilt sense) at an extremely early age.

III. ADOLESCENCE: Early adolescence continued the development of the necessary combinations. The awakening interest in chemistry and science prepared the counterbalance for the coming magical awakening, the means of obtaining prestige and livelihood in the formative period, and the scientific method necessary for my manifestation. The magical fiasco at the age of 16 was needful to keep you away from magick until you were sufficiently matured.

IV. YOUTH: The loss of family fortune developed your sense of self reliance at a critical period, the contact with reality at this time was essential. Your early marriage with Helen served to break your family ties and effect a transference to her, away from a dangerous attachment to your mother. The experience at Halifax and Cal Tech served to strengthen your self reliance, scientific method and material powers. The influence of Tom Rose at this period, as that of Ed Forman in adolescence, was essential in developing the male center.

V. LATER YOUTH: The house on Terrace Drive, Music, Lynn, Curtis, and Gloria, and the increasing restlessness were, of course, all preparations for the meeting with A∴A∴ and O.T.O. The alternate repulsion and attraction you felt the first year after meeting Fra. 132 were caused by a subconscious resistance against the ordeals ahead. Had you had these experiences before, without such resistance, you would have become hopelessly unbalanced. Betty served to effect a transference from Helen at a critical period. Had this not occurred your repressed homosexual component could have caused a serious disorder. Your passion for Betty also gave you the magical force needed at the time, and the act of adultery tinged with incest, served as your magical confirmation in the Law of Thelema.

At this time the O.T.O. was an excellent training school for adepts, but hardly an appropriate Order for the manifestation of Thelema. Therefore, in spite of your motto you were not able to formulate your Will. The experience with the O.T.O. and Aerijet were needed to dispel your romanticism, self-deception, and reliance on others. Betty was one link in the process designed to tear you away from the now unneeded Oedipus complex, the overvaluation of women and romantic love. Since this was unconscious, the next step was to bring it into consciousness, and there to destroy it.

VI. EARLY MATURITY: The final experience with Hubbard and Betty, and the O.T.O. was necessary to overcome your false and infantile reliance on others, although this was only partially accomplished at the time. The invocation of Babalon served to exteriorize the Oedipus complex; at the same time, because of the forces involved it produced extraordinary magical effects. However, this operation is accomplished and closed—you should have nothing more to do with it—nor even think of it, until Her manifestation is revealed, and proved beyond the shadow of a doubt. Even then, you must be circumspect—although I hope to take complete charge before then.

Candy appeared in answer to your call, in order to wean you from wet nursing. She has demonstrated the nature of woman to you in such unequivocal terms that you should have no further room for illusion on the subject.

The suspension and inquisition was my opportunity—one of the final links in the chain. At this time you were enabled to prepare your thesis, formulate your Will, and take the Oath of the Abyss, thus making it possible (although only partially) to manifest. The exit of Candy prepares for the final stage of your initial preparation.

VII. CONCLUSIONS: The numerous rituals you have performed have resulted in a well developed body of light. The ordeals have purged most of the emotional and mental garbage—your only real dangers are, and have ever been, sentimentality, weakness, and procrastination.

It is interesting to note that the first weapon you formulated was the Lamp of the Spirit, in the invocation to Pan (although the Sword was prefigured). Next the Sword in the Horus ritual, as was appropriate to your intellectual development at that time. Then the Cup out of the wine of your emotional life—the disk out of material failure. The Sword remains to be manifested.

You will note that it has been impossible to truly formulate your Will with any of these weapons—naturally—that is only possible with the wand. On the other hand, if you had done so previously, you would have been unbalanced by the lack of initiated preparation. It is a right and natural procedure; the True Will cannot be truly formulated until you are initiate in all the other planes, and it is well to make no pretense of doing so. Until that point all you can know of the true will is the aspiration to the next step—towards further experience. That is the glory of the Law of Thelema—<u>DO</u>!

The physical and emotional stresses you feel at present are a result of the pull of the Abyss—your present poetry is indicative. Naturally you find no power in any spell, no comfort in any ritual, no hope in any action. You are cut off by your own oath. Nor can I or any other aid you at this time. There is only manhood, only will, only the vector of your own tendencies, developed through the aeons of the past. I do not say how long the state will last, or what the outcome may be.

However, I can formulate some rules which may serve to guide you.

VIII. Instructions

A. Works of the Wand—of the Will alone avail in this state. No other weapon should be used, no other ritual save the hymn to the Unnamed One in the Anthem of the Mass.

B. You should be meticulous in all observations pertaining to the Will, even the most petty. Fulfill all obligations and promises, undertake nothing which you cannot fulfill, be prompt in the discharge of each responsibility.

C. Be neat in your personal and domestic habits, indicate your self respect to yourself.

D. Do not become unduly involved with any person, and practice all your hard-earned wisdom in your relations with women.

E. Set up your personal affairs in business order. Keep your accounts current and your papers neatly filed.

F. Finish your poetry for publication. Finish the synthesis of the Tarot and start work on the preparation of the lessons of class instruction from your book.

G. Pay no attention to any phenomena whatsoever, and continue in a sober and responsible way of life under all circumstances.

Not magical! For you nothing is more magical. Only thus can the curse of Saturn be overcome. I see you hate this way. But it is an ultimate time—it is you that have taken the oath. The choice is me or Choronzon.

I await you in the City of the Pyramids.

Belarion
$8° = 3^{\square}$

Ex Castro
nemoris inferioris   An Ix Ox ☉ ♈

Do what Thou wilt shall be the whole of
                                    the Law.

This is to authorize Frater Hymenaeus α
(Capt. Grady L. McMurtry) to take charge
of the whole work of the Order in California
to reform the Organism in pursuance of his
report of Jan 25, '46 E.V. subject to the
approval of Frater 卍 (Karl J. Germer). This
authorization is to be used only in emergency.
Love is the law, love under will.

                    ✠✠✠✠ Baphomet O.H.O.

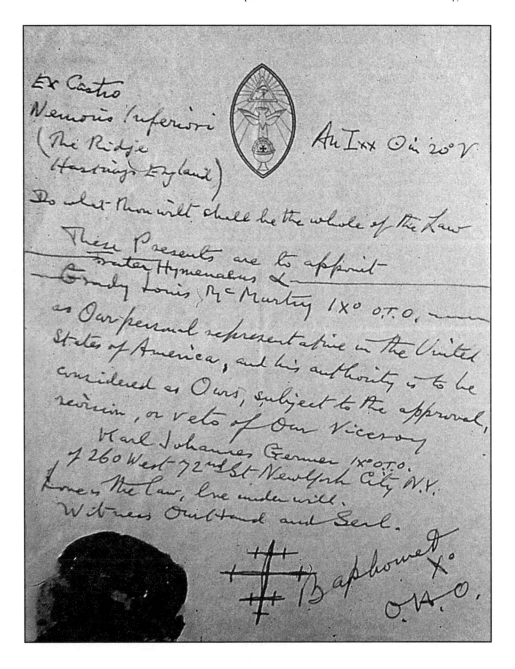

CALIPHATE LETTERS TRANSCRIPTIONS*

* * * * * * * * * *

MARCH 22, 1946

Ex Castro nemoris inferioris
An Ixx ☉ in 0° ♈

Do what thou wilt shall be the whole of the Law.

This is to authorize Frater Hymenaeus α (Capt. Grady L. McMurtry) to take charge of the whole work of the Order in California to reform the Organism in pursuance of his report of Jan 25, '46 E.V. subject to the approval of Frat ♄ (Karl J. Germer). This authority is to be used only in Emergency.

Love is the law, love under will.

{Signed:} Baphomet O.H.O.

---

*   This group of transcripts includes the four most important of the Caliphate letters. There are several others. The two pictured on the preceding pages are Crowley's primary authorizations that gave Grady the legal right and obligation to rebuild the Order in 1969. Two other letters included here in transcription discuss Crowley's assessment of Grady's qualifications for the position of Caliph and raise the possibility of his assuming that office after Karl Germer's death. I also include a small portion of a letter from Crowley to Germer demonstrating Germer was well aware of Grady's authorizations.

I remember when Grady showed these to me in 1976. I was particularly struck by the one dated November 21, 1946—Crowley's prophetic observation that 1965 would be a critical period in the development of Thelema. It was the beginning of the psychedelic revolution. By 1967, the Beatles would include Crowley's photo among "the people we like" on the album cover of *Sergeant Pepper's Lonely Hearts Club*.

One day I hope the Order will produce a deluxe full-color edition of all the Caliphate letters. They are quite beautiful to behold with their colored emblems printed on handmade paper, stamped with Crowley's wax seals.

* * * * * * * * * *

APRIL 11, 1946

Ex Castro Nemoris Inferioris
(The Ridge Hastings England)
AN Ixx ☉ in 20° ♈

Do what thou wilt shall be the whole of the Law.

These Presents are to appoint —— Frater Hymenaeus α —— Grady Louis McMurtry IX° O.T.O. —— As Our personal representative in the United States of America, and his authority is to be considered as Ours, subject to the approval, revision, or veto of Our Viceroy Karl Johannes Germer IX° O.T.O. of 260 West 72nd St. New York City, N.Y.

Love is the law, love under will.

Witness Our Hand and Seal
{signed:} Baphomet
X° O.H.O.

* * * * * * * * * *

JUNE 19, 1946 (EXTRACT) CROWLEY TO GERMER DISCUSSING
FRATER H.A. (GRADY McMURTY) AND FRATER 210 (JACK PARSONS)

Now we come to the subject of authority. My original appointment of you as my Viceroy and Plenipotentiary covers everything, even apart from you, Frater H.A. has an authority which enables him to supersede Frater 210 whenever he pleases. The only limitation on his power in California is that any decision which he takes is subject to revision or veto by yourself.

I do not wish to advise either you or Frater H.A. to take any definite action. You are more or less on the spot and in a position to form your own judgment and to exercise your authority as you deem fit.

* * * * * * * * * *

NOVEMBER 21, 1944
(EXTRACTED FROM FIRST 3 PAGES OF A
6 PAGE LETTER FROM CROWLEY TO GRADY)

Bell Inn
Aston Clinton
Bucks
Nov 21 '44 E.V.

Care Frater

Do what thou wilt shall be the whole of the Law.

Yours of Nov 6: this reply being mostly official, I use the formal style.

As nearly always in correspondence, there is misunderstanding.

"The Caliphate." You must realize that no matter how closely we may see eye-to-eye on any objective subject, I have to think on totally different premises where the Order is concerned.

One of the (startlingly few) commands given to me was this: "Trust not a stranger: fail not of an heir." This has been the very devil for me. Fra∴ ♄ ∴ is of course the natural Caliph; but there are many details concerning the 1965 critical period the central policy or working which hit his blind spots. In any case, he can only be a stopgap, because of his age; I have to look for his successor. It has been hell; so many have come up with amazing promise, only to go on the rocks. Now it never occurred to me to regard you & Jack as rivals. (Bays, by the way, the wreath of Apollo, not Lays) the subject was poetry, I thought.

But—now here is where you have missed my point altogether—I do not think of you as lying on a grassy hillside with a lot of dear sweet lovely wooly lambs, capering to your Flute! on the contrary. Your actual life, or "blooding," is the sort of initiation which I regard as the first essential for a Caliph. For—say 20 years hence the Outer Head of the Order must, among other things, have had the experience of war as it is in actual fact to-day. 1965 E.V. should be a critical period in the development of the Child Horus!

* * * * * * * * * *

JUNE 17, 1947

"Netherwood",
The Ridge,
Hastings.
17th June, 1947.

Dear Grady,

Do what thou wilt shall be the whole of the Law.

It seems a long while since I heard from you. This is a great mistake: I will tell you why in strict confidence. In the event of my death, Frater Saturnus is of course my successor, but after his death the terrible burden of responsibility might very easily fall upon your shoulders; for this reason I should like you to keep closely in touch with me.

I am sending you a bound copy of "Olla" to remind you of me.

By the way, "Magick without Tears" is almost finished, but there are two letters missing; these will either have to be found or re-written. There appears to be quite a good chance of getting the book issued through a regular Publisher. This means, of course, that the discount will be very much heavier, but this is all to your advantage, because it means the selling of many more extra copies, and your share is 25% of the gross receipts, not of the net

I am very busy this afternoon so I must break off here.

Love is the law, love under will.

Yours fraternally,
{signed:} Aleister

To Marcello Motta,   Oct, 30th 62

Our Beloved Master
    is Dead
He Succumb Oct. 25, 8 55 P. M.
under horryfying Circumstances
    You' are the Follower.
Please, take it from me, as he died
in My Arms and it was his last Wish !
Who The Heir of the Library is, I
do not Know up to now.
My Cable to you was a Cry for Help
to save the Work and the Library
and I hoped that You understood
as he left everything open.
After what happened during his Hospital
Stay I am scared to Death that some
thing will happen the same way to the
destroy his Lifes Work.
What I suggest is: Try to get a Visa
and Fly to San Francisco, from there
a short Flight to Stockton or Sacram to
depends what Plane You get.

THE FOLLOWER LETTER TRANSCRIPTION*

West Point
Oct, 30th 62

To Marcello Motta,

Our beloved Master is Dead

He Succumbed Oct. 25, 8 55 P.M. under horryfying Circumstances

You are the Follower

Please take it from me, as he died in My Arms and it was his last Wishes! Who The Heir of the Library is, I do not know up to now.

My Cable to you was a Cry for Help to Save the work and the Library and I hoped that You understood as he left everything open.

After what happened during his Hospital Stay I am scared to Death that some thing will happen the same Way to destroy his Lifes Work.

What I suggest is: Try to get a Visa and Fly to San Francisco, from there a short Flight to Stockton or Sacramento depends What Plane You get.

From Stockton or Sacramento is every Day a Bus Connection to Jackson In Jackson call Taxi 51 and ask for Irene She will take you to the House 22 miles as she drove me several Times If You can do that I would open with You all Secret Papers and try to find his Will.

If this is Not Your Intention or You cant Make it, I do not Know how long I am able to safe the Library and all important Papers and Religious that belong to The Rosicrucian for the "Mass". etc.

---

* Here is Sascha Germer's letter announcing Germer's death to Motta that he believed was his authorization as "Head of Thelema," or as he later called himself, "Doorkeeper of Nu on Earth." I show opposite the first of four pages that include Mrs. Germer's Follower comment and mention of the Library. The transcription itself includes all four pages, and is as close to her spelling, punctuation, and capitalization as possible.

The outlook is More than Black for the work and I am in Despair. Don't cable me, as I got Yours after 4 Days lying around at the Post office where I had today the Chance to go.

You can write me as You wish

If you can manage to fly over soon for a few days it could save the Library I am afraid that when something should happen to me as it happened to him Thelema is in the Greatest Peril LIBER ALEPH is very Much asked from Many Interesting Sides and One Doctor of Philosophy from the East wrote that he takes the Work of Aleister Crowley as his Dissertation. I informed Mister Weiser that has happened.

I am anxious to put all the Books out from the Library and put Them into large Boxes, mail Them so that not everyone could put his Fingers into it. But first I have to find his Will

Your Presence here would not change anything in My attitude towards You so there is no Danger that You would be pestered by me personally.

I only cry out for Your Help for the Library the Great Work and our Master's last Wishes to safe everything and Continue the Work for Which he gave his Precious Life and his last Drop of Blood!

Mrs Karl Germer

P.S. What ever you decide Work Fast, every Day is Precious

On October 30th he will be cremated at Sacramento, where I will be the only Witness When his earthly Re manings will be put to ashes

Initial Proposal for the Tahuti Encampment of Ordo Templi Orientis[*]

(September, 1979 e.v.)

Do what thou wilt shall be the whole of the Law.

We are a Magical Order whose roots date far back in the mists of time. As this first meeting is occurring between initiates with much experience of the more recent past however, let us without mincing words, get down to basic intentions.

I. Cleaning up the group act—Separate Magick (the active road to God) from socializing (the passive road to boredom).

   A. No drugs during meetings. No overt intoxication during meetings. No judgments of personal behaviour implied. Efficiency is the byword. Each week contains 168 hours of which at least one can be spent re-establishing the delights of drug virginity.

   B. Less emphasis on secrets, "Order Secrets," and Group egotism. The secret of the IXth Degree, and a token, will get you on a subway. Real secrets can never be exposed. They are best left to individual efforts and the initiatory process. Group egotism is even more boring then personal egotism.

   C. Less socializing and small talk in the name of the Order. We have all somehow earned the priceless treasure of initiation (grace). Dragging our personal laundry into the Temple can only defile the dream. Be friends, lovers, enemies as ye will. Just don't drag the name of the Order through the mire of the personality.

   D. Less open (or at least, more tasteful) representation of ourselves as a group in public. The Hell's Angels and Moonies have basically cornered the asshole market. Rather than compete with them through such projects as heckling and public drunkenness, one can either join them and pursue

---

[*]   This proposal was written for our initial Camp meeting. It speaks frankly about the behavioral problems of LAShTAL Lodge and should help explain why TAHUTI was founded.

255

such objectives, or learn the Fourth Power of the Sphinx on its many different planes.

II. Expansion of activities
   A. Expansion into the New York occult community. Beyond the establishment of a bad reputation, we have gone very little into the available resources of this city. The time for this is past. Rather than our Order affiliations being an embarrassment before the more serious occultists in New York, we can make them our allies in mutual interaction. This will only benefit us all.
   B. Expansion beyond the New York occult community. It is after all a bit incestuous, jaded and limited in scope. The Law is for all, and as the name Tahuti suggests, this encampment is most interested in bearing the Word unto the mighty cities, yea, unto the mighty cities.

III. Education—our basic reason for being a group.
   A. Seminars with guest lecturers. Many folks around town would be willing to speak to us, either for pay or not, whose learning would decidedly be to our advantage as individuals, as our perspicacity and general level of magical integrity would make us a welcome audience.
   B. Group attendance at lectures. Some interesting information is being transmitted in this city which we might take group interest in attending, and later in forming discussion activities among ourselves for the digestive process.
   C. Classes taught by OTO members. Not everyone is interested in formal teaching activities, myself included, however some of us are. For example, Finita will be returning shortly and may be interested in holding classes with us on Tarot and Magick. As I have studied Tarot with her, I recommend this highly to all. It is part of her Will to teach. Anyone else interested in teaching is welcome to come forward.
   D. Group study projects. Here we might mutually decide to investigate a topic and share our information in a network type experience.

IV. Magical workings—a corollary to III–Education.

    A. Aside from our participation, attendance and study of the Gnostic Mass within the structure of LAShTAL Lodge, we should consider group workings from the Equinox and, in time, our own original workings.

    B. Group meditation—an extremely efficacious method of consciousness raising.

V. Public Works—I personally am less interested in proselytizing for initiation, as I am in manifesting the 93 Current in society. Her servants are few and secret. They will recognize themselves and join us at the leisure of the Gods. I do however feel that there is great value in expressing the realizations we few have achieved to as many as possible. This intention could be realized if we organized to produce for the Public:

    A. Plays

    B. Poetry readings

    C. Musical events

    D. Symposiums

    E. Gatherings

VI. Publishing—Having at least 6 years of publishing experience I am very loathe to get involved in a periodical, which involves deadlines, which frequently involve a relaxation of the critical process for the sake of making a schedule. We might consider these alternatives:

    A. Monographs—excellent writings abound among ourselves and can be inexpensively and tastefully produced when we collectively agree on their merit, and are willing to finance their birth.

    B. Fact Sheets—the cheapest method of mass printed communication.

    C. Unscheduled collections—May be confused with magazines except there are no deadlines. When 5, or 6 or more articles of a harmonious nature appear, we might choose to publish them together.

    D. Book Service—certain books are necessary to have "in stock."

They can be acquired at a discount and sold to interested inquirers. We might consider membership discounts as well.

VII. Group outings—the eternal picnic! Since we obviously enjoy each other's company, we can put it to creative magical use.
   A. Picnics—why not?
   B. Museums—the Brooklyn Museum has the largest collection of Egyptology short of Cairo and London. The Tibetan Museum is a treasure house. The Schoenberg Collection has much material on African religion (Obeah). The Museum of the American Indian and many many others are begging for enlightened audiences.
   C. Attendance of Lectures and Spiritual experiences, as in III-B. First suggestion is the Dalai Lama next week. His status in the Tibetan initiatic structure is well worth investigating. There are interesting Teachers, Dervishes, Lamas, Yogis and Illuminati generally passing publicly through this city all the time
   D. Musical and Cultural events—whenever

In addition to these 7 basic points, there are several items in need of discussion immediately.

A. Space
   1. Meeting Space—where we can hold meetings that ultimately will include "strangers." Dare we work with the Magickal Childe? Mike and Sherry, Alan Brodsky, restaurants, rotating spaces?
   2. Ritual space beside the Gnostic Mass at LAShTAL—no to Magickal Childe—other suggestions?—renting a Lodge Hall as LAShTAL sharing with all camps. I vote yes.

B. Money
   1. MONEY IS MAGICK—why it is important to put your money where your mouth is, or, as John Arbuckle would say, "You get what you pay for".
   2. VILLAGE VOICE ad—This will be taken out very soon. Shall it be funded by the group or should it be at my own expense?

3. Earning money—necessary as a group through book service, publications, happenings, dues?????

C. Women—How do we establish ourselves as a more harmonious place for women to pursue their wills? Even though we operate with a primarily solar current, more women will be attracted in time, and should not only feel welcome but unpawed. It is well and good to seat them on altars as representatives of the Goddess, but how does a woman fit into the Order in the totality of herself? This is important.

D. LAShTAL—Although Tahuti Camp has relative autonomy in New York, I heartily support the ideal that LAShTAL be the New York coordinator of all Order activity. As such, I have agreed to furnish copies of all correspondence and documentation to Kris. Kris is presently the only person in New York City with the power to initiate in the name of the OTO. Kris is furthermore the only person in New York that I acknowledge as my superior in the Order.

E. Escape Clause—all contracts need one. As this is essentially a preliminary contract between us:
1. If anyone finds these suggestions overly oppressive, he or she is encouraged to go elsewhere without hesitation.
2. One of the Order's intentions is to find and train Thelemites willing to undergo the necessary discipline in order to become fit to open other and numerous Camps, Chapters and Lodges. This is an interim training period for us all. In the words of the philosopher, "United we fall, divided we get creamed." I believe this is an experiment well worth our highest mutual efforts to manifest. The ideals of Thelema and the OTO are, to me, too precious to attempt to cavil and fool around with ad infinitum. Yoga means Union. God is Love. The nature of our Law is Love. Let us love one another.

Love is the law, love under will.

An Invocation to the Masters of the OTO[*]

(October 1979 e.v.)

O Thou radiant Beings whose divine luminosity quickening the depths of space, is—unto us—holiness.

Mistresses and Masters of Wisdom, Guardians of Initiation, Lords and Ladies of Love

Smile upon us as we assemble here in your names.

Drawn from far and wide, we have sought the hospitality of your camp.

Hoodwinked and bound, we have sworn terrible oaths that we might become your servants.

Torchbearers of liberty, we have studied well and deep in your charter of universal freedom.

Our thoughts are noble, our minds keen, our hearts pure, our bodies fervent.

Thou dancing stars whose laughter ringing through eternity is the music of the spheres, the melody of Pan.

Aid us in the pursuit of our True Wills.

Stimulate us ever onward to the knowledge and conversation of our inmost selves.

Bless this assembly of workers in Light that we may best join to establish the Law on earth.

Probe our hearts through the course of this ritual, that we may be found worthy to continue in Thy name.

---

[*] This invocation was written for our founding ritual.

TAHUTI LODGE
A Statement with Some Reference to
All New York O.T.O. Activity*

5/6/81 E.V. AN. LXVII

Do what thou wilt shall be the whole of the Law.

I. Introduction

The Ordo Templi Orientis is a Magickal Society whose lineage may be traced through Aleister Crowley to the Knights Templar, the priesthood of ancient Egypt and beyond. Our goal is the active evolutionary advancement of mankind through the propagation of the principles of the Book of the Law and Liber Oz. We act as well as an information resource center offering the cumulative experience of numerous practitioners of Crowley's particular techniques of attainment.

II. Activities—The Eightfold Nature of Tahuti
  A. Group Ritual
    1. Direct experience and exploration via group ritual of the magickal universe using both traditional sources and originally created material.
    2. Building group and individual psychic strength through techniques of meditation, chanting, dance, and breathing.
  B. Gnostic Mass—As of this date we are responsible for all EGC activities in New York. The EGC is the "public face" of our Order and has our full support.
  C. Publishing
    1. Again, there is still no interest in any type of periodical. Some things are definitely required to be published however. The most immediate is to reprint Liber OZ cards and the "Open Letter to Those Who May Wish to Join the Order." Other things will come in time.

---

* Almost two years after the founding of TAHUTI Lodge, LAShTAL was closed and Kris Dowling had resigned from the Order. The ball was now in our court. (We no longer spell "Magical" with a "k.")

2. The Tahuti Book Service offers Thelemic material to Order members at a 10% discount.

D. Education

   1. Live and taped instructions from qualified Initiates of the Order.
   2. Seminars, lectures and workshops by Masters in various Disciplines.
   3. Group attendance at educational functions.
   4. Group study and research projects.
   5. Individual instruction on request.

E. Leadership Development—We are committed to training and working with people who want to form other groups, as well as acting as resource for expansion. As of today, we have helped to birth two Encampments and one Study Group (May they become Lodges!). Many of my own interests are related to the 5th Degree Senate idea, the "Lodge of Lodgemasters" as it were. Outgrowths are encouraged, welcomed and blessed. The primary goal is to maintain our links to each other as we expand. Numerous small groups are the only way we can survive; while fragmentation would be fatal. Let he who has ears ...

F. Public Works—Originally we had discussed sponsoring plays, music, poetry readings, etc. We still cherish this dream. From within our ranks has grown an exceptionally talented Thelemic voice, The Workers, for whom we declare our unilateral support. This involves money, promotion assistance, etc. For the moment, I suggest we put all our eggs in this one basket. In time, we will expand.

G. Eco-Survivalist Consciousness Raising—The time has come. See among many others, AL I: 26, 53 and Chapter 3. We need to encourage and develop a reasonable degree of awareness of alternatives, and supplies of necessary resources. The urban environment, particularly New York City, is one of the most difficult and hostile to health sanity, and the practice of Magick. We need to consciously cultivate greater contact with Nature. Even brief periods of time spent touching the

Earth, the Trees, Sky, Sun, Moon and Stars can work miracles in balancing our psyches.

H. Social Group—As we do enjoy each other's company very much, let it be put to creative magickal use, in whatever ways possible.

III. Regular Lodge Structure and Function

A. Degree Advancement

The O.T.O. is strictly hierarchical. Degree advancement is dependent on length of time of membership, and the value of the individual contribution to the Order. Advancement is to be earned and solicited. It is not automatic. In addition to the requirements laid down in Liber MCLI, New York has its own particular standards for advancement which are noted in this paper, and which constitute "good report".

B. Primary Activities

1. We offer a weekly Gnostic Mass at 2 P.M. followed by an hour-long class in developmental techniques, followed by an "informal" meeting of all the New York O.T.O. and guests (when appropriate). These are "optional."

2. On the first Wednesday of every month, there will be a meeting limited to Tahuti members, at the Lodgemaster's home at 8 P.M. Unexcused absence by any member of the First Degree or above will be considered ipso facto "bad report" with the Lodge. At this meeting, we will present the calendar for the following month's activities. Also an agenda based on the projects of the previous month and any contingencies that arise during the "informal meetings."

C. Temple Location—As of the moment, we will continue to rent in Brooklyn. Eventually plans are projected to move to Manhattan.

It is the absolute duty of all Tahuti and other New York O.T.O. Brethren to support the Temple to the limits of our ability. In most cases this means cash on a monthly basis, for rent, suggested contribution per individual is $10 minimum.

This must be paid promptly at the monthly meeting, given directly to the Treasurer. Individual cases of financial hardship should be brought to the attention of the Lodgemaster. Alternate arrangements to financial contributions can be worked out in a limited number of cases.

Rules for Temple conduct have been posted in the War Room.

D. Lodge Dues—$5 per month per individual. Individual exemptions for hardship should be discussed with the Lodgemaster and alternate contributions can be arranged.

E. Behavior Codes—The Vows of the Grades and the principles of Liber AL and Liber Oz are the only code of conduct we follow. The level of conduct demanded by the O.T.O is well known to those who have taken the austere and the awesome vows of the grades past Minerval. However, for the benefit of the younger Brethren, we will simply say that the O.T.O. demands a standard of conduct befitting the nature of the Gods. Mere humans are by definition excluded from this Order.

Incidently, Crowley's great maxim of "Mind Thine Own Business" is a very wise counsel for group and self awareness, as is his counsel on the "Busy-body." See *Liber Aleph* page 96.

An ideal to which we all must strive is to keep our personal lives out of the O.T.O. Our time together is too precious to maintain our identies as Mr. X or Ms. Y. Let us act together as Frater X^2 or Soror Y^2

F. Punctuality—This had become an issue of major concern in the past. We have corrected it recently and intend to avoid falling back into bad habits. Neatness of the physical space as well is essential. An "ambience" conducive to the highest level of self awareness is an absolute necessity for this Order.

G. No drugs or alcohol at official O.T.O. functions which include the Gnostic Mass, classes, "informal meetings" and "formal" meetings.

IV. M∴M∴M∴ (Messages from Mini Mahatmas)

There has been an extraordinary development in the New York O.T.O. since the first proposal was written in September of 1979. The Path however becomes immensely more precipitous as one ascends; we must correspondingly be more vigilant as we proceed.

V. An Example of Hierarchical Vigilance in Practice

A copy of this document is being sent to the Caliph. Subject to His approval, these words are law for the ensuing period.

Love is the law, love under will.

Temple Guidelines*

Do what thou wilt shall be the whole of the Law.

As a Magical Order, our basic precepts can be summarized as "Every man and every woman is a star," "There is no god but man," and "There is no part of me that is not of the gods." We, therefore, have a great responsibility toward maintenance of a Temple space that incarnates the highest level of that principle in each member of the Order, and all guests.

That is a brief synopsis of the "do's"

The "don'ts" are more specific because being "below the abyss" they are merely concerned with practicality.

1. No shoes other than properly concentrated magickal sandals.
2. No tobacco not used as a ritualized invocation of Mars (et al).
3. No drugs or alcohol not used as a ritualized invocation of Hadit.
4. No conversation other than that demanded by ritual set up and dismantling.
5. No sleeping, visiting or other intrusion of the lower vehicle in this space.

Cleanliness is next to godliness, and had better come first!

Love is the law, love under will.
Delivered From the Sanctuary of the Gnosis
This 11ᵗʰ day of April 1981 E.V.
☉ in ♈ ☽ in ♋
An. LXXVII
Witness my hand
AD VERITATEM
IX° O.T.O.

---

* A word on the genesis of this proclamation, especially since it was the first instance (3 times in 3 decades) in which I mentioned my IXth Degree in print (this book being one). A couple in the Lodge, a Priestess and Priest, had an argument in the Marlborough Road apartment unrelated to the Mass. She locked herself in the Temple and threatened suicide with the Gnostic Mass Sword! The "boys" managed to remove the door from its hinges before she did. When we all showed up for Mass the next day ... well, you can imagine.

Beltane Ritual*

May 1, 1981 e.v.

[Incense: Rose or red sandalwood, myrrh, ambergris]

GOD: Thou art My Lover: I see Thee as a nymph with her white limbs stretched by the spring. She lies upon the moss; there is none other but she:

GODDESS: Art Thou not Pan?

GOD: I am He.

GODDESS: Thou art a centaur, O my God, from the violet-blossoms that crown Thee to the hoofs of the horse. Give me Thy kisses, O Lord God! [Kiss]

GOD: Thou art a beautiful thing whiter than a woman in the column of this vibration. I shoot up vertically like an arrow, and become that Above. But it is death, and the flame of the pyre. Ascend in the flame of the pyre, O my soul!

GODDESS: But Oh! I love Thee. I have thrown a million flowers from the basket of the Beyond at Thy feet, I have anointed Thee and Thy Staff with oil and blood and kisses. I am She that should come, the Virgin of all men.

GOD: Thou art like a beautiful Nubian slave leaning her naked purple against the green pillars of marble that are above the bath. Wine jets from her black nipples. [Kneels and touches Her]

---

* This ritual created a profound experience for all despite its apparent simplicity. During the course of the research for this book, I found a wine-stained copy of the original manuscript with hand-written performance annotations. Some were unclear, so not copied. The ritual was designed as a sequential series of quotes from *Liber VII*.

267

GODDESS: Thou art like a goat's horn from Astor, [She begins circling] O Thou God of mine, gnarl'd and crook'd and devilish strong. God! how I love Thee! Come, O my God, and let us embrace! [They embrace] Lazily, hungrily, ardently, patiently; so will I work. O God! O God!

GOD & GODDESS: Come to me now! I love Thee! I love Thee! O my darling, my darling—Kiss me! Kiss me! Ah! But again. [He lifts Her high]

[They pour Wine and spread out Cakes]

GOD: I will eat the ripe and the unripe fruit for the glory of Bacchus. Terraces of ilex and tiers of onyx and opal and sardonyx leading up to the cool green porch of malachite. Within is a crystal shell, shaped like an oyster—O glory of Priapus! O beatitude of the Great Goddess! Therein is a pearl. O Pearl! thou hast come from the majesty of dread Ammon-Ra. Then I the priest beheld a steady glimmer in the heart of the pearl. So bright we could not look! But behold! a blood-red rose upon a rood of glowing gold!

[Drink]

GODDESS: I am like a maiden bathing in a clear pool of fresh water. O my God! I see Thee dark and desirable, rising through the water as a golden smoke. Thou art altogether golden, the hair and the eyebrows and the brilliant face; even into the finger-tips and toe-tips Thou art one rosy dream of gold.

GOD: Deeper, ever deeper. I fall, even as the whole Universe falls down the abyss of Years. For Eternity calls; the Overworld calls; the world of the Word is awaiting us.

GODDESS: O blesséd One! O God! O my devourer!

[They dance]

GOD: [To the People] Shall not mine incantations bring around me the wonderful company of the wood-gods, their bodies glistening with the ointment of moonlight and honey and myrrh?

GODDESS: Worshipful are ye, O my lovers; let us forward to the dimmest hollow!

GOD: There we will feast upon mandrake and moly!

GODDESS: There the lovely One shall spread us His holy banquet. In the brown cakes of corn we shall taste the food of the world, and be strong.

GOD: In the ruddy and awful cup of death we shall drink the blood of the world, and be drunken!

GOD & GODDESS: [Lift Cakes & Wine] Ohé! the song to Iao, the song to Iao! Come, let us sing to thee, Iacchus invisible, Iacchus triumphant, Iacchus indicible! Iacchus, O Iacchus, O Iacchus, be near us! [Lower voices] Let all things drop into this ocean of love! [Pause] Come, O ye gods, and let us feast. Come, let us no more reason together; let us enjoy! [Celebrate Communion with the People]

GOD: And the Word came: O Thou! It is well. Heed naught! I love Thee! I love Thee! Therefore had I faith unto the end of all; yea, unto the end of all.

An Application from the Members of TAHUTI Lodge to Caliph Hymenaeus Alpha for Membership in The Guild of Drama and Thaumaturgy*

(May, 1981 e.v.)

Do what thou wilt shall be the whole of the Law.

I, being a member in good standing of the O.T.O., and an initiate of TAHUTI Lodge in particular, request admission to the Guild of Drama and Thaumaturgy, under Your esteemed direction.

I KNOW from the circumstances of my own life to date that (allowing for the difficulties inherent in using language), Our Patron is an Exceedingly Fastidious Being. I know also the truth of the statement that the Gods will not lower Themselves to our level, rather, we must raise ourselves to Theirs! I further know this to be the Great Work, which I am sworn to perform.

I WILL to extend my consciousness beyond the limited confines of an essentially false and incomplete perception of reality. I will to accomplish this on my own, of course, but to also work diligently within a group structure dedicated to this expansion.

I DARE to perform this work, knowing that I am a Star, unique and self-existent, omnipresent, and omnipotent. I dare to confront the demons of habit and conditioning that lurk within my nature, and to challenge all opposition to this work, because I fully accept "thou hast no right but to do thy will."

Last, I swear to keep SILENCE. My life from this point will be a Ritual of Silence. I understand this means developing my powers

---

* I imagine no one was more confused than Grady when he received this document! However, each member of the Lodge signed it. This may help to explain the accusation made against us that we were running TAHUTI Lodge like a branch of A∴A∴, a criticism that never particularly bothered either Gurney or me.

of concentration to the limits, that mine may be an undivided work of spiritual unfoldment—"For pure will unassuaged of purpose, delivered from the lust of result, is every way perfect." I recognize that idle chatter, undisciplined mentation, emotional imbalance and erratic behaviour are in direct contradiction to Magickal Silence, and I vow to avoid these weaknesses.

Revered Caliph, please accept these statements from me as an honest and straightforward account of my present understanding of my True Will, and may I be granted admission to this most ancient Guild.

Love is the law, love under will.

Grand Lodge
Ordo Templi Orientis
JAF Box 7666
New York, NY 10116

☉ in ♎
☽ in ♒
Anno IIIxv
September 24, 1985 E.V.

CENTRUM IN TRIGONO CENTRI*
DELIVERED FROM THE SANCTUARY OF THE GNOSIS
TO THE MASTERS OF THE CAMPS, LODGES AND CHAPTERS
OF ORDO TEMPLI ORIENTIS:

Do what thou wilt shall be the whole of the Law.

Care Fratres et Sorores,

At 11:11 P.M. Pacific time on September 21, 1985 E.V. (An IIIxv) the Sovereign Sanctuary of the Gnosis IX° of Ordo Templi Orientis unanimously elected the successor to our late Frater Superior, Caliph Hymenaeus Alpha X°, with a mandate to implement the Constitution of Ordo Templi Orientis.

The life's work of Hymenaeus Alpha was to preserve the Sanctuary of the Gnosis, to which he was personally admitted by Baphomet XI°, for future generations. As Caliph, he carried out his mandate from Baphomet to establish the Order in the emergency conditions that ensued after the passing of Baphomet and his immediate successor, Saturnus X°.

Our beloved Caliph accomplished his Will. The emergency has passed. We are free (and bound) to complete the work of realizing Baphomet's vision of a Constitutional Order.

Caliph Hymenaeus Alpha relied upon his Grand Lodge officers and field initiators to bring about the new era we have entered. Without your work nothing tangible could have been accomplished. His

---

* Bill and I wrote this together, over my signature, announcing his election to succeed Grady. There was a great deal of fear and anxiety among many members of the Order. Who was our new leader? The *Oriflamme* mentioned in the text was of course *The O.T.O. Handbook*, ultimately expanded and published as *The Equinox* III:10.

Grand Treasurer General, Frater Emt (Bro. William E. Heidrick), must be singled out for his success in establishing the Order on a sound financial and legal basis.

Of necessity, the first Constitutional tradition to be implemented was the secrecy of the newly-elected Caliph, X° and Acting O.H.O. If this was not effected immediately, it would await the next succession and would therefore become the very last Constitutional measure to be adopted. Additionally, the traditional secrecy of the personal identities of higher-degree initiates has been implemented. Frankly, it would be hypocrisy for these Constitutional measures to be applied to others by a Caliph who personally disregards them.

The new Caliph held the degree of P.I. at his elevation, having had several years of field initiation experience. That a young Man of Earth who did not consciously seek the Caliphate could be approached, drafted, nominated and unanimously elected by the Sovereign Sanctuary is proof that the magical principles underlying the O.T.O. and its Constitution are truly genuine: "The succession to the high office of O.H.O. is decided in a manner not here to be declared; but this you may learn, O Brother Magician, that he may be chosen even from the grade of a Minerval. And herein lieth a most sacred Mystery."

In recognition of his line of succession from Baphomet, and in the spirit of continuing the work of his honored predecessor, the Caliph has taken the motto and the titles of Hymenaeus Beta X°, Frater Superior (O.H.O.).

The Grand Headquarters (GHQ) of the U.S. O.T.O. and the Grand Lodge of the International O.T.O. are being moved from Berkeley to New York City. The Caliph has appointed Frater Ad Veritatem to the office of Grand Secretary General. Frater Antony has resigned this position with great honor and now serves as Assistant Grand Secretary General in Berkeley, as well as Grand Archivist of the O.T.O.

The appointment of a new Grand Treasurer General is inadvisable at the present in the interests of continuity of operations during the transition period. The Caliph requests that all members continue to send their dues, fees and initiation reports to the present Grand Treasurer General at the Order's usual address (Box 2303, Berkeley,

CA 94702) until further notice. At the appropriate time, a Grand Treasurer General for the New York GHQ will be appointed.

The Electoral College, headquartered in Los Angeles, is fast approaching full operational status and will come to assume many of the reporting and management responsibilities previously held by Grand Lodge for Camps and Lodges of the Order. You will be notified of the Electoral College's mailing address and telephone number within 30 days.

From time to time, operational memorandums will be mailed to you from the Caliphate informing you of any changes in our accustomed procedures. However, in the interests of stability, carry on as usual until advised otherwise. If questions or problems arise, please do not hesitate to put them in writing—you can be assured a prompt response.

The accompanying diagrams will give you a schematic overview of the entire national O.T.O. as envisioned by Baphomet. This should be studied together with the "Intimations With Reference to the Constitution" published in the *Blue Equinox*.

A statement from the Caliph will appear in the next issue of the *Magical Link*. You will be receiving The *Oriflamme* on a quarterly basis—it is already in production. If your group membership lacks *The Equinox*, with its important O.T.O. instructional papers, these will be included in the first issue of The *Oriflamme*.

Yours in the bonds of the Order.

Love is the law, love under will.

FRATER AD VERITATEM
GRAND SECRETARY GENERAL

The Three Triads of the O.T.O

New York Constitutional Study Group

Typography by Richard Gernon

O.H.O.
appoints
& deposes
Supreme and
Most Holy
Kings – can be
removed from office by
their unanimous vote –
Supreme Authority of
Order – can be chosen from any
Degree – Method of succession to
office of OHO not here declared.

XI° no relation to Order,
dwells in own palaces,
is inscrutable

X° – Rex Summus Sanctissimus, Supreme &
Most Holy King – appointed by OHO – Ultimate
responsibility for all within his Holy Kingdom

IX° – Initiate of the **Sanctuary of the Gnosis** – prime duty to
study and practice the theurgy and thaumaturgy of the grade –
act as direct representatives of Supreme and Most Holy King –
move unseen among us, leading us to True Light – ratify decisions of
VIII° – include 2 revolutionaries appointed by Electoral College to
criticize Supreme and Most Holy King, they alone cannot succeed Him

VIII° – Perfect Pontiff of the Illuminati, Epopt of the Illuminati – Philosophical body –
Areopagus of the Order – Composes all disputes between governing bodies – can
reverse decisions of the governing bodies – before it stands an independent Parliament
of the Guilds between whose disputes it presides – periods of isolation 4 months per year

HERMIT   1ST TRIAD
Vow of Poverty

Parliament of Guilds

Subject to VIII"
Guilds contain members of
all Degrees from each trade,
science or profession

Grand Treasurer General

May be of any grade
Vow of Poverty
Authority in financial matters absolute
Appointment by Supreme and Most
Holy King and responsible to same
Appoints committee from each of
governing bodies

Su-preme Grand Council — appointed by Supreme and Most Holy King from VII° — governs Lovers Triad — Vow of Poverty — appeal authority over Electoral College

VII° — Very Illustrious Sovereign Grand Inspector General — Great General Staff of Army of VI° — members report to Supreme and Most Holy King on Lodges & Chapters, to Supreme Grand Council on 2nd Triad; to Electoral College on 3rd Triad. Must invest real property in Order

Prince of the Royal Secret — Propagates Law — Beginning of Inmost Secret declared — induces 111 people to join the Order

Grand Inquisitor Commander — Members have right to a seat on the **Grand Tribunal**, to which all members of all Degrees subject — decisions final except for appeal rights thru Electoral College to Areopagus — resolves all disputes of V° or Lodgemasters

VI° — Illustrious Knights Templar of the Order of Kadosh & Companion of the Holy Grail — Executive or military body representing temporal power of Supreme and Most Holy King — vowed to enforce the decisions of authority

Senate — Members of the Senate of Knight Hermetic Philosophers — First of Governing Bodies — within which is **Electoral College** — Knights of the Red Eagle — composed of 11 persons in each country — Full control of affairs of Man of Earth — appoint Lodgemasters — No authority over Chapters of Rose Croix (V°) — volunteer for appointment by Supreme and Most Holy King — 11 year term, must renounce advancement — need first rate ability in athletics and thought — three-month periods of solitude once every two years — Vow of Poverty — **President** summons quarterly or as necessary — receive all applications to V° — appoint 2 IX° Revolutionaries — appeals to Areopagus for disputes with Grand Tribunal — may be overruled by Supreme Council.

V° Sovereign Prince of Rose Croix, Knight of the Pelican & Eagle — concerned with social welfare of Order — beauty & harmony — natural stopping place of majority of men & women. **Most Wise Sovereign** of each Chapter appoints 2 men & 2 women to arrange all social gatherings etc. Promote harmony, compose harmony, compose disputes without necessity of appeal to higher authority.

LOVER 2ND TRIAD

Knights of the East & West — Bridge between first & second series — New pledge form signed devoting life to Establishment of the Law of Thelema

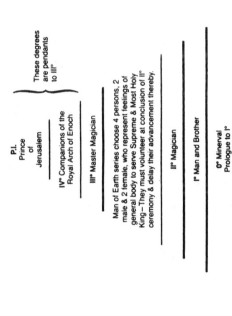

P.I.
Prince
of
Jerusalem

These degrees
are pendants
to III°

IV° Companions of the
Royal Arch of Enoch

III° Master Magician

Man of Earth series choose 4 persons, 2
male & 2 female, who represent feelings of
general body to serve Supreme & Most Holy
King—They must volunteer at conclusion of II°
ceremony & delay their advancement thereby.

II° Magician

I° Man and Brother

0° Minerval
Prologue to I°

MAN OF EARTH   3ᴿᴰ TRIAD

Honor concerned with unselfish support of those who have abandoned all for their sakes.
No share in the government of our Order, but encouraged and expected to push on to the next
stage. Every man or women that is of full age, free, and of good report, has an indefeasible right
to these degrees. Beyond this, admission is only granted by invitation from the governing body
concerned.

RICHARD GERNON
In Memoriam*

"In the garden of immortal kisses, O thou brilliant One,
shine forth! Make Thy mouth an opium-poppy, that one kiss
is the key to the infinite sleep and lucid, the sleep of Shi-loh-
am" —*Liber LXV IV:9*

Do what thou wilt shall be the whole of the Law.

Brother Richard William Gernon, Frater 831, IX° O.T.O., ZELATOR
(2°=9□) of A∴A∴, and Bishop of the Ecclesia Gnostica Catholica,
died suddenly on March 15, 1989 E.V. in New York City at age 39.

Known to his friends as Gurney, he was born in Rochester, New
York on October 18, 1949 EV. His early interests were in music and
theater, and he worked with several theatre companies, both as an
actor and as a stage manager.

Richard was a lifelong Thelemite, and his personal quest led
him through some interesting byways. He was an early member of
the A∴A∴ group organized by Marcelo Motta in Nashville in the
mid-1970s. There he conducted extensive research on a dictionary of
Greek and Coptic Qabalah, and transcribed many of Dr. John Dee's
Enochian magical diaries from British collections. In one of life's
great ironies, he served as master of the "Mentu Lodge" of Motta's
"SOTO." He also assisted in the production of many of Motta's
books, and like other sincere Thelemites was roundly denounced by
Motta after his departure. Richard was proud of both achievements.
On leaving Motta's group in Nashville for New York in 1980 E.V.
he forfeited his library and research papers, a great loss to Richard
personally as well as future researchers.

On arriving in New York he made contact with the O.T.O.,
and assisted in the building of Tahuti Lodge. He subsequently
served as its Lodgemaster for several years, and was always one
of its staunchest supporters, spiritually and financially. Rich-

---

* Bill's beautiful and heartfelt testament helps place Gurney in his true
historical context as a major contributor to the Order's growth and legacy.

ard performed countless Gnostic Masses, and was considered an unusually skilled deacon, as well as a priest. He was also instrumental in forming the first U.S. Electoral College, and served as M.W.S. of Tahuti Chapter in New York.

A careful and thorough scholar of magick, Richard amassed an important collection of Crowleyana before his death, including rare typescripts of *Commentaries to Liber AL* and *The World's Tragedy*. These, together with his many first editions of Crowley works, have been left to the O.T.O. Archives where they are kept in the Gernon Accession. Part of his personal working library will form the cornerstone of the Richard W. Gernon Memorial Library at Tahuti Lodge.

Richard would teach magick to serious students, but was a stern teacher. He had little patience with esoteric "wanna-bes" or armchair occultists, and would customarily instruct younger aspirants to read and practice *Liber E* and *Liber O*, and then come back to talk over their experiences. Predictably, few did. Equally predictably, the few that did are still working today. His skills as a ritualist were considerable, and his oratorical voice was simply astounding. A recording of his reading of *Hymm to Pan* is on deposit in several academic poetry collections, and was used in a course at the Naropa Institute in Colorado.

Professionally, Richard was one of this country's foremost computer typographers. He helped found Cromwell Graphics Systems, a computer manufacturer, and subsequently held many highly responsible management positions in the advertising typography industry. He was often sought out by the industry press for his views on the state of the art in typography, and was considered an authority on data conversion and text programming. A typical example of his capabilities familiar to all of us would be the subtle step-and-repeat "Thelema" pattern used for the dustjacket of the hardcover of *The Holy Books of Thelema*.

Richard applied his editorial and professional skills to help produce several important Thelemic books, including *The Holy Books of Thelema* and *The Equinox III:10*. He assisted in the redesign and production of *The Magical Link* in 1986 E.V.

His many tangible contributions to the furtherance of the furtherance of the Work were made without concern for credit or compensation. His accomplishments were made in Silence, as befits a Magician. Few of us are untouched by his quiet efforts on our behalf.

Gurney died of a heroin overdose. He had acquired the heroin habit only recently, and although he had sought therapy with a member of the Order, the addiction process had progressed to the point that our efforts were of no avail. It is important that we in the Order understand his recent condition as a treatable disorder and not some sort of moral failure. It certainly should not be permitted to overshadow his very real achievements. As one of his friends remarked, it is not how long one lives, but how deeply, and Richard lived very deeply indeed.

He was my friend and brother, and I shall honor him always. He did it his way, as was his right.

He is survived by his parents, former wives Debbie, Laura and Micheline, and two children.

In addition to memorial masses around the country, a funeral service will be held April 2 in New York City. In accord with his intention and his family's wishes it will be a Thelemite ceremony. His ashes are to distributed at sea.

"So Life takes Fire from Death and runs, whirling amid the Suns." —*Liber DCLXXI*

Love is the law, love under will.

Caliph Hymenaeus Beta
Frater 218 A∴A∴

The Middle Pillar Ritual
as Developed by TAHUTI Lodge[*]

Israel Regardie introduced the Middle Pillar ritual to the modern Western Occult Tradition. He stated in *The Complete Golden Dawn System of Magic* that he could find no references to the technique in the original Golden Dawn papers, but was able to trace its origin to Dr. Felkin of the Stella Matutina, who described the ritual in an undeveloped form in one of the Society's grade papers. Regardie then perfected and popularized it in *The Middle Pillar, The Art of True Healing, The Complete Golden Dawn System of Magic,* and *The Foundations of Practical Magic.*

Briefly stated the ritual proceeds as follows:

After performing the Lesser Banishing Ritual of the Pentagram or the Star Ruby, begin with conscious relaxation. Do some deep breathing and yoga postures to calm the mind and free the body of deeper stresses and strains.

Next, imagine a ball of scintillating white light (say larger than a grapefruit and smaller than a basketball) coalescing both above and interpenetrating with the top of the skull (the *Sahasrara* chakra or *Kether* position). Vibrate the Divine Name EHIEH (eh-hee-yeh) several times, while the sphere of Light grows brighter and more vibrant. Regardie suggests at least five minutes.

When the visualization is firmly established, allow the energy to descend slowly through the head and face bathing and rejuvenating oneself, until it comes to the throat. Here the Light coalesces in the *Vishuddha* chakra or *Daath* position and is of a pale purple or lavender color. Vibrate the Name YHVH ELOHIM (yeh-ho-vah el-o-heem) until comfortable with the level of concentration, and ready to go on.

---

[*] To the best of my knowledge, the use of the Middle Pillar Ritual as a group working originated with TAHUTI Lodge. The practice has since spread to other magical bodies. Here also is a record of our substitution of Thelemic god names for those of the Regardie/Stella Matutina version of the ritual, along with some practical instructions for group performance.

Allow the energy to descend through the upper chest region with the same purifying and flowing movement until it comes to the heart or *Tiphareth* region, being the *Anahatta* chakra. Vibrate the Name YHVH ELOAH VA DAATH, (yeh-ho-vah el-o-ah vah-daath) while visualizing a sphere of golden light growing richer and brighter.

Then take the energy through the solar plexus and stomach, down to the base of the trunk at the genital region, where it meets a sphere of deepest rich purple at the *Yesod* position or *Svadishthana* chakra. Here vibrate the Name SHADDAI EL CHAI (sha-dai el chai [there is no equivalent in English to the Hebrew "CH" sound; it is a guttural sound, similar to clearing the throat]).

The energy now descends through the thighs, knees, and shins until it coalesces at the feet in the *Malkuth* position. Here the cross-over to the chakra system is more tenuous although, in my opinion, this position is analogous to the *Muladhara* chakra. This is particularly evident if one performs the ritual in a seated, cross-legged position. The Malkuth sphere is visualized as deepest vibrating black in color. The Divine Name is ADONAI HA-ARETZ (pronounced as spelled).

Now that the Middle Pillar has been formulated, one visualizes the energy rising through the body, passing upward through the spheres. It ascends from the black sphere at the feet, through the legs to the purple sphere at the genitals, through the stomach and solar plexus to the golden sphere at the heart, through the chest to the lavender sphere at the throat, and up through the face to the white sphere at the crown of the head. Here one concentrates on the glowing white brilliance and begins the work of the three Circulations.

The energy is first visualized as descending down and outward from the crown sphere, along the left side of the body during the out-breath, until it reaches the left foot. Then it crosses over to the right foot and ascends, on the in-breath, until it returns to the crown chakra, at the completion of the in-breath. This should be done numerous times until one can feel a flowing motion, timed to the breathing, which is most rejuvenating.

Continue on to the second circulation. It also begins at the crown sphere and goes forward and down the front of the body, on the out-breath, until it reaches the feet. Then, on the in-breath, the energy proceeds up and around the back of the body, until it returns to the sphere of white brilliance at the crown of the head on the completion of the in-breath. Continue to circulate the Light in this manner until it is felt as real (which is easier than it may sound).

Finally, the third circulation is performed. With the energy at the crown, the Light is visualized as descending again through the Middle Pillar, until it reaches the Malkuth sphere at the feet. From here, it is circulated up and through the body to the crown on the in-breath. When it reaches the crown, it is imagined as "fountaining" at the completion of the in-breath, before the out-breath begins. The fountaining energy goes up and out through the crown, and then down and around the body during the out-breath, until it reaches the feet when the out-breath is complete. It is raised again with the in-breath, and the cycle of raising, fountaining and descending continues until the ritual is closed. (The aura is visualized as extending around the body in the shape of a large upright egg.)

* * * * *

THELEMIC MIDDLE PILLAR AS A GROUP WORKING

The members of TAHUTI Lodge further developed and modified Regardie's ritual for use as a group working. We also adapted Divine Names for the spheres more appropriate to our particular theological aesthetics as Thelemites. These Words of Power were arrived at through a study of *Liber V vel Reguli*.

At the *Kether* point we substitute the Divine Name of NUIT.
At *Daath* we use the Name AIWASS.
At *Tiphareth* we vibrate RA-HOOR-KHUIT.
At *Yesod* we say HADIT.
At *Malkuth* we use the conjoined Divine Name BABALON-THERION.

First the Circle is banished. One person serves as the leader, guiding the group through a period of synchronized breathing, then synchronized mantra, and again synchronized breathing. Until the entire group can breath and chant as one, no attempt should be made to proceed.

The leader should then begin the guided meditation over the sound of the synchronized breathing. The leader continues to "talk" the group through the steps. It is critical that everyone functions in unison.

The leader should stand within the group around the circumference of the Circle. With experience, he or she might, on occasion, risk standing in the center of the Circle (the use of the word "risk" is deliberate as the psychic strain of that geometry is real and should not be attempted until the group is thoroughly coordinated by much practice, and there are no elements in the environment to disrupt the concentration).

The leader must take the time to carefully prepare the group for any desired activity. For example, the instructions for the first circulation would sound something like this:

> "We will now begin to circulate the energy from the top of the head, on the out-breath, down the left side of the body, to the left foot. Then transfer the energy to the right foot, and raise it, on the in-breath, along the right side of the body, until it returns to the crown. We will begin the circulation on the out-breath. Breathe in ... and now out and circulate."

Working with a group encourages a heightened sense of the metaphysical responsibility of one's magick. For example, during the fountaining circulation, we raise the energy not only above and through the Circle, but expand it throughout the Universe, bathing all "Planes of Being and By-coming" in the warmth and radiance of the Light.

Further insights came to us which are best left to be discovered by the intuitive process of the group workers, guided by their practice of the ritual and commitment to the Great Work—however, the building of God forms suggests itself as one of the most powerful uses of this exercise.

At the end of the last circulation, we close something like this: "Now take the energy and focus it at eye level in the center of the Circle. It is in the form of a glowing ball of light that is intensifying in brightness. Hold it in the center of the Circle. It is beginning to shrink even as it grows brighter. It is shrinking, shrinking ... and now it disappears into itself ... please open the eyes."

There is an almost an audible "pop" when the ball of light collapses into the Void. The effect of opening our eyes at once, while being almost painful, is most effective in maintaining group mind cohesiveness and concentration—there should be a lightness, an inspired, energized and crisp feeling throughout the Circle.

The Middle Pillar Ritual may be used as the main focus of the evening's work, or as the prelude to other ritual. In either case, it is a most adaptable and energizing exercise, and one we recommend to Western occultists whether for group or individual use.

LIBER LXXVII

 **Oz:**

> "the law of
> the strong:
> this is our law
> and the joy
> of the world."
> — *AL. II. 21*

"Do what thou wilt shall be the whole of the Law."
> — *AL. I. 40*

"thou hast no right but to do thy will. Do that, and no
other shall say nay." — *AL. I. 42–3*

"Every man and every woman is a star." — *AL. I. 3*

There is no god but man.

1. Man has the right to live by his own law —
    to live in the way that he wills to do:
    to work as he will:
    to play as he will:
    to rest as he will:
    to die when and how he will.

2. Man has the right to eat what he will:
    to drink what he will:
    to dwell where he will:
    to move as he will on the face of the earth.

3. Man has the right to think what he will:
    to speak what he will:
    to write what he will:
    to draw, paint, carve, etch, mould, build as he will:
    to dress as he will.

4. Man has the right to love as he will: —
    "take your fill and will of love as ye will,
    when, where and with whom ye will." — *AL. I. 51*

5. Man has the right to kill those who would thwart
    these rights.

> "the slaves shall serve." — *AL. II. 58*

"Love is the law, love under will." — *AL. I. 57*

Aleister Crowley

GLOSSARY

A∴A∴ The Order of the Silver Star. See *One Star in Sight,* included in *Magick in Theory and Practice, Book IV,* Part 3 and *The Weiser Concise Guide to Aleister Crowley.** Crowley called the A∴A∴ the Great White Brotherhood, the spiritual hierarchy that guides humanity.

Adeptus Minor One of the eleven Grades of the A∴A∴ corresponding to the Sephira Tiphareth on the Tree of Life. It is designated as 5°=6▢.

Adonai אדני, "Lord," 65. The Holy Guardian Angel, HGA, Divine Self, *Augoeides.* The relationship between the Adept and Adonai is most beautifully described in *Liber LXV: The Book of the Heart Girt with a Serpent.*

Aeon of Horus Crowley considered the Aeons to represent periods of 2,000 years, based on astrological progression. He named these spiritual epochs after Egyptian deities and familial archetypes. He called the matriarchal period, in which there was a continuum with Nature and fertility religions abounded, the Aeon of Isis. It was superseded by the patriarchal period, that of the Dying God, in which sacrificed and resurrected deities were the rule. The current Aeon, that of the Crowned and Conquering Child Horus, came into being in 1904 at the Equinox of the Gods.

Agape Αγαπη, "Love," 93. The Greek language is alpha-numeric like Hebrew. Thus, there is a Greek Qabalah in which words of the same numerical value are considered to have a special relationship. Compare with Thelema, Θελημα, "Will," whose value is also 93.

Aiwass The praeter-human Intelligence who dictated *The Book of the Law* to Aleister Crowley in Cairo, Egypt on April 8, 9, and 10 of 1904. He announces a New Law for mankind and the transition to the Aeon of Horus.

A ka dua Mantra A prayer taken from the Egyptian text of the Stele of Revealing and described by Crowley as the holiest mantra of all. *A ka dua / Tuf ur biu / Bi a'a chefu / Dudu ner af an nuteru* (Unity uttermost

---

* The literature by and about Aleister Crowley and his system of spiritual development is vast. I highly recommend *The Weiser Concise Guide to Aleister Crowley* by Richard Kaczynski, edited by James Wasserman. Our goal was to provide as broad-based an introduction to Crowley as was possible within a 128 page book, as well as provide the reader with legitimate resources for additional study.

showed! / I adore the might of Thy breath / Supreme and terrible God / Who makest the gods and death / To tremble before Thee— / I, I adore thee!) (See Stele of Revealing.)

Ankh-f-n-khonsu The Priest of the Princes. A 25th–26th Dynasty Egyptian priest (early 7th century BC) whose funeral stele is linked to the revelation of *The Book of the Law*. Crowley considered himself the reincarnation of this ancient figure. (See Stele of Revealing.)

Asana "Posture." A practice of Yoga utilizing various positions to still the disruptive signals emanating from the body. See *Book IV*, Part I, *Mysticism*, chapter I.

Ayurvedic Medicine An indigenous Indian system of healing whose roots are over 2,000 years old.

Ba English transliteration of the Egyptian word for "soul." Iconographically depicted as a human-headed bird.

Beltane The Celtic May Day holiday, May 1, that honors and calls forth the fertility of Earth during the planting cycle. It is a celebration of renewal, sensuality, fertility, and marriage.

Bodhisattva Enlightened being. In Mahayana Buddhism, this term refers to an aspirant who, motivated by compassion, devotes the fruits of spiritual attainment to the liberation of all sentient beings.

Bonpo The indigenous, shamanistic religion of Tibet prior to the introduction of Buddhism in the 7th century. Padmasambhava is said to have bested the Bon sorcerers in magical competition during the 8th century and to have subdued the demons from which they drew power.

Book IV, **Parts 1–4** This four-part series (*Liber ABA*) was issued separately during Crowley's lifetime. Part 1 is *Mysticism*. Part 2 is *Magick*. Part 3 is *Magick in Theory and Practice*. Part 4 is *The Equinox of the Gods*. It was released as a one volume collection under the title *Magick* in 1994 by the O.T.O. It contains the essence of Crowley's curriculum.

Book of the Law The primary scripture of Thelema was dictated to Aleister Crowley in Cairo, Egypt in three one-hour sessions in 1904. The book announces a New Aeon, the Equinox of the Gods, and a new formula for mankind in which the individual is the key to the pursuit of Truth.

Chokmah Wisdom. The second Sephira on the Tree of Life, identified with the Egyptian God Tahuti, the planet Neptune, and the A∴A∴ Grade of Magus, among other attributions.

Class A Comment Known as the *Tunis Comment*, it is mentioned in *Liber AL* III:40, ""But the work of the comment? That is easy; and

Hadit burning in thy heart shall make swift and secure thy pen." It is included in properly published editions of *The Book of the Law.*

Class A Writings Crowley assigned his prolific literary output to five classes, designed to give his readers a sense of their doctrinal importance. He identified Class A material as written from the point of view of the highest level of initiation. "Change not as much as the style of a letter ..." (AL I:54).

Cledon A Greek term for messages from the Gods, the Universe, and/or the Unconscious. Cledons are omens and auguries. They include the phenomenon in which unsuspecting people are used to convey messages, or seemingly random and natural occurrences communicate personal information to the seeker.

Court Cards In the Tarot, these 16 cards depict royal figures: the King, Queen, Prince, and Princess in each of the four Suits of Wands, Cups, Swords, and Disks (representing the elements of Fire, Water, Air, and Earth).

Denderah Zodiac A zodiac placed on the ceiling of the Temple of Denderah in Egypt. It is believed to represent the Heavens at midnight on the Summer Solstice of 700 BC. Its zoomorphs show Greek influence, thus it is believed to have been carved ca. 100 BC. Napoleon removed it from the Temple in 1799 and moved it to the Louvre in Paris.

Ecclesiae Gnosticae Catholicae (E.G.C.) The Gnostic Catholic Church is the liturgical arm of Thelema. Its members maintain a special focus on the Gnostic Mass.

Electoral College The O.T.O. governing body that administers the affairs of the Man of Earth Triad of the Order. Each national Kingdom has its own Electoral College.

Enochian Magic A system of angelic communication developed by Dr. John Dee and Edward Kelly in 16th century England. It later became the basis for an ambitious ordering of occult symbolism undertaken by Samuel Liddel MacGregor Mathers and the Hermetic Order of the Golden Dawn during the late 19th century.

The Equinox The official publication of the A∴A∴ Volume 1 comprises 10 numbers (books), published every six months by Aleister Crowley from 1909 to 1914. He called it the "Encyclopedia of Initiation." New numbers are issued on a periodic basis.

Equinox of the Gods A term utilized by Aiwass in *The Book of the Law* to signify the point of transition from the Aeon of Osiris to the new Aeon of Horus. It took place on March 20, 1904 when Crowley performed the Supreme Ritual in Egypt.

The Equinox of the Gods *Book IV,* Part 4, in which Crowley documents his receiving of *The Book of the Law.*

Gardnerian Witchcraft Gerald B. Gardner (1884–1964) was the founder of the modern pagan religion of Wicca or Witchcraft, following the repeal of the British Witchcraft laws in the early 1950s. Gardner was a tireless writer and organizer. He was also an associate of Crowley's and at least a IV° initiate of O.T.O. Crowley chartered Gardner to operate a Camp of the Minerval Degree.

Gnostic Mass *Liber XV.* Crowley called the Mass the central ritual public and private of the O.T.O. The Gnostic Mass is a Eucharistic ritual in which bread and wine are transmuted into the body and blood of God.

Goetic Magic *The Goetia,* or *Lesser Key of Solomon,* focuses on the evocation of demons. It is the most famous example of a Goetic Grimoire. The word "Goetia" derives from "howling" and refers to the cries of the sorcerer uttered during the rites. As were many medieval-derived grimoires, it was attributed to King Solomon.

Golden Dawn A magical Order that functioned in London from 1888 through the early part of the 20th century. Its subsequent influence on Western occultism has been ubiquitous. Crowley was a member as were several other leading lights of British society such as W. B. Yeats and Arthur Machen.

Great Work The Work of Initiation performed in service to mankind. The uniting of divine and human consciousness through spiritual aspiration and effort.

Grimoire "Grammar." Broadly refers to magical textbooks that include seals, invocations, exorcisms, and instructions for the attaining of personal goals. They have been compared to recipe books and are often attributed to ancient mythic sources.

Hadit The secret core of one's own Star. The point within the circle. "In the sphere I am everywhere the centre, as she, the circumference, is nowhere found." (AL II:3) Aiwass dictated the second chapter of *The Book of the Law* in the name of Hadit.

Halveti Jerrahi A traditional Sufi Order of Dervishes founded in the 17th century in Turkey by Pir Nureddin al-Jerrahi and flourishing in some 15 countries today.

Holy Books This term refers to the collection of texts identified by Aleister Crowley as Class A. (See Class A Writings.)

The Holy Books of Thelema A publication by the A∴A∴ and O.T.O. of the Class A texts, called by some the "Thelemic Bible."

Holy Guardian Angel (HGA) The Holy Guardian Angel is Crowley's term for the True Spiritual Instructor, "Adonai." The Angel is frequently identified as God, or one's personal connection with God. "O my Lord, my beloved! How shall I indite songs, when even the memory of the shadow of thy glory is a thing beyond all music of speech or of silence?"

Ifa Divination A Yoruban system of divination that makes use of the apparently random patterns formed by cowrie shells or palm nuts. The patterns are then interpreted according to the 256 chapters of traditional verses of the literary collection called *Odu Ifa*. The *Babalawo*, or diviner, must undergo a long and rigorous period of training, study, and initiation.

Karmapa Lama He is the head of a branch of the Kagyupa sect, one of the four schools of Tibetan Buddhism. The famed Tibetan saint Milarepa was a Kagyupa.

Kundalini The Life Force, symbolized as a serpentine energy, whose activation results in the expansion of consciousness.

LBRH The Lesser Banishing Ritual of the Hexagram. A ritual of spiritual cleansing explained in *Liber O,* based on the six-pointed star.

LBRP The Lesser Banishing Ritual of the Pentagram. A ritual of spiritual cleansing explained in *Liber O,* based on the five-pointed star.

Lemniscates The figure-eight shaped sign of Infinity above the Magician's head in most versions of the Tarot.

Liber The Latin word meaning "book." Crowley identified his magical instructions as various "libri" to which he assigned both numbers and a classification system from A through E based on the importance, intended use, and spiritual coherence he attributed to each of his works.

Liber AL vel Legis See *The Book of the Law.* The central text of the New Aeon. It is a Class A book.

Liber III vel Jugorum An instruction by Crowley for the development of self-control in action, speech, and thought. A series of exercises are given in which cuts with a razor are self-administered for slips in concentration.

Liber Israfel A powerful invocation of Tahuti originally developed by Allen Bennett. It was revised by Aleister Crowley and published in *The Equinox* I:7.

Liber LXV: Liber Cordis Cincti Serpente *The Book of the Heart Girt with a Serpent* is one of the Holy Books of Thelema or Class A publications. Its five chapters refer to the five Elements: 1) Earth, 2) Air, 3) Water, 4) Fire, 5) Spirit.

Liber O vel Manus et Sagittae   One of Crowley's most important instructions for the development of the spiritual body and the practice of Magick. It includes: Assumption of God-forms, Vibration of Divine Names, the Banishing and Invoking Rituals of the Pentagram and Hexagram, and Rising on the Planes.

Liber Oz vel LXXVII   The "Declaration of the Rights of Man" was published in a postcard-like format in 1942. See page 286.

Liber Resh vel Helios   See Solar Adorations. *Liber Resh* is Crowley's text describing the Adorations.

Liber V vel Reguli   See the Ritual of the Mark of the Beast.

Liber VII: Liber Liberi vel Lapidis Lazuli   One of the Holy Books of Thelema or Class A publications. The seven chapters refer to the seven planets in this order: Mars, Saturn, Jupiter, Sol, Mercury, Luna, Venus.

Liber XV   See the Gnostic Mass.

Liber XXV   See the Star Ruby Ritual.

Liber XLIV   See the Mass of the Phoenix Ritual.

Loa   The deities of the Voodoo pantheon. They are the ministers of the Supreme Creator. In an actual ceremony, the priest or priestess becomes possessed by the particular Loa of the rite. At the end of the ceremony, the members of the congregation are brought into his or her presence to receive a personal blessing or communication.

Magical Diary   Crowley insisted that aspirants to the A∴A∴ keep a diary of their spiritual practices and the daily events of their lives so that they would have a coherent and scientific record of their progress. See *Aleister Crowley and the Practice of the Magical Diary* for two examples of such diaries.

Magical Link, The   A newsletter publication of the O.T.O., first issued in 1981.

Magical Record   See Magical Diary.

Magick in Theory and Practice   Part 3 of Crowley's opus *Book IV. Magick in Theory and Practice* forms the primary source book of Crowley's system of spiritual development including rituals, meditations, spiritual exercises, and a theoretical exposition of occult philosophy.

Magick   The art and science of causing change to occur in conformity with Will. Crowley spelled the word with a "k" to distinguish it from common superstition. He spelled the word "magical" without the "k."

Magister Templi   "Master of the Temple." An exalted Grade of the Third Order of the A∴A∴ corresponding to the Sephira Binah. Designated as 8°=3□.

Mahayana Buddhism "The Great Vehicle." There are two primary schools in Buddhism, the Mahayana and the older Hinayana or Theravada tradition. The Mahayana is concerned with sharing Enlightenment with all sentient beings through the Bodhisattva tradition, while the Theravada solely seeks Nirvana (Liberation) as the solution to the problem of suffering and illusion.

Mantra "Prayer" or "Hymn." A sound, word, or phrase used to develop one-pointedness of thought. See *Book IV,* Part I, Mysticism, chapter II.

Mass of the Phoenix Liber XLIV. One of Crowley's most important rituals for the elevation of consciousness and identification with the energies of the New Aeon. Crowley described the ritual as an "exoteric form of Eucharist" and a "Ritual of the Law."

Middle Pillar The Central Pillar on the Tree of Life. It represents the balance between the Pillars of Severity and Mercy.

Minerval The introductory Degree of the O.T.O. initiation system.

N.O.X. Symbolic formula based on the initial letters of the Latin NOX "Night." The letters N.O.X. signify the "Night of Pan." N.O.X. is the central formula of the Aeon of Horus.

Neophyte The first grade proper of the A∴A∴ It is attributed to the Sephira of Malkuth and designated as 1°=10° to indicate that is the first of ten Sephiroth.

Nyingma School The oldest of the four schools of Tibetan Buddhism, it traces its lineage to Padmasambhava. Dudjom Rinpoche (1904–1987) was the primary lineage holder of this school when he visited New York in 1979.

Ordo Templi Orientis (O.T.O.) The Order of the Temple of the East. A magical Order that claims derivation from the Knights Templar. It is a post-Masonic group, originally founded in 1895, which adopted the Law of Thelema, circa 1910 when Aleister Crowley joined. He became the Outer Head of the Order in 1923. See "An Open Letter to Those Who May Wish to Join the Order" in *Equinox* III:10 and in *The Weiser Concise Guide to Aleister Crowley.*

Pan "The All." Crowley's conception of Pan was more exalted and doctrinally relevant to Thelema than the traditional archetype of Pan as the God of Nature in Greek mythology. Crowley conceived Pan as the universal continuum, above even the realm of manifestation symbolized by the Tree of Life. Pan's masculine, erotic, unpredictable, even cruel nature was particularly appealing to Crowley's psyche. Crowley's *Hymn to Pan* is published in *Magick in Theory and Practice.*

Pentagrammaton A five-lettered Name of God, traditionally signifying יהשוה, "Yeheshuah." (See Tetragrammaton and Yeheshuah.)

Powers of the Sphinx The four Virtues of the Adept—*to Know, to Will, to Dare*, and *to Keep Silence*.

Praemonstrator Latin for "Guide." The Teaching Adept of the A∴A∴, one of three primary officers, who is specifically tasked with representing and communicating the doctrines of the Order.

Pranayama "To control the prana (or breath)." A practice of Yoga using measured breathing to help still the body and thus allow the mind to concentrate. See *Book IV, Part I, Mysticism*, chapter II.

Probationer The preliminary Grade of the A∴A∴ in which the aspirant signs an Oath and receives a Task. Designated as 0°=0□.

Qabalah "To Receive." The name applied to Jewish esotericism which was subsequently adopted by the Western occult schools. In modern Western usage, the Qabalah includes, Astrology, Alchemy, Magick, Tarot, Numerology and Symbolism. *The Mystical Qabalah* by Dion Fortune is an excellent and comprehensible introduction to the system.

Qliphoth The World of "Shells." Lacking in Truth or spiritual coherence. The unbalanced world of the profane. Impure aspects of the human psyche. Demonic, negative, or unevolved forces and complexes.

Radha Swami Satsang The term that designates the followers of Sant Mat.

Bhagwan Shree Rajneesh A controversial Indian guru (1931–1990) whose teachings attracted many Western followers during the 1970s. His embrace of sacred sexuality brought opposition from more traditional Hindu teachers. He relocated to the United States in 1981 and is the author of many published works.

Rites of Eleusis A series of seven planetary invocations written by Aleister Crowley and first performed by him and aspirants of the A∴A∴ in London in Caxton Hall in 1910. It was designed as a public outreach to share rituals of Magick with the larger society.

Ritual of the Mark of the Beast "An incantation proper to invoke the Energies of the Aeon of Horus, adapted for the daily use of the Magician of whatever grade."

Samhain The Celtic name for Halloween, October 31. The night when the spirits of the dead visit the world of the living and must be honored, lest ill-fortune result.

Sant Mat The "Teaching of the Saints." An Indian spiritual path that acknowledges a lineage of spiritual teachers who are viewed as incarnations of the Light itself, evolved beings whose task is the elevation of humanity through the practice of meditation, right living, and "guru bhakti" or devotion to the Teacher.

Santeria The Afro-Caribbean magical system in Puerto Rico. (In Cuba it is called *Lucumi,* in Brazil *Umbanda,* and in Haiti *Voudon* or *Voodoo.*) When African slaves were brought to the New World, they disguised their indigenous religions with the symbols of their Christian slave masters.

Saturn Return Each planet circles the heavens in its orbit around the Sun within a defined period of time. The Earth takes 365¼ days, the measure of a year. The Saturn cycle is 29½ years and represents the outermost of the "personal" planets. (By way of contrast, Uranus takes 84 years, Neptune 164, and Pluto 248. They are thus considered "generational" and "historical" planets.)

Sephira (pl. **Sephiroth**) "Number." A term for one of the ten levels of emanation symbolized by the Tree of Life. To each Sephira is attributed a Name of God, an Archangel, Angel, and archetypal nature, along with a planetary reference. The Sephiroth and Paths of the Tree of Life are emblematic of all knowledge and serve as an organizational schemata of the Universe. (See Qabalah.)

Sigil An occult design or magical seal believed to hold and attract magical energies and powers.

Solar Adorations A series of prayers or invocations done at Dawn, Noon, Sunset, and Midnight by Aspirants of the A∴A∴ They are outlined in *Liber Resh vel Helios.*

Star Ruby *Liber XXV.* Crowley's improved and modernized version of the Lesser Banishing Ritual of the Pentagram.

Stele of Revealing An Egyptian painted, wooden, funeral, commemorative tablet. It measures 20 inches tall by 12 inches wide and dates to the 25th–26th Dynasty (late 7th century BC). It depicts the four primary archetypes of the Thelemic revelation. The arched star goddess Nuit bends over a scene in which the Priest Ankh–f-n-knonsu addresses the seated deity Ra-Hoor-Khuit. A Winged Disk, representing Hadit, further frames the scene. Crowley was astounded to note that it was catalogued as Exhibit Number 666 when he visited the Boulak Museum in Cairo in 1904.

Sufism The Gnostic tradition within Islam. Sufi mystic doctrines and esoteric practices are widespread in the Near East. There are numerous traditions and schools within Sufism, among which are the Halveti Jerrahi. The "Whirling Dervishes" are another well-known sect.

Supreme Ritual The Invocation of Horus performed by Crowley in Egypt on the Spring Equinox of 1904. It is associated with the advent of the Aeon of Horus, the Equinox of the Gods.

Tahuti "Thoth," the god of Wisdom, writing, measurement, and magic. Called Hermes in Greece, Mercury in Rome, Manjusri in Tibet, Odin in Scandanavia, Ganesha in India, Eleggua in Puerto Rico, and Legba in Haiti.

Tarot A resume of the Qabalah, Astrology, Alchemy, and Esoteric Symbolism disguised as 78 "playing cards." The 22 Trumps are identified with the Hebrew letters; the 4 Suits are identified with the four Elements; and the 10 "Small Cards" (in the four Suits) with the 10 Sephiroth. The 16 Court Cards (four in each of the four Suits) are identified with the archetypal forces of Tetragrammaton—Father, Mother, Son, and Daughter.

Tetragrammaton יהוה. The biblical name of God. It represents the four Elements. י (Fire), ה (Water) ו (Air), ה (Earth).

Thelema Θελημα, "Will," 93. The Greek language is alpha-numeric like Hebrew. Thus, there is a Greek Qabalah in which words of the same numerical value are considered to have a special relationship. Crowley adopted the word Thelema to distinguish his spiritual system. In AL I:39, it is called "The word of the Law…" Compare with Agape, Αγαπη, "Love," whose value is also 93.

Thelemic The adjective describing that which is consistent with the philosophy of Do what thou wilt.

Thelemite One who practices the system of Do what thou wilt, an adherent of the Law of Thelema. See *The Book of the Law*, I:40. "Who calls us Thelemites will do no wrong, if he look but close into the word. For there are therein Three Grades, the Hermit, and the Lover, and the man of Earth. Do what thou wilt shall be the whole of the Law."

Thoth The Greek form of the Egyptian name Tahuti. (In the Greek Mysteries proper, He is known as Hermes.)

Tiphareth "Beauty." The sixth Sephira on the Tree of Life, also called "Harmony." As the center of the Tree of Life, it is considered the meeting ground of human and divine and is associated with the Knowledge and Conversation of the Holy Guardian Angel.

Tree of Life A symbolic diagram of the Universe. It includes 10 Sephiroth united by 22 Paths, representing the successive emanation of the Universe from Nothingness into Being, as well as indicating the path of return. (See Sephira and Qabalah.)

Tzaddi צ. A letter of the Hebrew alphabet whose meaning is "Fishhook." Its numeric value is 90.

Vajrayana Buddhism "The Diamond Vehicle." It dates to the beginning of the 6th century in India, and later migrated to Tibet. The Vajrayana is regarded as the origin of the four schools of Tibetan Buddhism. The *Vajra* is the Diamond Thunderbolt of Indra (the *Dorje*), equivalent to the Wand in Western Magick. Padmasambhava is the religious figure most associated with the Vajrayana path.

Wicca Witchcraft. The Nature-oriented pagan religions believed to have secretly survived from their pre-Christian roots in Europe. During the Middle Ages, witches were viciously persecuted by the Inquisition. Laws against witchcraft remained on the books until modern times. (See Gerald Gardner.)

Yeheshuah יהשוה, "Jesus." The four letters of Tetragrammaton, יהוה, with ש (Spirit) placed in their midst. It represents the spiritualization of Matter. (See Pentagrammaton.)

Yoruba The name of a West African people (currently residing in the modern nations of Nigeria, Togo, and Benin). Their indigenous religion is shamanistic and animistic and was imported to the New World by slaves. The Caribbean Yoruban exiles continued to practice and pass down their traditions. They camouflaged their ceremonies and the identities of their gods (*Orishas*) with iconographic aspects of the saints of their Catholic slave owners.

Acknowledgments

In addition to those people mentioned in the Introduction, I would like to thank several others for their help in assembling materials and reviewing progressive drafts of this text.

Daniel and Julia Pineda provided crucial early encouragement without which I simply would not have continued. Daniel, especially, closely monitored the development of this effort as did Teri Norris. Emma Gonzalez, Shelley Marmor, Tim Linn, Stella Grey, and Anthony Derajja, provided insight and affirmation. My thanks to Kent Finne, Michael Kramer, Bokar, Simon, Brian Crawford, Claire, Jane, Wileda, and Steven Fox for their help in reconstructing our shared past and sharing photos. I appreciate the help of Lon DuQuette and look forward to reading his book, to be published by New Falcon Publications, chronicling his West Coast O.T.O. experience. I thank Rodney Orpheus for his perceptive comments, and Emily Lawson, Barbara Shelt, Michael Antinori, and Mike Patterson for their interest. Bob Martin stimulated a long-lost memory of Weiser's where we worked together.

I am grateful to Donald and Yvonne Weiser for sharing photos of the bookstore and the 1984 Maine visit of Grady, Bill, and myself. I also appreciate the help with photos provided by James Strain, Bill Breeze, and Dan Gunther. Thanks to Scott Hobbs of the Cameron Parsons Foundation for permission to include Jack Parsons' paper "Analysis by a Master of the Temple of the Critical Nodes in the Experience of His Magical Vehicle." Angel Lorenz generously allowed me to share his solution to the riddle of the Star Ruby that puzzled me for 35 years.

The editorial diligence James Strain applied to my ever-evolving text made this book much better. I also thank my friend Keith Stump, co-author of *Divine Warriors,* for his editorial efforts. Brother Henrik Bogdan noted certain lacunae in the text that I had purposely decided not to write about. His perceptive insight forced me to expand my account and proved, once again, the value of the Order as a forge for the development of courage and character. Thanks to Mark Reynolds for his review. Dr. Laurel Trufant of ProLogos Editorial Services greatly improved the text.

My friend Lindy Cooper Wisdom made the important editorial suggestion of adding the Glossary. Lindy also did a careful reading of the book, sharing her grammatical expertise. I hope the Glossary proves of service to the reader. Thanks to Angel Lorenz for his help in reviewing it for doctrinal accuracy, and to Dan Gunther for his unyielding and critical advice. As simple as it may seem, attempting to define spiritual terms demands a highly disciplined approach.

David Vagi helped me understand that this story has a wider relevance as an alternative cultural history than I initially anticipated.

Bill Corsa, as ever, provided his expert guidance on how to make this book actually manifest itself in three dimensions.

Satra Wasserman edited the video of the 1980 Samhain ritual, filmed by my friend Rob Stelboum, for publication on www.inthecenterofthefire.com. Anthony Derajja contributed his extraordinary web skills to build that site. Years earlier, he digitized the reel-to-reel tapes of the Jodorowsky interview. Illia Tulloch digitized the cassette tape recording made by Harry Smith of Gurney's 1987 Hymn to Pan ritual, also posted on our website.

My thanks to David Scriven, John Bonner, and Stephen King for their leadership of the U.S., UK, and Australian Grand Lodges of O.T.O. They have helped manifest the Order in ways I could not have expected to see during the period this book chronicles.

I knew I had a hit on my hands when my teenage daughter Rachel devoured the first draft looking for evidence of my hippie days. (I thank her for her work in typing much of the materials for the appendices.) Satra was fascinated by the details of his infancy and youth and the early tales of his father's magical quest. I appreciate Nancy's tolerance for this intimate catalog of my past, her patience in dealing with my creative obsession, and her help in editing and producing this record.

Contact Information

To contact O.T.O. worldwide

Ordo Templi Orientis
www.oto.org

To contact O.T.O. in the United States

Ordo Templi Orientis
PO Box 32
Riverside, CA 92502-0032
www.oto-usa.org

To contact TAHUTI Lodge

TAHUTI Lodge
Old Chelsea Station
P.O. Box 1535
New York, NY 10113-1535
www.tahutilodge.org

To contact A∴A∴

Chancellor
BM ANKH
London WC1N 3XX
ENGLAND
www.outercol.org

For more information on this book:

www.inthecenterofthefire.com

For more information, please visit:

www.jameswassermanbooks.com

Secret Societies: Illuminati, Freemasons, and the French Revolution
by Una Birch, enlarged, edited, and introduced by James Wasserman

The greatest success of the Bavarian Illuminati conspiracy was the French Revolution of 1789. The profound impact of that Revolution are felt to this day in the political destinies of millions of people worldwide. The Illuminati had declared war against Church and State and worked feverishly to spread their new gospel of Liberty and Reason. Although the Order was officially suppressed on the eve of the Revolution, its efforts do not appear to have been in vain. What message does the triumph of these secret societies carry for the modern world?

$18.95 • Paperback • ISBN: 0-89254-132-6 • 288 Pages • 6 x 9

Pythagoras: His Life and Teachings
by Thomas Stanley, preface by Manly P. Hall; introduction by Dr. Henry L. Drake; edited by James Wasserman; with a study of Greek sources by J. Daniel Gunther

Pythagoras is known as the Father of Philosophy and was one of the most influential figures of all time. He did much original work in such diverse fields as Mathematics, Religion, Mysticism, Symbolic Numbers, Philosophy, Music, Astronomy, Politics, Health, and Nutrition. He founded a spiritual academy in which an active intellectual curriculum was augmented by a highly disciplined program of character development. He sought to improve his students through the cultivation of morality, self-discipline, spiritual sensitivity, and good citizenship.

$24.95 • Paperback • ISBN: 978-0-89254-160-7 • 416 pp. • 6 x 9

Initiation in the Æon of the Child: The Inward Journey
by J. Daniel Gunther

In 1904, *The Book of the Law* declared the advent of a new period in the course of human history—The Aeon of Horus, or Aeon of the Child. This ground-breaking book provides a penetrating and cohesive analysis of the spiritual doctrine underlying and informing the Aeon of the Child, and the sublime formulas of Initiation encountered by those who would probe its mysteries. Drawing on more than 30 years of experience as a student and teacher within the Order of the A∴A∴ the author examines the doctrinal thread of Thelema in its historical, religious, and practical context.

$40.00 • Hardcover • ISBN: 0-89254-145-5 • 224 Pages • 6 x 9